HITLER'S WARTIME PICTURE MAGAZINE

HITLER'S
WARTIME
PICTURE
MAGAZINE

Signal

EDITED BY S. L. MAYER

PRENTICE-HALL, INC.
Englewood Cliffs, N.J.

 A Bison Book

Signal: **Hitler's Wartime Picture Magazine**
Edited by S. L. Mayer

This book was prepared and produced by
Bison Publishing Company, London, England

First U.S. Edition published by Prentice-Hall, Inc., 1976

Copyright © 1976 by Bison Books, London, England

Second impression 1976
Third impression 1976
Fourth impression 1977
Fifth impression 1977

Sixth impression 1977

Printed by Dai Nippon, Tokyo, Japan

ISBN 0 13 810051 9

Library of Congress Catalog Card Number: 75-28749

Signal had the largest sale of any magazine published in Europe during the years 1940-45. Although produced by the Wehrmacht under the authority of the German Ministry of Propaganda, it only had a small circulation inside Germany (except among the military) as it was intended for export to sell the Third Reich to the peoples it conquered and to nearby neutral states. *Signal* was published fortnightly from April 1940 to March 1945, in as many as 20 languages. Its circulation reached a peak of 2½ million in 1943.

Germany's attempts to publish foreign language periodicals in the pre-war years had been a dismal failure. Although Hitler had his admirers in Austria, Czechoslovakia and Eastern Europe, the virtually exclusive German appeal of the Nazi creed and its characterisation of most Eastern Europeans as 'Untermenschen' (sub-humans) limited the extent to which Nazi propaganda could succeed before 1939. In Western Europe proto-Nazi movements like Mosley's British Union of Fascists, the Rexists in Belgium and the Croix de Feu in France were considered the lunatic right-wing fringe. Thus when Hitler's conquest of Europe began, there was considerable interest in promoting a propaganda magazine for popular consumption abroad to make the occupation, or at least German domination of Europe, seem more palatable.

Dr. Paul Joseph Goebbels, chief of the Propaganda Ministry in the Third Reich and one of the greatest propagandists of the 20th century, foresaw the Nazi take-over of most of Europe and made preparations accordingly. Once non-German subject peoples came under the Nazi domination, they had to be convinced that resistance to the New Order was futile and that they would be better off than in the decadent days of democracy and self-determination. The initial impact of racist propaganda on Germanic peoples was critical, since they were expected, as co-members of the 'master race', to co-operate with the New Order and support German hegemony in Europe. For the Slavic and Latin peoples of Europe, they had to be convinced that German rule was best too. This propaganda mission was a formidable one, but essential to permanent Nazi mastery of Europe. Goebbels sought to obtain the collaboration of the German Army in this propaganda mission, since they were the spearhead of German power. For that reason *Signal* was placed nominally under the control of the Wehrmacht, although censors from the Propaganda Ministry oversaw and vetted every issue prior to publication.

The image *Signal* hoped to create was that of Germany as the great benefactor of European peoples and civilization. Heroic and humane deeds of the Wehrmacht were idealized; a rosy picture was painted of Europe's dynamo, Germany; an exaggerated enthusiasm of the occupied peoples for German 'liberation' was reported and photographed. *Signal* became the leading journal in Europe and was described by *Life,* the American pictorial magazine, as 'the great arsenal of Axis propaganda'.

To achieve this success, German racial supremacy, one of Hitler's major doctrines, was played down. Anti-semitic propaganda, so virulent in the Reich itself, never appeared in a blatant manner; in fact the Jews were hardly ever mentioned. The impression given was that the Jewish problem had been solved, for according to *Signal* there were no problems in Nazi Germany. In the same way anti-Slav propaganda did not appear even when Operation Barbarossa, the invasion of Russia, was at its height. Even greater efforts were made to win an English-speaking audience, and the British were often portrayed as noble opponents who were foolishly led to oppose Germany – their natural ally. The United States, however, was depicted in harsher colours. Its racial diversity doomed it to decadence from the start, and when America became a belligerent, *Signal* portrayed the United States as purveyors of a new barbarism which threatened to engulf European culture.

Under the command of General Jodl, the Wehrmacht propaganda machine was responsible for the *Signal* project. Major-General Hasso von Wedel ran a sub-department, the foreign unit, which actually worked on journals and magazines. But these men did not possess journalistic professionalism which was provided by a publicity man, Fritz Solm. The Oberkommando der Wehrmacht or German High Command (OKW) chose the name *Signal* largely because it had the same meaning in virtually every European language. The layout was copied from *Life* and no expense was spared in either the launch or its continued publication. The OKW considered *Signal* their brainchild and when paper shortages – indeed shortages of every description – began to be felt in Germany in 1943, Albert Speer, then in charge of the German economy, made certain that the magazine received not only sufficient quantities of paper but the highest quality available. The OKW paid for the publication of *Signal* as well as for the salaries of all the editors, who were army men. The annual bill for salaries alone was estimated at ten million Reichmarks, roughly $2\frac{1}{2}$ million dollars at the prewar exchange rate. Thus money was no object for *Signal* and it sold at comparatively low prices, and in some areas, at least initially, was given away free.

The editorial offices were located in the building of Deutscher Verlag in the Kochstrasse, Berlin. There the editorials were written and the articles and pictures were chosen by a small team of 10-15 editors. The German language edition was a model for the others. There were approximately 120 translators, all of whom were foreigners who voluntarily joined the team. Some had come to Germany before the war; others had joined foreign units in the SS or Wehrmacht and were later transferred to the department. The editor-in-chief checked the foreign texts to make sure they corresponded with the German original. The professional journalists who were on the translating team were dedicated Nazis who believed in their work, which helps to explain the exceptionally high quality of the translations. The editorial staff, ironically, was drawn largely from former employees of the Ullstein publishing firm, whose Jewish connections in the Weimar period and earlier were well known.

Although the magazine had several editors, perhaps the most important was Dr Giselher Wirsing, later editor of the Stuttgart weekly *Christ und Welt*. Wirsing wrote the leading articles in almost every issue from May 1943, although he did not become editor in name until 1945. Franz Hugo Mosslang was in charge of production. After the war he edited the popular illustrated *Quick,* and is now head of the German School of Journalism in Munich.

Many freelance journalists, economists and historians contributed to *Signal* including Professor Dr Heinrich Hunke, later head of the Finance Ministry in Lower Saxony, and Dr Heinz Grauper, now a well-known writer of medical paperbacks. The quality of the articles and the subtlety of their editorial approach were a great help in making *Signal* a best seller. The other outstanding quality was the photography, especially the colour. The war photographs came from PK (Propaganda Company) which followed the soldiers on all fronts. The PK was established by the Wehrmacht in 1938 so that the OKW had its leading war photographs ready when fighting began.

Approximately a thousand cameramen were available to the editors of *Signal*. Working for the propaganda units of the three major armed services, they could be placed in key positions on the front as the German Army advanced through France, the Low Countries and the Soviet Union. Supplied with the latest and most modern equipment available, and with the development of the Agfa-Gevaert colour cameras, *Signal* photographers were allowed generous funds for photographs in colour. Furthermore, ample space was made in the usual 48-page format for colour pages. During the heyday of *Signal* about eight pages of four-colour positioning was allotted, with the use of two-colour on several more pages. As the economic stringencies of the war reduced the number of editions in 1944, the number of colour pages were reduced as well, but in mid-1944 full colour covers were introduced when the specifications of the interior of the magazine were cut. *Signal* still retained a large if declining readers ship even when the number of issues printed in 1944 was reduced. By 1945, with most of Europe already liberated by the Allies, the number of editions in translation which appeared was markedly less than in the peak year of 1943.

Signal was first sent to Hitler's allies; the Italian version came out in April 1940 and the last ally to receive copies in its tongue was Slovakia in July 1942. The French edition which sold as many as 800,000 copies an issue came in 1940 and was followed by versions in English, Danish, Dutch and Norwegian. In 1941 more editions proliferated: Spanish, Bulgarian, Swedish, Hungarian, Rumanian, Croat, Portuguese and Greek. Finally in 1942: Finnish, Slovak, Serbian, Russian, Turkish and Arabic, making 20 foreign editions in all. Although the type was set in Berlin, not all editions were printed there. For instance, the French and English editions were printed in Paris. The English edition, though sent in small quantities to the US before Pearl Harbor and to the Republic of Ireland, only had wide circulation in the Channel Islands of Jersey and Guernsey, occupied in 1940 when France fell.

Signal was never a news magazine. Since it was severely censored with every word studiously poured over by Nazi officialdom, German victories were discussed well after the event. The picture one gets from the early years of *Signal* is that Germany had already won the war. Later, when setbacks were obvious, they were tacitly admitted but disguised as temporary and tactical withdrawals. As the victories slowed to a halt and reverses were suffered, *Signal* devoted itself to more and more gossip about film stars in the Reich, sporting events, theatre and fashion. By 1943 some defeats were reported weeks or even months after they took place, but the contrast with the smiling blonde film stars suggested subtly that despite the reversals all was well in Germany and optimism for inevitable victory still high. In any event, thanks to Allied bombing of Berlin, the editorial team moved to a village some 70 kilometres from the capital. The last issue contained rather cold-blooded forecasts of the future which remind one of the aphorism current towards the end of the war: 'Enjoy your war; peace will be much worse'.

In March 1945 the last issue of *Signal* appeared. The foreign editions had been dwindling in numbers for some time as their markets were absorbed by the advancing Allied forces. Giselher Wirsing managed to organize a special train for the editorial and translating staff and their families, which brought them and their luggage from Berlin to Wattendorf near Bamberg. After all the propaganda they had produced about the barbarous Bolsheviks and the racially impure Americans, they chose to be captured by the Americans on 13 April, 1945. The era of *Signal* had come to an end just a few days before the fall of the Third Reich.

The blitzkrieg in Poland had no *Signal* to publicize it. Hitler had expected the war against Poland to be brief, to be followed by further appeasement on the part of Britain and France in the spirit of the 'phoney war' and ending in Western acceptance of the New Order in Eastern Europe. Despite Germany's peace overtures in October and November 1939, Britain and France refused them. The Propaganda Company was alerted, so that when Operation Weserübung, the attack on Denmark and Norway, was launched in April 1940, photographers would follow the troops on their mission. *Signal* was launched in April 1940 to coincide with Germany's supreme effort in Western Europe. The spring of 1940 and the first issues of *Signal* were the salad days of the Third Reich and its propaganda organ. The easy victory over the Low Countries and France were covered in the grandiloquent manner which Hitler made his trademark. Every aspect of the victories in Scandinavia and Western Europe was covered by *Signal* reporters and photographers, but when the Battle of Britain brought Operation Sealion, the proposed German invasion of the British Isles, to a standstill, *Signal* encountered the kind of problem which the editors in the Kochstrasse faced for the rest of the war.

Defeat in the Battle of Britain was never acknowledged. Anti-British propaganda, played down by the editors of *Signal* in the first months of the publication in the hopes that a peace with Britain might be forthcoming, now was given full vent. There were no fresh victories to publicize in 1940, so the editors were forced to reproduce more stories of the spring blitzkrieg throughout the rest of the year. *Signal* was designed for propagandizing Nazi triumphs. When victories did not materialize, old ones were rehashed, and a more strident, less confident tone appeared. The take-over of the Balkans and Greece provided a shot in the arm to the propaganda team, as so did the early victories in the Soviet Union in 1941. Oddly enough the Desert War was not covered well, even in the offensives of 1941 and 1942, when all seemed to be going well for the Afrika Korps and its Italian ally. The Russian campaign was the over-riding concern of Germany, and it received by far the greatest coverage in the pages of *Signal*.

The turning point in the Desert War, the Battle of El Alamein, was never mentioned in *Signal*. Neither was the long retreat to Tunisia by Rommel's forces. In *Signal* Axis armies were fighting in Cyrenaica. After several months of silence in late 1942, by 1943 they were suddenly in Tunisia. Then, somehow, they were in Italy, another campaign which received scant coverage. When the fight against Britain and America was mentioned, it was largely to indicate the inhumanity of Allied strategic bombing of population centres as well as to encourage fear of the expected terrors of invasion by British and American forces when it came. The strength of the Atlantic Wall was over-emphasized, and by the time D-Day took place in June 1944 *Signal* as well as the Third Reich were already on their last legs. By July 1944 publication of the English and French editions halted and the Paris office of *Signal* was hurriedly closed down as Allied forces approached to liberate the French capital.

The campaign which received more *Signal* coverage than any other was the struggle against Russia. Operation Barbarossa was the blitzkrieg that failed. Preceded by the un-expected takeover of the Balkans, precipitated by Mussolini's attack on Greece, which surprised Hitler as much as the Allies and whose failure forced him to come to the aid of Il Duce, the invasion of Russia was by far and away the most ambitious venture at-tempted by the Third Reich. The easy victories in Poland, Scandinavia, the Low Countries and France had convinced Hitler as well as the General Staff that an attack on Russia would bring as speedy a victory as the successes of 1939-40. *Signal*, which was still praising the Russo-German alliance in March 1941, shifted position rather slowly. But within a fortnight of the invasion of Russia on 22 June, 1941 the initial border clashes were vividly portrayed in black and white and colour by Wehrmacht photographers. The speed and ease of the operation were as daring as *Signal* indicated, and rationales for the invasion were invented by its editors and their masters in the Propaganda Ministry. But as the invasion slowed *Signal* faced a fundamental problem with which they were forced to cope for the balance of the war.

Signal was created as an instrument of boosting the war effort by publicizing German victory to conquered peoples and the army itself. When victory was not forthcoming, former glories were stressed in the absence of fresh battle photographs or victorious portrayals of Nazi troops marching through cities taken recently. The Wehrmacht was stopped before Moscow in December 1941. Despite the ferocity and intensity of the attack on Leningrad, the city did not fall, and held its lines of defense until 1944. Although the summer offensive of 1942 extended German supply lines further in the southern sector or the Ukraine, the Soviet armies held once more in their epic defence of Stalingrad in the last months of 1942. At the end of January 1943 the German Sixth Army was forced to surrender at Stalingrad, the turning point in the European as well as the Eastern war. *Signal* at first glossed over the end of the blitzkrieg offensive. Then it began to stress the heroism of the soldiers on the front who fought on in spite of all difficulties, such as the poor Russian roads and supply-line problems.

But *Signal* expected a great German victory at Stalingrad. Thus the first stages of the battle were widely publicized. The fall of the city to the Soviets was never mentioned and for some months not acknowledged. Then, as the summer of 1943 approached, and a new German offensive was launched at Kursk, Stalingrad was first mentioned in its true context, but only as a temporary setback on the road to victory. Although several photographs of Kursk appeared later, taken in the first stages of the giant offensive which turned out to be the biggest tank battle in history and Germany's greatest defeat, which forced a thousand-mile retreat back to Poland, they were never identified in their proper context. The bitter retreat was also never acknowledged, except in oblique references to the difficulties of fighting in the East.

Signal had lost its *raison d'être*. Editions in some foreign languages were dropped as the readership returned to the bosom of Stalinism. The editors, starved for news that they could publish, resorted to long, tendentious historical articles about the first years of the war or German or Prussian victories in other eras. When an Allied landing was expected in the West in 1944, articles meant to strike terror in the hearts of the Germans and French portrayed the Americans as brutal savages who had even destroyed their own country in the Civil War (1861-65) and who would show no mercy on Western Europe. The brutalities of strategic bombing of the RAF and USAAF were shown as an example of indescriminate Allied destruction. Fashions, concerts and other non-military subjects were emphasized as the number of pages in the magazine were reduced when supplies of paper became less readily available.

But *Signal* put a brave face on the increasingly desparate situation, and tacitly admitted Nazi setbacks. Pictures taken in 1941 or earlier were shown as part of 'counter-offensives' in 1944 which were entirely imaginary. Covers in colour were introduced in 1944, but even *Signal's* courageous and inventive editors could not make deprivation and carpet bombing of Germany seem good. The final issues of the magazine, published solely in German by the beginning of 1945, even speculated on the state of the world after the war was over, ironically predicting many of the postwar indelicacies and struggles between the victorious Allies. *Signal*, once the herald of glorious victory, wrote the obituary of the last days of the Third Reich.

Blitzkrieg 1940

Blitzkrieg in the North and West may have caught the neutrals and France by surprise, but *Signal*, like the Wehrmacht, was ready for action. These extracts from the first issues of *Signal* are among the most impressive ever produced by the magazine. Starting appropriately with the Pzkw-IV tank, the most modern armoured fighting vehicle in Germany at that time, with its short 75-mm. gun, it is interesting to note that the principal armoured weapons used in the campaign of May-June 1940 were the Mark I and II. *Signal*, like all good propaganda, is a subtle mixture of truth and fiction. The German allegation, refuted during the war years, that Britain intended to make amphibious landings on the Norwegian coast to block shipments of Swedish iron ore through Norwegian ports, now appears to have been true. The attacks on Norway and Denmark were as much precautionary as they were offensive measures. But the impression *Signal* tried to make of German troops being warmly greeted by their fellow Aryans in the North is belied by the hard fighting against the Norwegian and British forces in rugged terrain.

The conquest of the Low Countries and France in only six weeks beginning on May 10, 1940 was the most stunning and overwhelming victory of the war for the Third Reich. This was the high noon of *Signal*, and the photography and overall coverage of these great events speak for themselves. The PK could not resist a touch of heavy racial progaganda in its coverage of French African and Indo-Chinese prisoners, but the poignancy of the suffering of French civilians is depicted as well. The contrast drawn between the photographs of the German entry into Paris and the text by Captain Sir Basil Liddell Hart, Britain's foremost military historian, describing the German surrender at Compiègne in 1918 is a brilliant touch. In their moment of triumph the Germans were not magnanimous. The class struggle within Britain is said to have contributed to the ignominious retreat from Dunkirk.

The Battle of Britain is hardly mentioned after early August 1940. The pursuit of a Spitfire by an Me-109 was a common enough sight over Britain, but the picture shown by *Signal* was probably faked, since the terrain below indicates that the photograph was taken over France. A fine sarcasm expressed over the destruction of the French Fleet by the Royal Navy to prevent it falling into Nazi hands is followed by an analysis of why World War II was inevitable. It is often forgotten that Germany saw herself as a unifier of Europe in the Napoleonic manner, sweeping away the anomalies of the past and introducing a new era of social justice and equality of opportunity. As in Germany itself, capitalism and its attendant evils are depicted in lurid terms in the pages of *Signal*. Actually, international cartels and their interests in Europe were protected by the Third Reich. Although the German economy was directed by the government, as was almost everything else, monopoly capital worked hand in glove with the authorities. Social reforms were in fact instituted, but the aristocracy of merit never really saw the light of day under the swastika. In France, at least, the aristocracy of blood was supported, and in turn it largely backed the New Order. In Germany itself, the last stand of the old order of the Wilhelmine period was in the hands of the Wehrmacht, where the landed aristocracy still kept its influence. Hitler, jealous of any institution which was not completely controlled by him, was busily undermining the independence of the Army by creating the Waffen-SS.

In monetary policy, Hitler wanted to link every currency in Europe to the Reichsmark. Gold, the recognised international standard for centuries, is the enemy of the imperialism of any paper currency. Therefore gold is attacked by *Signal*, for in the period between the two world wars and during the war, there was a significant gold drain to the United States. But in monetary policy as in all other things, the Third Reich was supreme in Europe in 1940 and Hitler was its overlord. Berlin was the

Knights of our times...

Tank units, mobile, fast and hard-hitting, and directed by wireless from headquarters, attack the enemy. This armoured machine paves the way to victory, flattening and crushing all obstacles and spitting out destruction

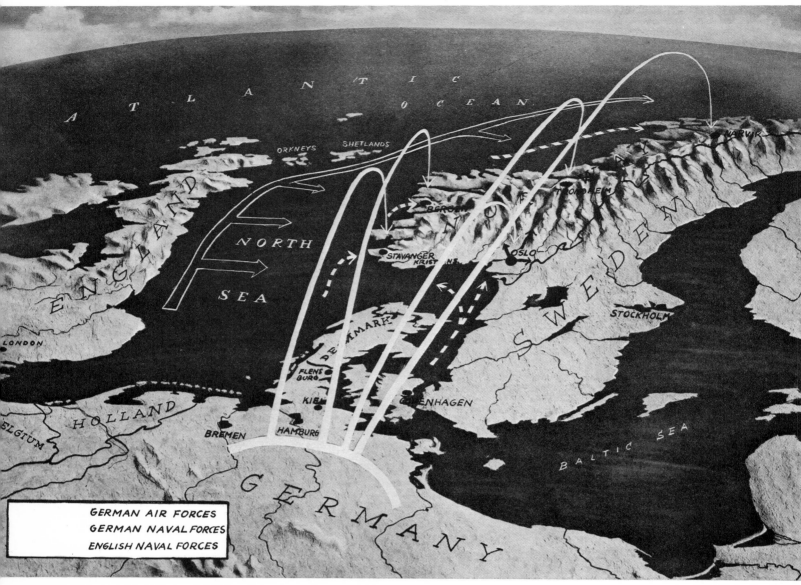

GERMAN AIR FORCES
GERMAN NAVAL FORCES
ENGLISH NAVAL FORCES

This was the course of our lightning expedition to Denmark and Norway which was too quick for the British invasion

Long before the 9th April English freighters had been bringing war material to Norwegian harbours. After that England proceeded to lay mines in Norwegian territorial waters and on the 9th April English troopships accompanied by units of the Royal Navy were already on their way to land in Norway. Then there was the sudden roar of German fighter machines over Norwegian aerodromes, and German warships appeared suddenly in the entrances of the harbours of Oslo, Bergen and Narvik, being followed by troopships. The most important points were occupied like lightning by German troops. At the same time German forces also took over the defence of Denmark against any attempts at invasion by the English. The map shows the progress already made in occupying the country immediately after the 9th April

Ten hours too soon

The last parade before the enterprise

The officers and men of a German landing party have their tasks exactly explained to them before going into action; their eyes eagerly follow every movement of the officer's lips

German flying units arrive

Units of the German air force appeared at dawn on the 9th April over Norwegian territory; they came to reconnoitre, and to transport material, and to employ force in the event of resistance

In Denmark also

Bodies of troops were landed from troopships, and co-operated with the detachments, which marched in from the south. The troops were ready in field-service order for landing

Marines to the front!

The advance detachments of marines in their blue uniforms were the first to land, and began with the systematic occupation

At 3,30 a. m. on the 9th April in the office of the German Embassy in Oslo, the First Secretary von Neuhaus was awaiting the Ambassador Dr. Bräuer. He entered the room with instructions that had been brought from Berlin by special courier

At 5 a. m. acting according to these instructions the German Ambassador proceeded as plenipotentiary of the Reich to the Norwegian Foreign Office, to hand over the memorandum of the German Government

The first German aeroplanes having appeared over Oslo and landed at 10 a. m., the first troops arrived about 2 p. m. before the premises of the German Embassy, and mounted guard there

OSLO
9th April

The new German military plenipotentiary for Norway, General von Falkenhorst, discussed with the German Ambassador and plenipotentiary of the Reich the measures to be taken for the defence of Norway

At 3 p. m. the main body of the German troops marched into Oslo. At the same time other Norwegian towns such as Bergen, Trondheim, and Kristiansand were occupied. The German soldiers systematically advanced into the country from the towns

On 10th April, one day after the German army had taken over the defence of Norway against the intended aggression of the Western Powers, complete quiet reigned in the capital of the country. Life went on in the usual manner, and in the parks the inhabitants were enjoying their spring sunshine

On the way over
Mountain riflemen detailed for service in Norway being instructed in the use of swimming-jackets

Hastening towards the destination
A divine fighter machine flying to Hamar

A centre of interest
Here we see a motorised unit resting and how heartily the German troops and Danish population are associating together

Photographed on April 12 in the morning
King Christian of Denmark enjoying his usual morning ride in the streets of Copenhagen

IN COPENHAGEN

A familiar sight these days in Oslo: German infantry is landed

Large German troop-ships arrive in the Norwegian harbours in a ceaseless stream. Soldiers, arms, and ammunition pour forth from the ships. For the first time German troops land on Norwegian soil; they are on guard against England as far as the Arctic Circle

England's Plans Frustrated

Pictures of the Occupation of Norway

Crowds line the roads to see . . .

German troops march through the Norwegian capital. New weapons, German songs and unfamiliar music arouse their interest. They know now that these well-disciplined colums have not come to oppress and besiege them, and that a great power is behind them

All coastal batteries are surrendered

Coastal defence against attacks by English air and naval forces is taken over by the Germans in systematic cooperation with Norwegian military officials

At army headquarters

Here the Commander is explaining plans to his staff with the aid of a map. He gives the orders for the advance towards the west and north. Messages come and go. Orders are given—in short, headquarters are the brains of the army

With his automatic pistol cocked . . .

A soldier on the lorry guards his comrades on the march. The enemy lurks on the roads, in the dense woods and on the steep rocks. Isolated Norwegian groups, uninformed of the political situation, continued to resist the Germans

High above the reefs and fjords:
A German sentry before a Norwegian coastal fort

Tanks thundering forward
On the road from Oslo to Sönefoss they light on battlements and trenches, and meet with resistance . . .

In Norway's fjords, on rocky coast and islands:

Everywhere German soldiers are on guard, all coast batteries, even beyond the Northern Polar Circle, are fully manned and ready for the enemy

German anti-aircraft guards the air regions over Norway

The eyes of the men at the fast-firing guns follow the horizon tirelessly from West to North, peering through the breaks in the clouds — ready day and night for enemy flyers

Under the German war flag

The crews of the coast fortifications communicate constantly by means of safety signs, blinklights or radio

On guard
in the North

When evening falls on Norway's fjords...

comes the most dangerous hour of the day. The attentiveness of the men at the guns
becomes still sharper, for this is just the time when enemy flyers often attempt an attack

There has been shooting...

A special correspondent in Norway describes the fight for a burning village occupied by the enemy:

A German tank halts at the entrance to the village . . .

Its advance covered by a tank, an infantry detachment proceeds Toward the suspected village. There has been some shooting. Houses are burning, having been set on fire by Norwegian troops. Every nerve is strained. Have enemy forces established themselves here for defence? The detachment halts, and gets well under cover . . .

The advance becomes more cautious . . .
The men jump from fence to fence, from yard to yard, with their fingers continually on the triggers of their guns. Apart from the collapsing of the red walls and roofs and from the crackling of the fire, there is nothing to be heard . . .

Then there is more shooting . . .
Enemy machine-guns are shooting out of a half collapsed barn. The detachment immediately gets into position, and its leader sights the enemy gives an abrupt signal and . . .

Right through a hell of smoke, heat and snow . . .

the German soldiers take this nest of resistance by assault at the point of the bayonet. The enemy is taken prisoner and disarmed

After the fight: „Rally"

The village is free of the enemy and the advance can continue. The detachment rallies behind its tank at the entrance of the village on the other side, and continues its march in the direction ordered. The small isolated bodies of Norwegian troops continue falling back

Holland

The German march over the Dutch, Belgian and Luxemburg frontiers began along a wide front on May 10 in order to forestall England and France. The first decisive breach was made with the storming of Fort Eben Emael. Holland capitulated after 5 days. The Maginot Line was pierced along a front of 100 kilometers in length. German tank divisions thrust through France rapidly as far as Abbéville, Boulogne and Calais and then turned East. In the North the Shelde River positions were overpowered. The Belgian army capitulated on the 18th day. Just as in the case of Poland, a new type of weapon and corresponding tactics decided the outcome.

The flying artillery completed its task: *On May 10, the German Air Force systematically destroyed 72 Dutch, Belgian and French airports, and demolished several hundred enemy planes on the ground (picture above) thus assuring German supremacy in the air from the first day of the campaign. This air supremacy is the preliminary condition for the ensuing air attacks on the enemy's reinforcements, and for successful reconnaissance work*

Lightening action of parachute troops. *They occupy important airports and make it possible for air units to land. They also prevent the destruction of bridges and railway junctions on the German roads of advance. They interfere and confuse the enemy forces behind the front*

Belginm in 18 days

Man after man they fall out of the thundering machines ... *The planes fly in close formation, engines throttled, over the jumping place. The men jump in quick succession so that the group reaches the ground in as close a formation as possible*

Head first toward the ground. *The planes are especially equipped for parachute jumping (picture at right). The body has only one wide door opening without doors. The parachutist uses the handles to give himself more clearance in making the jump. The first few seconds of the jump are a free drop — then the parachute opens*

On a bridge in Rotterdam. *A parachute with ammunition is salvaged*

In a Rotterdam street: *Reinforcement material has been landed by parachute*

On a roof in Rotterdam: *A parachute sharpshooter levelling his gun*

Buildings of tactical importance *at road crossings are at once occupied by the parachutists and taken under fire from vantage points*

Rotterdam on fire: *Sections of the retiring Dutch army erected barricades all over the city, making it a stronghold of resistance. German "stukas" therefore attacked the city and broke down all resistance*

An emissary arrives: *Rotterdam has surrendered*

The tanks roll on. *Skirmishing tanks and light armoured units are already on the other side. The heavy tanks follow on ferries built by the engineers*

In five days:
Advance to the Belgian-French frontier

Strong armoured units gather on May 14 at the Maas River crossings while the infantry is still engaged in widening the bridgeheads. The tank battle begins — the greatest in the history of this modern weapon. Between the 14th and the 28th of May the towns of Dinant, Givet, Valenciennes, St. Quentin and Abbéville fell in rapid succession. The shores of the Channel were reached

The great tank battle in France

For the first time in this war *strong units of German and French tanks meet. The German attack is assisted by the "stuka" planes (diving fighters). Heavy anti-aircraft is also put into action and subdues the enemy by direct firing*

Air view of the tank battlefield. *Ruined French tanks cover the field as far as the eye can see*

above: **Way for the storming party**

A passage has been made in the wire closure by a concentric charge. At the same moment when it explodes the German skirmishing party charges forwards, and before the enemy realizes what has happened hand-grenades are already bursting in the enemy position

below: **There is no means of coping with the flame**

The sapper has worked his way right up to the wire obstacles protecting the m. g. po tion. A few spurs of flame and the deadly stream of burning oil has put the versary out of action. The flame throwers must be fearless men with nerves of st

Sedan in flames

After the German occupation French artillery bombarded the town setting whole streets on fire

The first coloured photographs
of the
great battle in the west

**The enemy's
lines of retreat — Germany's lines of advance**

Burnt-out motor-cars, abandoned equipment, broken glass and rags . . . . On the roadside thousands of French prisoners, an assortment of the coloured races of the earth

In the far north *an aeroplane is circling above the snow-covered landscape. Men jump from the machine, parachutes open — reinforcements for the brave men in Narvik* P. K. Böttcher

The soldier with the camera

Unexampled documents from the Propaganda Companies

II. The unknown P. C. man

Many people will have wondered how it is possible that detailed P. C. reports can be read or vivid eye-witness accounts can be heard on the wireless on the day following an event which has occured several hundred miles inside enemy country.

The deeds of the men who make these things possible deserve to be recounted. One example may serve for many:

A mixed reporter unit belonging to a Propaganda Company had been detailed for duty with an advancing tank division. The open, unprotected cars contrasted strangely with the armoured reconnaissance cars and tanks, but the unit, in spite of the fact that its cars were by no means meant for cross-country driving, kept well up with the foremost troops. The French front had been successfully penetrated. The advance into the hinterland was proceeding rapidly. In the evening, the division was more than 60 miles ahead of the old front.

The oral reporter belonging to the unit had taken advantage of a short halt to describe the manner in which the line had been penetrated and to outline the victorious events of the day. The two photographers had "shot" 15 spools of Leica films, and 8 spoken folios by the wireless reporter were also ready, descriptions of the course of the battle and the questioning of prisoners which provided much useful information. All that remained to do now was to convey this material to the rear. Eightly miles back through the darkness!

. . . advancing into France! *Columns of German troops marching along the roads of Artois, Burgundy and the Ile de France . . . pictures as such as this one, which in itself has no tense dramatic element. nevertheless convey the swinging rhythm of the great historical event* P. K. Huschke

The war is over for him. *The poilu has left his giant of steel and goes towards the German infantrymen with upraised arms. They have silenced his "firebreathing fortress". Human courage is harder than steel—the picture convincingly symbolizes this truth*   P. K. Utecht

Everything goes well for the first few miles. Now and again the motorcyclist despatch rider encounters supporting units belonging to his division and piquets from his own troop. After half an hour he is alone. There is no sound but the roar of his engine. A village is burning a long way off. For miles the road runs straight as a die towards it. The leaping flames throw a ghostly light across the road.

He has now reached the entrance to the village. The heat is tremendous. He must make his way through. Part of the village is still undamaged. An ambulance car is drawn up in front of a small farm. He stops and asks for water. He is given a glass of wine. He asks if there are any French in the neighbourhood. None have been seen. He sets off again along the straight road! Suddenly an invisible power knocks the handle-bars out of his hands. He is thrown from the cycle. His machine lands in a ditch. He slowly pulls himself together, quite shaken by his fall. His hands are bleeding. His machine is undamaged as is also the courier's bag with the reports. He switches on his torch. He had crashed into a dead horse.

After another three miles, he is subjected to fire from the left. Lights out and full throttle! Suddenly he hears a huge crashing and rending a few hundred yards in front of him. The French have just blown up the bridge. He jams on the brake, leaps from his machine which he pushes up to a brush by the side of the road and takes cover. He hears voices. He releases the saftey-catch of his rifle. The voices die away in the distance.

With his courier's bag across his shoulder, he resumes his road after half an hour's wait. He leaves his motorcycle behind for the time being, and goes reconnoitring. The bridge has been completely demolished. The river is more than thirty yards wide. He tests how deep it is with a plank which he makes loose. It is impossible to wade through. He creeps under

Britain's departure from the Continent. *The roads along which the British retreated towards the Channel ports were lined by tall pillars of smoke; towns and villages belonging to their "Allies" were pillaged and set on fire*
P. K. Schmidt

Rouen in flames. *The French fought desperately to hold the opposite bank of the Seine at Rouen, but the bastions were forced and the burning town was captured*
P. K. Wehlau

The spectacle of "total" war. *After Warsaw, it was Rotterdam that, issuing a challenge, learned how hopeless it was to resist the German Luftwaffe —and paid for the lesson by the destruction of the centre of the city* P. K. Carstensen

The tanks storm forward: *The streets of Orleans are cleared of the enemy* P. K. Kipper

The roads of the vanquished. *Who could look at this scene in a mighty tragedy without feeling deeply moved? Refugees making their way homewards hurry past the never-ending columns of prisoners. The boy on the perambulator who is tired to death causes the prisoners to forget for a moment their own fate*   P. K. Weber

a bush behind the embankment of the bridge and gets out his map and his torch. The nearest bridge is five miles away. It lies to the right of the road. The voices which he had just heard had gone off towards the left . . .

The magic of weapons. *A huge mortar during the battle. It towers up in the smoke of the battle-field like some prehistoric monster*   P. K. Bauer

Back to the motor cycle. He stows the bag away in the side-car. But he does not dare to start the engine. He is afraid of betraying his whereabouts. The French cannot be very far off yet. So he pushes his machine the 300 yards down to the blown-up bridge. Then he turns to the right and follows the course of the river. The dawn is beginning to break in the east.

A frightful moment? No: psychological moment. *As the German troops reach an enemy cupola a shell bursts. The PK man—takes first his photo and then cover*   P. K. Grimm

He starts his engine and drives off. He reaches the next bridge in a quarter of an hour. It is undamaged, sentries are posted on the other side of the bridge. He is just about to shout to them, when he sees that they are French. Without increasing his speed he drives on through the village. It is occupied by the enemy, but nobody recognizes him. He turns off the left and comes on to the main road. There is movement here: a column on the march, pushing its way forward. German soldiers! He is safe. He makes his report to the first officer whom he encounters and an hour later he has reached the information centre of his company. He has carried out his instructions . . .

The hand of death. *A German bomber has challenged a British motor torpedo-boat. The crew has left the ship after a number of M. G. bursts. Their boat is heading towards the coast which lies at a distance of six miles. Bombs now rain down—the next, a direct hit amidships, sends the vessel to the bottom of the sea* P. K. Wundshammer

Captured in the inferno of Dunkerque. *Exhaustion and hopelessness have furrowed the face of this British soldier* P. K. Titz

Compiègne — the last act! *At the spot where in November 1918 the conditions of a humiliating armistice were dictated to Germany in a most offensive manner, the German guard of honour parades in June 1940 at the commencement of the historic ceremony which for ever obliterated the "crime of Compiègne"* P. K. Borchardt

Historical Hours Around Paris

In his book "Foch, the Man of Orleans", the famous English author Liddel Hart describes the decisive hours in the Wood of Compiègne in November 1918 in following words

The first half-hour of the 7th November had barely elapsed when Foch received a radio message from the German High Army Command giving the names of the negotiators and requesting that a meeting-place should be named. The message went on: "The German Government would be pleased if the arrival of the German Delegation could be made the occasion of a temporary cessation of hostilities, in the interests of humanity." Foch disregarded this request and simply invited the Germans to come to the outposts of the Debeneys front.

July 14, 1919: The Triumph of France

The victors of the World War 1914/18 march under the Arc de Triomphe. On top, the "Conqueror of the Marne", General Joffre and Commander-in-Chief Foch

June 14, 1940: Marching-in of the Germans in Paris

A German train section crosses the Place de l'Etoile in front of the Arc de Triomphe. On the foreground an anti-tank gun

March 1, 1871: The Victorious German Troops Marching into Paris

Bismarck ordered that most of the troops should not march under the Arc de Triomphe but besides of it. An armistice was stated under the condition that the town of Paris was to be occupied by German forces until the conditions of peace were accepted by the National Assembly

The Marshal took Wemyss and Weygand aside for a moment to examine the credentials, signed by Prince Max of Baden, by which Erzberger, Count Oberndorff, Major-General von Winterfeldt and Captain Vanselow were given full powers to negotiate an armistice, and to arrive at an agreement subject to the assent of German Government. Two somewhat younger officers completed the deputation.

After the papers had been inspected the Marshal took his place at the table, with Weygand on his right, Wemyss on his left. Erzberger sat opposite Wemyss and Winterfeldt opposite Foch. True to his principles, Foch took the initiative by asking: "What is the purpose of your visit? What do you want from me?" Erzberger replied politely that he had come to receive proposals from the Allied Forces regarding the signing of an armistice. "I have no proposals to make."

Taken aback by such an answer, the Germans maintained silence. Finally Count Oberndorff asked: "How shall we express ourselves? We are not bound to observe any particular form. We are ready to say that we wish to learn the conditions of an armistice." "I can name no conditions."

Erzberger now began to read out the note of President Wilson. Foch quickly interrupted him: "Do you wish to request an armistice? If so, please say so . . . formally." "Yes, that is so, we desire an armistice."
„Very well, then we will read out to you the conditions under which it may be granted."

Weygand now read the chief clauses out, and they were translated one after another. Grave and immobile, Foch sat there listening. Now and again he tugged sharply at his moustache. Wemyss toyed with his monocle. Winterfeldt's face revealed increasing dismay.

When Weygand had finished, Erzberger proposed that military operations might cease immediately. The revolution had broken out, and the soldiers would no longer obey. He feared that Bolshevism would overrun Central Europe, and should that occur, it would be very difficult for Western Europe to avoid being affected. The German Government needed to be relieved of the pressure of the Allies, in order to restore discipline in the Army and order in the land.

At 5 p. m. Foch, accompanied by Admiral Wemyss, left Senlis in a special train for Rethondes which lies in the Forest of Compiègne. The train was shunted on to a siding which had been built for the heaviest rail artillery. Foch retired into his sleeping-car. It was not until 7 a. m. the following morning that the other train slowly glided up alongside. The Germans had been held up by barriers after emerging from their own lines. Weygand climbed up on to the train and informed them that Foch would receive them at 9 o'clock or shortly afterwards.

When the Delegation appeared at the appointed time in the saloon car, they were received by Weygand and Admiral Hope stiffly but politely. Weygand said that he would inform the Marshal. A few minutes later Foch appeared, accompanied by Admiral Wemyss. The officers saluted one another. The stern face of the Generalissimo betrayed no sympathy for the humiliated enemy. Erzberger received from him the impression of a small man, full of vitality, whose first glance revealed that he was accustomed to command. Erzberger, speaking in low tones, presented his suite, upon which Foch remarked briefly: "Have you any papers, gentlemen? We must verify your credentials."

Sixty - Nine Years Ago
Barricades on the Grand Boulevard. To day the Parisians had prepared entirely for street-fights against the German troops. In 1871 these sort of barricaeds were erected by the Government against the Parisian mob

Twenty-two Years Ago
"What's the purpose of your visit?" "What do you want of me?" With this words general Foch and his staff received the German delegation in his Pullman Car in the Forest of Compiègne. General Weygand (second from left) read aloud the conditions of the Armistice of the Allies

This reference to the internal conditions in Germany came as a revelation to Foch. Facts began to give support to his belief . . . and his bluff. Harshly he rejected Erzberger's proposal. "You suffer from an illness which only attacks the loser. I am not afraid of it. Western Europe will find ways and means of averting the danger."

Winterfeldt now produced a paper and declared that he had been charged by the Government and the High Army Command with a special duty. He read out the paper, the wording of which was: "The armistice conditions of which we have just learnt, require careful consideration. In view of the fact that it is our intention to arrive at an understanding, this examination of the conditions will be completed as soon as possible; nevertheless, this will require a certain time. During this time hostilities between our Armies will continue and many victims will be claimed as much amongst the soldiers as amongst the civil population. They would fall needlessly at the last minute, although their lives could be spared for the benefit of their families." In short, the German Government and the Army Command repeated the proposal that hostilities should cease.

Awaiting the Parade on the Avenue Foch
I mounted-band in front of the Arc de Triomphe, awaiting the beginning of the march

Burning Oil Tanks in the Northern Paris
Heavy smoke clouds witness the activity of German Dive bombers still after the marching in of the German Forces

Life in Paris Is Going On
The day after the capitulation of the city. Parisians at the Champs Elysées are observing the approaching cars of the German reinforcements

Compiègne in June 1940
German soldiers in the Memory Hall, looking into the Pullman car of generallissimo Foch. In this car the German negotiators got the conditions-of-armistice on November 7, 1918

Foch replied inexorably: "No. I represent here the Allied Governments, who have laid down their conditions. Hostilities cannot cease before the armistice has been signed."

"Would it be at least possible to prolong the present truce by twenty-four hours? We need time to communicate with our Government."

"We will grant you facilities as regards contact with your government, but the time has been decided upon by our Governments and cannot be prolonged. It amounts to 72 hours and will expire on Monday, 11th November at 11 a.m."

Defenders of —

French culture

Even during the war of 1914—18 France used coloured troops to defend her interests. The continual annual decrease of population of the country was at that time such that the French Army could not be kept up to strength. Even for the occupation of the Rhineland black troops had to be called upon. And again today France confronts German soldiers with her coloured troops: Berbers, Moroccans, Arabs, Senegalese and Bantu negroes, Cingalese — a variegated mixture of peoples and races

A view across the Avenue Foch during the parade on the occasion of the troops' entry into Paris

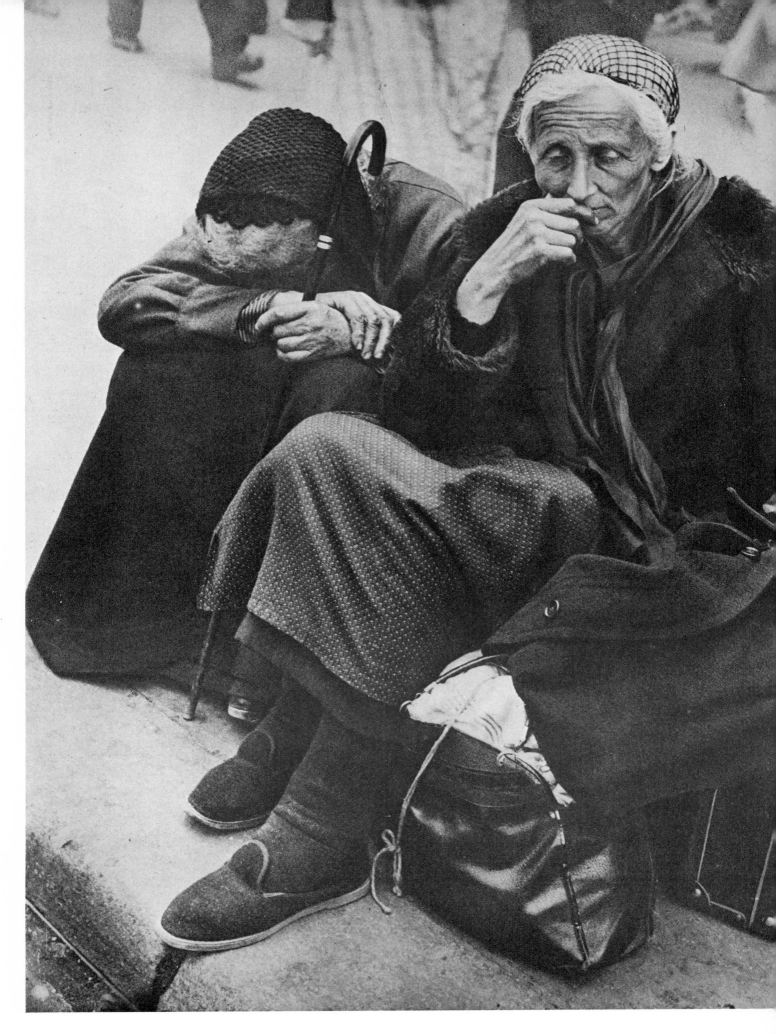

These poor old women, driven from hearth and home by ruthless propaganda, haunt the highways of France

Just as in times of absolute peace the Parisians are sitting in front of the cafés in the Champs-Elysées drinking their apéritifs. Among them are German soldiers, and the population of the capital of France seems to have become accustomed to seeing them

PARIS, 24 hour after the occupation

Regiments of Poilus and their coloured auxiliaries
proceeding between the famous arcades in the Rue de Rivoli and the Louvre on their way to the prisoners of war camp

A Mars-la-Tour veteran
this old Parisian who fought in the war of 1870 is conversing with a German corporal

An experience which many Parisians have not had: ascending the Eiffel Tower
German soldiers taking the first opportunity of getting a bird's eye view of Paris, which has been left intact

Poilus who have been taken prisoner — at liberty
The German speaking Alsatians taken prisoner in Paris have received permission from the German command to proceed alone to the rallying camps. Their relatives accompany them on the way

Paris policemen and German military
The unaccustomed sight in their streets causes the Parisian policemen controlling the traffic to have a good look at the German soldiers

In the cloud-covered sky over England

The same spectacle every day: A M
The R.A.F. pilot dives in an attempt

tt fighter has discovered a Spitfire and steers towards it. The British plane, from being the pursuer, now becomes the pursued.
but the Messerschmitt follows, hurtles towards him, spraying him with machine-gun fire until the enemy plane crashes to the ground

The Road
to
Dunkerque

*On the Structure
of English Society*

It is a hot June afternoon in London. Heat-waves rise from the sea of houses and rob the sun's rays of their wholesome effect. We are standing in the stifling, sooty hall of Waterloo Station waiting for a train which will take us out to a spot somewhere between green fields. Suddenly two trains arrive at the same instant, one on either side of the platform. An invisible hand opens all the doors as though with a single turn of the wrist, and immediately two streams of men begin to merge into one another and pour from the platform out into the main hall of the station—two very different groups indeed: one train emits a dark stream of workers—dirty, sweaty, tired and dejected—the other a bright stream of gay gentlemen, with light, measured step, in grey cut-aways and grey top-hats, white spats, small silver-knobbed walking sticks in their hands, their monocles dangling from ribbons, flowers in their button-holes.

These two streams join for an instant, then separate again. The gloomy men trudge home to their dismal quarters on heavy legs; the gay gentlemen stride towards the long row of limousines parked outside. Those were rather tense moments for us as the two groups mingled and jostled together. With so much provoking elegance brushing against them we were afraid that one of these sullen-looking men might give vent to his feelings and quite unnoticed rub a small blotch of grease on one of these immaculate cut-aways, creating a critical situation. But nothing of the sort occured. All of these men drew back from the gay gentlemen to a respectful distance and hardly glanced at them. Two castes — each one untouchable by the other: the men in overalls and the gentlemen returning to their town palaces from the races in Ascot ...

A young English student tells us his tale of woe. He had been living for two years in an Oxford college—not one of the very old and famous ones, to be sure, but nevertheless a real college—and in spite of his unusual qualities as a sportsman he had not succeeded in getting a place in one of the first teams. And why not? Because he didn't "belong". Not because he didn't have the financial means which Oxford demands of one, if one wishes to keep in the run socially; his father, a major-

general in the British army, had not skimped with his education. He had seen to it that he had attended the fest schools and travelled abroad; he was intelligent and industrious; he had those pleasing, polished, rather reserved manners which we have come to recognize as characteristic of a gentlemen. Nevertheless, as he pointed out to us, he was not considered as such. This annoyed him not so much for his own sake, as he had enough stamina to build up his life on his own responsibility, but because the injustice which he had experienced caused him to worry about the future of his country, and because he saw that in this way many able youths were prevented from getting on. We asked him what requirements must be fulfilled by a young man before he is admitted to this chosen circle.

"You must have graduated from one of the public schools—the source of all bliss—Harrow, Eton or Rugby, perhaps a few others," he answered, "and then again you are accepted only if you belong to one of the families which go to make up 'society'. You are either

born a gentleman or you have practically no hope of becoming one."

This statement sounded rather embittered and one-sided to us and we would have preferred to take it with a pinch of salt. In this connexion we recalled a delightful reply which we had recently received from a learned scholar. He had been citing many examples of English statesmen, both living and dead, pointing out to us that political ability in England was always founded on a thorough, in fact, often even on a specialist's conversance with classical antiquity. When we tried to shake his faith in this theory by mentioning the case of Ramsay Mac Donald, who certainly did no dishonour to British statesmanship, although he had never attended a classical university, he answered, "Yes, but MacDonald had a clas-

sical soul." And so we expressed hypothetically to our student the consoling possibility that perhaps eventually one might be admitted to this chosen circle if one had what one might call the soul of a gentleman. But we were disappointed. "To have the soul of a gentleman", our young complainant replied, "you must be enormously rich."

Of course he exaggerated very much in his youthful indignation, our young social critic from Oxford, for it is generally known that newly-gained wealth, no matter how great it might be, is by no means an "open sesame" to the portals of English society; not even when it is used to court admission in the form of openly extravagant endowments. As, for instance, the failure of Courtauld, the artificialsilk king, in obtaining the longed-for title of nobility, in spite of his having enriched the public art collections of England with a great number of magnificent masterpieces of French painting, which he had gathered together in the Tate Gallery, built by himself. Those bitter words of our young student were not completely unjustified, however, for it has often happened during the past decades that industrialists have been ennobled, meaning that by the grace of the King, they have been given a position of equal rank with the ancient families. Louis Philippe's classical answer to the lower French bourgeoisie who were grumbling about their being politically neglected: *Enrichissezvous!"* (then you will also "belong"—one must add in one's imagination) remains as an unexpressed challenge to those who were not born gentlemen.

And we can well believe another statement of our disappointed Oxford man because it has been verified by many other observations. The dividing line between the "gloomy" and the "gay" classes is found much higher up in the social scale than we on the Continent are accustomed to think of it, namely, above that which the English call the upper middle class—what we would term the "best-situated bourgeoisie". There is something strange in connexion with this—in English there is no original word for "bourgeoisie". Whatever lies between the leading families and the lower classes is simply classified as "the middle classes"—a sign that the Englishman himself considers the social structure of his country as hierarchy in form with the definitions upper—lower—middle. In such a system there is of course no room for that unique class-consciousness which is peculiar to the patrician families of the German cities and which has produced its own special traditions.

The contrary would also be wrong, that is, to put the leading classes on the same level as the aristocracy, thereby placing English nobility on a parallel with that of continental countries. Prussian nobility and army service are inseparable, whereas among the ancestors of the present peers (not to mention the gentry—the lower aristocracy) only a few are yet to be found who owe their titles to soldierly merits. The number of aristocratic families which can trace their lineage back to the period of knighthood is also very small. As far as pedigree is concerned, the Duke of Norfolk is the leading English duke in spite of the fact that in his family his title dates only from the year 1483. A typical illustration of the contrary, however, is the case of the Cecil family's rise to power, whose famous ancestor descended from country landowners. Some of them gained great influence in the service of the State under Queen Elizabeth, and since then members of the family have repeatedly succeeded in obtaining influential positions, the best known case being that of the Marquis of Salisbury.

We shall be better able to understand the character of the upper classes, if we consider the elements of which Parliament is composed. According to tradition this is divided into the House of Lords and the House of Commons, the latter representing the middle-classes (comparable to the "third estate" in France before the Revolution). In reality, however, the lower gentry has always been predominant in the House of Commons and even since the franchise was officially made democratic, their class has succeeded in keeping the leadership in Parliament. Above all it has created that grandfatherly, cautious, carefully rounded system of speeches, procedures, and technicalities which makes the parliamentary forms of address such a difficult jargon to learn, and which leaves the outsider in an atmosphere of ceremoniousness that he can hardly penetrate. And so the House of Commons has remained a "club for gentlemen", as someone has pointedly said—of course the word "gentleman" is not used in this case to express a moral criterion but only to denote that magical circle of those who have established the "rules of the game" and who act according to them.

"The rules of the game"—that is primarily the spirit which prevails over the upper classes in England. We on the continent are accustomed to each class fulfilling certain definite duties, which are at all times recognizable in their moral significance for the good of the community as a whole. Hence we are inclined to consider the word "gentleman" as implying as sort of moral ideal which the members of the upper classes live up to with more or less

success, but which in any case everyone holds in mind as a duty even though it be only in the form of a warning conscience. As a matter of fact, one supposes in this connexion that the English posses a keener sense of and readiness for self-criticism than is really the case. There are of course exceptions. Just as the essence of the service in the Anglican Church (to which the majority of the upper classes belong) is not so much the stirring sermon reminding one of the seriousness of life's problems, as the impersonal magical service of the Holy Sacrament and the Liturgy; the wordly life of those belonging to high society is likewise essentially the fulfilment of their duties only in the empty form of behaviour according to unbreakable rules of the "game". One does something or leaves it undone because it is or is not customary. Why it is good form is just as little to be delved into as it would be unseemly to question the infallibility of the Bible. From November to March is the season for fox-hunting; accordingly one has to go fox-hunting. Receptions at court, garden-parties, horse-races, cricket or rowing matches are hardly different from going to church—ceremonies into which the personal element scarcely enters, and in the performance of which one finds something like the peace resulting from having a good conscience.

Even their exclusiveness is one of the rules of the game. One is not exclusive in a pharisaical way because one considers himself better than the others (such a pharisaical attitude is rather a characteristic of the Englishman—in fact even far below the "middle classes"—compared with other people), but merely because there "must" be such a distinguished caste. One groans perhaps under the calendarlike monotony and excessiveness of social obligations, but one shudders at the thought of ridding oneself of them by taking a daring jump into a life of one's own as if it were a crime to do so. For the members of the middle classes it may be a pleasure or a hobby to engage in sports during their free time, to go to the opera or to visit each other. For the gentleman, however, the relation of duty and pleasure is differently proportioned. Military service, political activity, scientific work, all that belongs to the private sphere of the individual. Fox-hunting on the contrary, Ascot and the Covent Garden Opera during the "Season" in June, that is duty of a higher order, service for the welfare of a class which embodies the eternal life of England, the existence of which would be extinguished by the mere omission of a single one of its regular obligations—one is tempted to say of its sacraments.

The other classes of society may not be clearly conscious of these conceptions, but even the lowest members of society have at least an idea of them. Otherwise such an experience as the one we had at Waterloo Station would not be possible. Otherwise it would not be possible that in the side-streets off Piccadilly Circus in the evening, when the West-end theatres open their doors, the poorest of the poor stand in the narrow entrances to their homes, and watch with devout shyness the gentlemen in silk evening cloaks and the ladies with peal tiaras, making their way from their parked Rolls-Royces to the entrance of the theatres or elegant cinemas protecting themselves with cautious grandeur from the contact with the dirt of the street and its inhabitants.

Only one class of people are the real outsiders to this hierarchy. Those are they who believe in the arrangement of life according to different laws, such as, for instance, according to the laws of reason or social justice. To these belongs our Oxford student. His way of thinking was not that of a born gentleman (or perhaps not yet).

We shall not expect of a class which has shown hardly any willingness to revise the fundaments of their social structure that they will be able to compete with the onset of a young world. Germany has rearranged its forces in a revolutionary process. Britain reached Dunkerque on the well-worn tracks of its tradition.

Dr Ernst Lewalter

In the stern of the battleship "Bretagne", *which like most of the other French units was lying in the harbour of Oran on the morning of 3rd July 1940. She had been struck by a British 15-inch shell*

A last salvo *has hit amidships and finally has put the turret out of action*

The shameful work is accomplished: *the "Bretagne" heels over and sinks in the waves*

A presumptuous demand that was refused: *The British negotiator leaving the "Dunkerque" after the French Commander had refused to hand over or sink his fleet*

The end in the harbour of Oran, *taken from the deck of the "Dunkerque": under the fire of the British guns the French squadron tries to reach the open sea. In the foreground, the "Provence", behind on the right France's most modern battleship "Strasbourg" which succeeded in breaking through; the ship in flames is the unfortunate "Bretagne"*

The first pictures from

Oran!

The gratitude of the "comrade-in-arms"

A French defeat, the British triumph of Fashoda in 1899, was the overture to the Franco-British *Entente cordiale*, which evoked the Great War — the disgraceful attack on the French squadron at Oran was the end of this alliance which proved to be a catastrophe for France. On the morning of 3rd July 1940 powerful British naval forces appeared in the roadstead of Mers el Kebir, the naval base of Oran and demanded that the French war-ships should be handed over or sunk. The British squadron opened a devastating fire on the French, whose vessels were incapable of manœuvring at this time, the fires having been let out. Only the *Strasbourg* succeeded in breaking through and reaching Toulon. "Inqualifiable and odious" were the words employed in the official French communiqué in referring to this unparalleled, monstrous British crime against an ally of yesterday.

Thus ended the Entente cordiale: *The French squadron commander, Admiral Gensoul, delivers a funeral oration before the coffins of his fallen comrades, killed by British shells*

1914

1919

1941

The peace which could not last

Why 1939 had to follow 1919

"Is Czechoslovakia actually the same as Yugoslavia?"... This question was by no means asked by an 8-year old mission scholar in the Australian bush. No! It was posed by a British peer, a member of the House of Lords, and it was addressed to another peer in the year 1937 after a debate in the House of Lords. The former was not in the least worried about asking the question and the latter saw nothing wrong in repeating it. It would therefore appear that the old adage still holds good that the educated Briton knows more about Africa than Europe. During the great peace conference at Paris in 1919 Lloyd George often opposed the French with their unreasonable demands. The French politicians used then to annoy him by pointing out his lack of knowledge of geography, even in its simplest form. As a matter of fact the French were never very much better in this direction. Bismarck's sarcastic attitude towards the menacing demands made in Paris after 1866 when France declared that she would never tolerate the appearance of the Prussians on the Zuider Zee, was expressed in the following words: "The very fact that the spelling of this word was correctly given in the Paris newspapers is conclusive proof that this was a foreign and not a French suggestion." This was the way in which a man of authority at that time criticized the Frenchmen's knowledge of a European district of comparatively close proximity. In addition to this, in 1919 large numbers of the strangest petitioners insisted on presenting memorandums about the conditions in Bohemia and Moravia, couched in typical Beneš style, with the result that the little knowledge that the "Peace politicians" possessed was completely confused.

*On the left : **30 years'struggle for power*** *In 1914, when the Entente challenged Germany and Austria, diplomatic intrigue had reached its culminating point. In 1919 Germany was oblidged to allow herself to be checkmated at Versailles by a coalition of adversaries, created by Great Britain. The dire necessity of the post-war years was responsible for the rise of a National Socialist Germany. Britain again pressed for war. But this war's trial of strength resulted in the loss of her Allies. In 1941 the fight continues*

*On the right : **"Down with dictated peace"*** *This was the slogan used even in 1919 when the whole population of Germany protested against Versailles*

12,500 miles of new frontiers

In 1919 the new frontiers were all established as a result of lack of knowledge; of petitions of interested parties which could not be verified; of the ambition to make France, by nature and internal strength only a second-class European state, a predominating big power on the Continent; of Great Britain's pressure to limit the danger of France as a big power; and as a result of America's interference with her strange and bigoted theories. At a time when a greater number of people were converging towards the town and industrial areas, and when the rapid development of communications made a grouping of larger communities an urgent matter, if the former standard of living was to be upheld, the frontiers of states and customs were extended by 12,500 miles in a simple session of a few months! Many smaller and new states were created. If these were to exist, they would, to a certain

with flourishing industry and commerce, to become absolutely desolate. As an example, one need only take the neglect of the Corridor area, the decrease of production in that part of Upper Silesia ceded to Poland and the indescribable poverty of the Sudeten countries which had formerly been the seat of three-fifths of the whole of the Austro-Hungarian industry.

This was a particularly impressive example of the fact that the peace dictates were not only unjust in their final constructive decisions but were contrary to living requirements and incapable of existing. It was therefore natural that one day the demands of life would become the revisors of this enforced structure. This we experienced in Czechoslovakia. As a country, its position became untenable as soon as Germany had regained her normal healthy condition. In the early years after the creation of this state the Germans embodied in it were paying something more than 60 % of all its taxes; in the last years of the crisis they were still paying 40 %. In addition to this, and in spite of all efforts to the contrary, nearly half of the exports (46 %) from Czechoslovakia were sent to the Reich and Austria. If the amount is calculated that the Germans in the interior of the country paid in taxes together with the quantity of exported goods delivered to Germans outside the country, the total yearly sum amounted to double as much as the already very high military budget of Czechoslovakia. As a result people of German origin were paying nearly twice over for an army which was being maintained exclusively against them. A mere tax-strike in the interior or a commercial boycott outside would have been sufficient to upset the whole of this flimsy structure. This was the value finally placed on this state even by the British and the French.

Continued

The Peace Delegation behind the fence, a typical illustration of those days, when in 1919 peace was being "negotiated" with the Germans in Versailles

extent, all have had to endeavour to be self-supporting; and for this very reason, they became parasites of Europe's living substance, they lowered the general standard of living and diminished Europe's competitive ability in comparison with more uniform continents such as America. Through the greater number of states the general insecurity was increased to a higher degree, inasmuch as the areas of friction which had originally led to war had now increased more than the total extension of state frontiers. This effect made itself felt at once as soon as the general feeling of exhaustion which followed the Great War began to disappear. When these states started concluding a series of pacts for and against one another, the value of which was shown by the inglorious foundering of the Little Entente. The new frontier demitations caused former areas of great value to the whole of Europe,

1914

1919

1941

With the pressure of the war against Britain, the economic confederation of the European continent practically broke down economic barriers. The commercial treaties and clearing systems from government to government will be the forerunners of a vast European economic network

Leading men of Britain appointed themselves judges of Germany

*A picture from the year 1919 : British plenipotentiaries on their way to the Law Courts in
Leipzig for the trial of the German "War Criminals". This faked trial was part of "Peace".
The Allies were trying to put the blame for the outbreak of war on Germany's shoulders*

Continued

The peace which could not last

Today we are in a position to judge the practical value of the Peace Treaty of 1919. We need no longer worry about the numerous attempts of its originators to back out of their responsibility for an affair which had been of their own making, by condemning it with long-winded justifications. We have witnessed how the bastions of this enforced dictate crumbled away one after another without a gun being fired or a drop of blood being shed. All this was solely brought about by the fact that Germany recovered her inner latent strength and was able to make free use of it. This process of revision through life itself, which was eventually bound to return to its old and unalterable course need never have led to war, had it not been for Britain. As Britain wished to frustrate a sensible revision of Germany's eastern frontiers, and declared war, every serious-minded European was confronted with the gigantic question: Why war? When the last war only resulted in a kind of peace which became the fundamental cause for a fresh war. Do the British want hell on earth again!

What were the British motives for the Great War ?

Wars have been waged in the world's history for causes that could not be settled any other way. The campaign of Prussia against Austria in 1866 is a classical example of such a war, by which any justification of a war can be gauged. Viewed from this aspect, what were the main motives of the French for going to war in 1914? They maintained that their security was menaced by the unity of Germany representing a state of 20 million more inhabitants and a vastly greater productive capacity. If France did not succeed in 1919 in destroying this unity, it was not because she did not want to, but simply because she was incapable of doing so. She achieved just as little success in trying to get rid of 20 million Germans by depriving them of their nationality and handing them over to other states. This act defeated itself as it merely increased the sense of national self-assertion in the German nation. Meanwhile, this continued pressure has, to a great extent, resulted in transform-

ing a Germany of 60 million inhabitants into one solid united state of 80 million Germans.

The war aims of the French were a complete paralysis of Germany as a state. But to achieve this purpose they required the permanent assistance of half of the world, but especially that of Britain and America. As they never could and never will be permanently able to reckon on such assistance in peace-time, they were obliged to shoulder the burden alone of maintaining an adequate organization for the suppression of Germany. But for this they were not strong enough. This overtaxing of their strength undermined the artificial structure of France's preponderance. Since then we have seen the downfall of this giant.

What were the British motives for the Great War? What did they hope to gain from a war with Germany? They wanted to conquer Germany's ever-increasing ascendancy on the Continent and at the same time to eliminate her as a world competitor whose productive and commercial power was beginning to take the upper hand. Did they arrive at their goal? This question is answered by the very fact that after 20 years they considered themselves obliged to take up arms once more for the same cause. The Great War, which had only resulted in a marked weakening of Britain's position relative to America and the rest of the world, did not solve any of those problems which were represented as its aims. Are the problems of Europe as viewed by Britain and France in 1914 any different from those of today? Does this present war, which Britain dared to force upon Germany, offer any prospects of satisfying her most cherished desires? Not at all! The conditions which have been produced by the ever-progressing development of life in Europe are today far more advantageous to Germany and far more disadvantageous to the criminal minds of those who have thought fit to involve Europe in a fresh massacre as a solution of these problems.

Why? Because life, undeterred by peace dictates, has continued in its normal path, and because the whole of Europe still retains fresh in its mind the memory of the brutal attempts forcibly to suppress life. Everyone knows that in such times unemployment increases in all countries, that everything on our continent is closely interwoven and that it is impossible to limit a crisis to any particular country; in other words, how strong is the link of destiny amongst all European nations!

In many small countries the opinion was and is still held that Britain was

a friend of the liberty of nations because of its policy of splitting up the Continent into a number of small states. This applies particularly to certain classes in those countries who are dependent as small fry on what they can earn from Britain's so-called world trade and everything connected with it. But it does not apply to the broader masses and certainly not to those nations who are dependent on a system of close co-operation and extensive grouping for protection against competition in those world markets dominated by Great Britain with cheap nigger and coolie labour. As a result of the last war, during recent decades, world competition has assumed a form which necessitates the acting of European nations in close co-operation with one another, if they are to maintain their existence and their high standard of living. Up to this war Britain's interest consisted in creating buffer states opposite its shores and preventing Europe from ever presenting a united front.

Why is the existence of Germany necessary to Europe ?

Germany's political policy is different. Germany's mode and code of living can never come into conflict with the general order of life on the Continent as she has become a component part of this order of life itself. Britain refuses to recognize that it is linked up with the fate of Europe; on the other hand Germany cannot exist without recognizing this link in theory and in practice. This has also been proved by the development of the last decades. The opinion was held that Germany was open to robbery, extortion and impoverishment for an indefinite period. What were the consequences? All those who were determined to inflict permanent poverty on Germany fell into the pit they had dug for others, as both Britons and French were overtaken and shaken to their foundations by those same crises as they had provoked in Germany. Germany is and remains the heart of Europe. This portion of the globe can only be healthy if the heart is healthy, it is sick if the heart is ill.

All this has long passed the stage of mere assertions. It will be remembered with what bitterness the British fought against the high prices which Germany was paying to agricultural countries on the Continent for their farm products. This action of Germany placed the peasants of these countries in a position of being no longer dependent on the fluctuations of the Anglo-Saxon world markets for their

revenue. Mr Willkie now describes the position as follows: If ever German methods succeed in achieving a uniform representation of European economic interests in the world and if our gold is deprived of its despotic influence, then America will no longer be in a position to uphold her standard of living. Yes! This describes the attitude of the British when they started this conflict with an economic war and a financial blockade against Germany which, by the way, they have already definitely lost.

None know better than the British that Germany must defend Europe if she wish to defend herself. Germany cannot exist against Europe, and it fully realizes that it cannot count on any profits for itself from even the slightest damage done to Europe. It is therefore essential that the establishment of a new peace be basically constructed by Germany on the prosperity of the Reich being closely linked up with the future prosperity of the whole of this portion of the globe. The peace that Germany requires must be instrumental in giving Europe a totally new mode of life. For this life has undergone fundamental changes owing to industrial revolution and the creation of conglomerate states. If the existence of Europe is to be assured it can no longer rely on itself and its own trade but must consider the changed aspects of the world and competitive conditions. In this Germany's interests are analogous. The ingrained characteristics of Germany's entire attitude to civilization are not evidenced by the ideals tending towards some kind of abstract everlasting bliss in this world of worry, such as were propounded by the peacemakers of 1919 and renewed again today, but on the determination to fall in line with the dictates of the laws of nature. Germany's own existence is governed by a fixed principle to harmonize all the natural qualities in the life of European nations, which cannot be changed, with state conditions, and to recognize the claims of nations for the free shaping of their own lives as determined by world conditions in relation to the Continent.

The uniformity of Europe cannot be determined by mere discussion, as the British would have it, but by the participation of all those concerned in common aims. How sincere the aims of Germany to find protection and forms of expansion for political life in Europe are, is clearly demonstrated by those important sacrifices alone which she has made with the transfer of her small national minorities from the Baltic and other states. Furthermore, those beneficial acts must be recalled whereby since 1933 the German commercial policy in the whole of the south-east of the Continent has resulted in the development and improvement of the general economic situation and in such a way that it has not even been seriously influenced by the progress of the war. Reference must also be made to the elimination of interstate tensions by revisions and arbitrations, tensions which had often been purposely created in order to prevent Europe from ever coming to rest. Thus the primary outlines of a peace such as Germany is planning are now becoming visible in economic development. Such a peace cannot be set down on paper as first of all a realizable and suitable political form must be discovered for it which can be applied to the creative political nature of European nations and because it must be slowly derived from a realistic observation of European economic requirements. It is no wonder therefore that the existence of peace and a new Europe is far more advanced than most people can imagine.

Does abundance of gold create wealth?

"The flight of gold continues", "large shipments of gold to York", "American gold reserve increasing": These are only three instances out of the mass of reports continually appearing in the press all over the world. The flow of European gold to the United States has now been going on for years. The quantity and fluctuation is not constant, but the so-called "up stream" direction remains the same, and leads to a country offering an

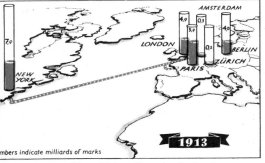

The gold is still evenly distributed
Shipments take place only occasionally

unusually low rate of interest and possessing a great surplus of capital.

The war has caused this flow of gold to increase. By the beginning of March of the current year the American gold reserves exceeded 18 milliards, and thus amounted to two-thirds of the world stocks. At the end of 1939 America had in her possession seventeen milliard dollars worth of gold, so that the last milliard flowed into the country within a period of three months.

Armaments for gold

This extraordinary flow of gold to America was originally caused by the Great War, and the result was the collapse of the gold currencies of the world, which shook the economic life of every nation concerned to its very foundations. The fight of Germany's enemies against her was so ruthless, that they were not able, even, approximately, to produce the amount of war material they required. Therefore they had to enlist the aid of America. The latter rendered this aid, because she had already invested too much money in the cause of the Allies. Guns, aeroplanes, rifles, oil, and food stuffs were supplied: these goods were paid for with gold, because there was no longer any confidence in the currencies of the belligerents and the latter were not in possession of enough money of countries still retaining the gold standard, in order to be able to pay their debts. Between 1915 and 1918 the United States made 1.13 milliard dollars out of this business, half a milliard of this sum coming into the country in the course of the year 1916. This amount of gold was, however, only sufficient to cover a fraction of the surplus of exports. The rest was delivered on credit, which was readily granted but never entirely repaid. France and Russia bore the brunt of these losses, their gold reserves in 1918 only amounting to 2.8 and 2.5 milliard marks respectively, whereas these were in 1912 5.04 and 4.2 milliards; the United States had the chief gain, and after them the neutral countries, the wealth of the latter in some cases very considerably increasing. For instance the gold reserve of Spain rose to 52,300% of the gold coming into the country between 1907 and 1912. The position of Germany was the reverse of that of her enemies, for during the Great War she was able to keep her gold reserves practically intact. The reason was that the peculiar geographical position of the Reich rendered far-reaching economic relations and large shipments of gold impossible from the very outset.

Between the years 1920 and 1930 this stream of gold to America gradually diminished. It is true that those who had been enemies during the Great War were

worn out and economically exhausted, and they still needed the economic aid of North America just as before; this ai dwas, however, henceforth rendered almost exclusively in the form of delivery "on tick", i. e. on credit. But was not until the year 1925 that there was any considerable change in the flow of gold to the United States; in that year a variety of circumstances led to an increased strain upon the money market of the United States. The cause of this was that Germany returned to the gold standard, and that therefore the 100 million dollars loan, which she had obtained, had to be put on the gold basis. A further reason was that the Asiatic princes again began to increase the fabulous hoards of gold and treasures with which they are wont to adorn their palaces and temples.

The gold reserves of the United States, which amounted to 18 milliard marks in 1923 as compared with 8 milliards in 1913, had therefore been more than doubled. On the other hand the European reserves had during the same period sunk from 24 milliard to 13 milliard marks.

The Trans-Atlantic Gold Chase

The second, one might say almost tidal, wave of European gold, which led into the armour plated safes of Fort Knox, began in the year 1934 immediately after the North American money reform, and about two years after the devaluation of the pound. These shipments, however, were quite different from the former ones. They consisted only to a small extent of capital arising out of export surpluses and shipping proceeds, or insurance policies and investments. The reason in this case was the anxiety about economic and political upheavals, and also fear of devaluation of currencies and the possibility of war. The chief result was that huge quantities of gold were, so to speak, chased over the Atlantic. The fluctuations in this flow of gold were more

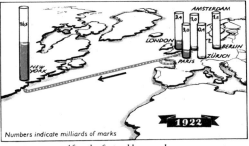

After the first gold — exodus:
Europe becomes poorer in Gold

confused, and it was less possible to put a check upon them than in the previous cases, because of the subsidiary influences arising from the continual collapse of currencies. The United States were regarded as an oasis, where there was no danger of war and where it was still possible to do business, bècause the price of an ounce of fine gold in America was 35 dollars and this was abnormally high. The extent of this transfer is well known: in April of the current year the gold reserves of the United States amounted to about 18.5 milliard dollars, in other words some 44 milliard marks, or more than two thirds of the entire gold reserves in the world.

The world in the throes of economic suicide

What happened in the interval between these two tidal waves of gold to the shores of the United States, brought about the financial collapse of the economic system throughout the world, and it was in vain that the supporters of it had maintained that it would work in spite of Versailles, of reparations, of an unfair distribution of gold and of every form of obstacle placed in the way of the mutual exchange of products between the different countries.

The agony of this economic suicide began shortly before 1930 with the breakdown of an outward prosperity in America, which had never been real. The failure of the banks in Germany in July, the introduction of state control of money exchange business there, the financial moratorium, and the devaluation of

the currency both in England and the United States were the next stages in this economic upheaval. The countries belonging to the so-called gold block—particularly France, Holland and Switzerland,—were the last strongholds of this obsolete system, but they collapsed too. Also during this period the relative amount of the gold reserves fluctuated very considerably; these fluctuations were, however, mostly confined to transfers between the countries of Europe. For instance, between January and December 1931 the Reichsbank lost 1.2 milliard marks in gold, which owing to the termination of credits chiefly flowed into the coffers of the Banque de France. Before the devaluation of the English Pound in September 1931, England had to transfer large quantities of gold, a part of which she was able to recover later. The same was the case with France, which country was, up to the end of 1933, in a position to import gold, but between 1935 and 1936 suffered correspondingly heavy losses.

The gold illusion

And what is happening at the present time? The United States are again supplying the Allies with war material, particularly in the form of aeroplanes, guns and rifles, and with food stuffs, payment again being made in gold. But this time our enemies are saying good-bye to their gold with less pain than during the Great War, when the problem of gold was not so clear as today. Our enemies will soon cease to be able to pay in gold. For the "riches" of England and France are melting away like snow in the sun. Amsterdam, Brussels and Zurich also have practically no gold left. Their "riches" are either already on their way to New York, or stored in London waiting to be sent by the next ship.

America is getting gold for her goods. But is she not really squandering her agricultural and industrial products for a metal the value of which has become extremely

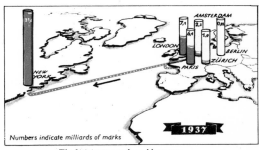

The USA attracts the gold masses
like a magnet

doubtful? What guarantee have the Americans that they will in a few years get back for their gold what they gave for it? What guarantee have they that they will not be left stranded with their gold, and "starve" like the legendary King Midas, whose prayer, that everything he touched might turn into gold, was so literally fulfilled, that even the food in his mouth became gold?

At the present time no one can answer these questions.

But no matter what happens to gold, one fact is sure, and that is that it only has a real value, as long as it supports production, and not as a means of controlling the fluctuations in economic life. The capacity of a people to produce, their social work, the brains of their leaders and the diligence of their workers are more valuable than gold. There are everywhere indications that other peoples are also beginning to recognize these facts.

Diether Heumann

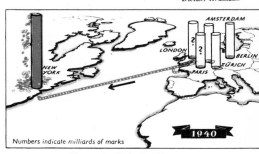

Too much gold in Fort Knox

The exploiter: *According to "Hansard's Parliamentary Debates" of 1936–37, a census taken on 12th December 1936 showed that 17,044 boys under sixteen years were employed underground in the coalmines of Great Britain. The English boast, says G. B. Shaw in "The Man of Destiny", that every slave is free as soon as he sets foot on British soil and yet they sell the children of their poor when they are barely six years old to factory owners and make them work under the whip like slaves, 16 hours a day*

The speculator: *On the exchanges of the world bread, wheat and foodstuffs are objects of speculation for private gamblers who —sanctioned by the principles of liberal economy —stage booms and slumps as it suits them, are responsible to no one and whose methods of competition have exposed whole countries to famine*

The landlord: *This picture shows tenants in Stepney, London, who have barricaded themselves in because one of their number was to be evicted. Often it is a question of a paltry week's rent of a few shillings. The houses are owned by companies such as the "London Property Investment Trust" which in 1923 paid a dividend of 250 pounds on 5-pound shares and in 1931 even 710 pounds. In nine years the shareholders pocketed a dividend of 80,000 %*

In the new Europe there is no place for such big businessmen

Has the big businessman a future?

By Professor Dr Heinrich Hunke, Berlin

Today this question is discussed with lively interest, here and there not without a certain anxiety. In the following article "Signa!" gives a clear and positive answer demonstrating at the same time by means of a number of characteristic examples which type of speculator has played out his rôle in Europe and for whom there are no prospects in the future

It is always difficult to predict future developments, for that implies recognizing the essential and distinguishing it from the non-essential. Everyone who has studied this problem thoroughly is in a position to confirm this fact. It is essentially true of problems influenced by the great revolution of our times and perhaps decisively modified by it, for the old point of view which has given the problems their meaning and significance has meanwhile become the object of bitter criticism. How is it possible to define the attitude to problems which, like the problems of economy, are complex questions the individual factors of which are difficult to isolate and still more difficult to evaluate in their relation to the whole?

Take as a concrete example of the preceding remarks the economy of Berlin. At the end of the Thirty Years' War, Berlin had 6,000 inhabitants. At the beginning of the 19th century the numbers had risen to 175,000. In the seventies of the last century the population had already reached the million mark. Subsequently Berlin developed more and more rapidly into a great metropolis although the process was in no way favoured by the presence of mineral wealth or other riches or even by a particularly favourable geographical situation. There is no doubt that the city became great solely because political energy, politico-economical foresight, business initiative, scientific research and the general industry of the population co-operated successfully in a very special way. The political development

laid the foundations for Berlin's greatness, for this city would have remained small if the German Reich had not become a world power over Prussia's head. The comprehensive politico-economic foresight of the Prussian kings had called into existence and strengthened the economy of Berlin. In the 19th century these beginnings flourished with the help of business initiative. Scientific research, too, and the intelligence of the worker have contributed their share to realizing, consolidating and promoting this growth.

That is the secret of the development of the economy of Berlin. Deeper study of the problem, however, leads to complex and lengthy analyses. Even the rôle of politics is differently interpreted. Liberalism saw in business initiative the driving force of the economic system. Planned economy of every description denies absolutely business initiative.

Now, however, a decision must be reached on this point, for the entire organization of economy depends on the answer given to this question. What is the truth? Is the big businessman an essential unit or merely a chance product of the economic organization of the present and the future?

The mask of the big businessman

In order to answer this question we must define the big businessman. It is necessary to emphasize immediately that the common definition of a big businessman as the person who bears the actual risk of an undertaking is far from satisfactory. Were this definition correct every person with legal rights, every hereditary community and at the same time every individual with a limited capacity for business could be a big businessman. It is clear that this is only a formal explanation of the problem which affords no insight into the nature of economy. The result can be judged in exactly the same way as when for example the doctor discovers that a patient can live with half a lung. For the real meaning of this institution is in no way clarified.

At the same time a number of types with whom the big businessman in general is identified exclude a real insight into the problem of his importance. That is to say, we do not doubt that there are such figures but the question is whether they reflect the essential character of the big businessman.

One observer sees the capitalist, the moneymaker who scents good business, who collects the treasures of the world and continues to multiply them. This identifies the big businessman with the classical burgher once described by Sombart and even though we deny him he is nevertheless surrounded by a certain romance. It would be pleasant to participate in this economic order without being exposed, however, to the danger of the liberal order, the crises and the struggles for power. An ideal comes in sight which confirms the advantages of this world and cancels the disadvantages: it is the medieval order of the guilds with their strict regulations for admission, means tests and the norm for sufficient food. People overlook the fact, however, that the achievements of the big businessman are dependent on a maximum energy and a maximum freedom and that when these conditions are not satisfied the quality of the capitalist is eliminated.

Another observer sees in the big businessman the employer, and in this connexion he usually thinks at the same time of the so-called unchanging wage law, the industrial reserve army and class warfare. The big businessman is the exploiter. Here, too, a new ideal tries to deal with him: the ideal of equality and the big businessman is replaced by the official, the functionary.

A third group, even though it refuses to acknowledge the intellectual foundations of this equality idea, also sees in the capitalist the administrator, that is the representative of the authorities. What the second group strives for is here noted with regret, but the development is regarded as unavoidable. And it cannot be denied that state intervention curtails more and more the freedom of the big businessman. The ecnomics of the entire world have been forced to develop either by necessity or by principle into planned economy thereby reducing the big businessman to the position of an instrument executing official regulations. The numbers and the power of the functionary are steadily increasing.

Finally there is a fourth group of observers who identify the big businessman with the technical expert. They point out that economics are

A TAYLOR SYSTEM MACHINIST "UP-TO-DATE"

An Argument Without Words

The working man as a machine: *The notorious Taylor system, the systematic mechanization of the working man invented by the American F. W. Taylor, could only come into existence under a business régime which aimed at unlimited profit and reduced the factory worker to the level of a robot*

Prototypes of the exploiter system

It is not by chance that the names of some of the most successful exponents of liberal economy have been connected with the greatest scandals of recent economic history, for these men were by no means exceptions in an otherwise healthy system; they were prototypes of the prevailing economic form. This type of businessman will not be able to exist in the new Europe, because the economic system which was the premise for his activity will have ceased to exist

Camillo Castiglioni, *the son of a rabbi in Trieste, obtained control of almost the entire Austrian aeroplane industry at the outbreak of the Great War. By delivering inferior machines and engines for which he obtained maximum prices he sent hundreds of gallant airmen to their death. When his infamous behaviour came to light he absconded to escape punishment*

Sir Victor Sassoon *is the youngest member of the Oriental family of the Sassoons who founded their fortune on the illegal import of opium into China. Collaborating with the British Government, they were largely responsible for involving China in the Opium War. Sir Victor inherited the Bombay firm and is known today as one of the greatest speculators in the world*

Sir Basil Zaharoff *was the largest supplier of armaments of all times. During the Boer War, the Balkan Wars, and the Russo-Japanese War he sold arms to both sides. He financed the 17 revolutions in Greece between 1910 and 1930 and the campaign against the Turks. He did his best business, however, in the Great War. From 1875 he was an agent of the Intelligence Service which in no way prejudiced his business interests*

A. P. Sloan, *President of General Motors Company, began the biggest instalment system racket in the world. He speculates deliberately on the recklessness of purchasers who normally are unable to afford luxury articles. Before the beginning of the war the firms doing business on the instalment plan sold 80% of all furniture, 10% of all jewelry, 90% of all cars and 90% of all radios in America extorting a profit ranging from 10 to 30% from their clients*

Alfred Löwenstein, *the Belgian financier who in 1928, under mysterious circumstances, fell out of his private aeroplane over the Channel, was a gambler. Fascinated by his prospectuses and promises, thousands of people with small saving accounts and small incomes entrusted their money to him and lost it. He was the typical uncreative financier who juggled with figures. All he knew about the factories he owned was how their shares were quoted*

The private office of the creator of the 5- and 10-cent store. *Frank Woolworth, who was a great admirer of Napoleon, furnished his private office with valuable pieces which had belonged to the emperor. Speculating with cents he won millions. He always tried to give his world-wide concerns a social note externally and liked to emphasize that shops stocked with the cheapest goods were a boon for the purchaser of small means. In reality with inferior goods he frequently damaged the small manufacturer and craftsman as well as the buyer*

Woolworth counting his dollars. *In the entrance hall to the Woolworth head offices this grotesque statue of the proprietor has been set up on one of the pillars*

unthinkable without modern technics, that in the past technics always played a subordinate rôle, but that this situation must now change. In addition, the task of business enterprise today —if there ever was such a thing—has been replaced by the distribution and planning of contracts by the State. It is clear that there is a kernel of truth in these arguments but on the other hand we must not overlook that as well as technics there is such a thing as an independent economic task and achievement. For technics can do much, yet the effects are not to be found in the world of technical enthusiasm but in technical intelligence, that is the world of economics in which the economic forces of labour, available raw materials and food supplies lay down strict frontiers which are indeed extended by technics but which cannot be avoided or violated. These popular views of big business could be multiplied indefinitely. But it would add nothing essential to our knowledge.

The truth about the big businessman

It is only possible to define the true character of the big businessman when we decide whether the capitalist, the employer, the functionary or the technical expert is in fact the big businessman or whether he has only adopted this mask by chance. An example will illustrate this point: the only practical form of organization to con-

trol the masses is undoubtedly by division into leader and led, officers, non-commissioned officers and rank and file. And this is valid for all times, in all types of states and regardless of opinions. In other words, the officer can be a captain of mercenaries, the militia commander or the modern officer, he may be either elected or nominated, he may draw financial benefit from the victory or not, one fact remains irrefutable: all control of the masses is unthinkable without leaders and subalterns and without the element of discipline. Applying this to our problem, the question must be answered whether the big businessman is a natural product of organized economic life and what is his essential importance.

Careful investigation proves that in fact big businessmen can possess all the above-mentioned characteristics separately or collectively, yet they do not form an exhaustive picture

It is possible for their material struggle for gain to be in many cases the only motive for their attitude to economics. But the assertion that the creative forces of personality are dependent on the material struggle for gain alone cannot, however, be proved. It is a bloodless construction born at a time when the economically active individual is isolated as the homo oeconomicus from the rest of life and its connexions. But life itself shows that industry, the joy in work, inventiveness, technical gifts and wisdom in economy are no less important than the struggle for gain: Alfred Krupp was once able to say to his workers: "I began with a few employees; they earned more and lived better than I;

for 25 years I had nothing but anxiety and difficult work and when I employed a larger number of workers my fortune was still less than that of many a worker in a cast steel factory." And his was no isolated case. To public economy, however, applies without restriction what the Führer said at the Hundred Year Jubilee of the German State Railways: "It is a warning against the exclusively private claims of capitalist teaching. It is the living proof that a community enterprise can be conducted without private capitalist leadership."

The function of employer, too, is

only one side of the big businessman's activity. Through the mistaken subdivision of workers into employer and employee we have become accustomed to seeing in the big businessman the employer. In reality, however, the primary task of the big businessman is the planning of an economic activity which then and then only legitimizes his function as employer.

Similarly it is impossible to consider that the big businessman is equivalent to the functionary, the official or the representative of the authorities. It is just as misguided to maintain that the big businessman is an official as

The new style of businessman

Ernst Abbe, *the physicist, later the head of the Zeiss Optical Works in Jena, took a step rarely taken by a businessman. He gave his fortune to the enterprise, creating the famous German Carl Zeiss Endowment. He himself continued to work as before. He introduced social measures and insisted on good wages being paid. In accordance with his wishes the profits were to benefit not the manager nor the workers but the whole undertaking*

Alfred Krupp, *the celebrated German industrialist, wrote a letter from England in autumn 1871 in which he said: "We want only loyal workers who are honestly thankful to us for offering them a livlihood. Let us treat them with humanity and let us care for them as well as for their families. They must be able to earn in our works the maximum that an industry can offer—or we must abandon an industry which starves its workers"*

The houses of London landowners. It is true they do not live here themselves, but they own the sites on which the notorious London slums stand. Twelve lords and dukes share the largest property in the city on the Thames and their vast fortunes are almost exclusively derived from the rents of wretched workers' dwellings. Incomes of 900,000 pounds are quite common. Over and over again plans for the clearance of the slums have been boycotted by the owners

it is to declare that the official cannot be a big businessman. Experience shows that everywhere, in the State and in private economy, decisive progress is the work of enterprising forces and the administrating official has the same task in administration and economy. The numbers and powers of these functionaries are steadily on the increase. But they all live by the initiative and creative achievements of individuals.

Neither are the big businessman and the technical expert identical. The technical expert, it is true, can be a big businessman, not in virtue of his technical gifts but of his business capacities. In the military sphere it would occur to nobody to place technical tasks and technical capacity on the same level as the problems of tactics and strategy and the qualities of leadership necessary for their solution. On the contrary, in the soldier's world technics have the rôle of helper. The same must be true for economics.

When all is said and done historical and scientific analysis teach that the big businessman is the personality responsible for conducting and shaping an enterprise. He is to be found in small and big undertakings, in private and State economy; he is irreplaceable. It is true that conditions and regulations, capital and inventions offer economic possibilities but always only to those who know how to turn them to good account. It is very difficult, therefore, to define the true figure of the big businessman and estimate his importance for individual enterprises and for economics as a whole. They have much in common with political figures

and great scientists. Like them they look for problems and struggle to solve them. They concentrate energy and open up new fields of activity for many.

This situation will never change, for the big businessman is the inventor, the discoverer, the organizer and the educator in economic life. He is the inventor in the economic sense. It is his task to build up production based on the technical discovery. Only someone who has himself experience of the long road to be covered and the difficulties to be overcome between the first technical experiment and large scale economic production can appreciate the responsibility and magnitude of the big businessman's task. Equally important is the opening up of new markets by the pioneer, the discovering and satisfying of new needs. To achieve both ends the big businessman must be able to see economic conditions as a whole. His organization will forge complete success for all out of the maximum of individual capacity. And all this is closely connected with the education of the entire concern to thrift, economy and skill. It is, therefore, not a presumptuous claim to declare that the big businessman is an indispensable member of every system of economy.

The importance of the private businessman

It cannot, therefore, be the task of economic policy to eliminate enterprising forces but to adjust economy in accordance with the two principles of performance and common profit and to further its activity in this direction.

The Barmat case in Berlin was a bribery scandal on the largest possible scale. The four brothers Barmat looked upon it as a "business enterprise" when they bribed officials in order to do gigantic business and inflicted losses of 39 millions on the German Reich alone. After the case against them in 1937 a new lawsuit in Holland brought to light further fraudulant speculaions of the Barmats in which the Belgian National Bank had lost 34 millions

The surprising arrest in 1938 of the President of the New York Exchange, Richard Whitney, was a big Wall Street scandal. He is a member of one of the ten richest families in America. As the proprietor of a well-known firm of stockbrokers, he had embezzled deposits and was condemned to a long term of imprisonment in Sing Sing. The evils of free competitive economy have repeatedly been laid bare by numbers of such scandals. In the economic system of the new Europe there will be no place for such businessmen

The Führer
and his Reich Marshal

"... Since the re-establishment of the German Armed Forces, Hermann Göring has been the creator of the German Air Force. It is granted to but few mortals in the course of their lives to create a military instrument from nothing and to develop it until it becomes the mightiest weapon of its kind. Above all he has instilled into it his spirit ..." (The Führer before the Reichstag on 19th July 1940.)

"... In the early morning, the squadrons of the German Air Force swooped down on the Soviet enemy. In spite of the numerical superiority of their adversary, they obtained the mastery of the air on the eastern front on the first day and inflicted a crushing defeat on the Soviet Air Force. During the battles in the air, 322 Soviet planes were brought down by chasers or by A. A. fire. Including the machines destroyed on the ground, the number of planes of the Soviet Air Force which were annihilated had reached 1,811 by the evening. The German losses on this day amounted to 35 machines ..." (From the special communiqué of the High Command on the operations on the eastern front on the first day of the campaign.)

THE NEW REICH CHANCELLERY

On 11th January 1938, the Führer commissioned Prof. Speer, Inspector-General of Building Construction, with the erection of the new Reich Chancellery. The building was to be completed by the 10th January 1939. The initial and necessary work of demolition was made difficult by heavy frosts. The actual construction was started in March. During the remaining 9 months fixed for its completion, the Inspector-General and his staff of architects, artists, workmen and artisans from all provinces completed this work, which represents the Reich in modern classical form

The door of the Führer's study

It is 20 ft high, made of mahogany and German marble, and decorated with the initials A. H. The huge door connects the Führer's study with the "Long Hall"

Crowned with the emblem of the Great German Empire: The west portal of the Reich Chancellery in Voss-street

҉҉ men are on guard in front, they belong to the life-guards of the Führer and wear black uniforms with white leather strappings

The "Long Hall" in the Reich Chancellery

The marble gallery is 480 ft long. The bright walls are made of marble stucco. Between the doors which lead to the Führer's study and the room of the aide-de-camp, the walls are hung with gobelins. Beautifully shaped tables and chairs together with gilded wall sconces of bronze give the gallery, in spite of its size, a harmonious character

The room, in which world political decisions are made:
THE STUDY OF THE FÜHRER

*The heart of the new Reich Chancellery is a high room 90 ft long, nearly 50 ft w
and nearly 33 ft high. The walls are composed of dark-red marble from the
Marches and the wainscoting of dark-brown ebony. The floor is made of marble,*

A view of the Führer's desk from the front. On the wall hangs a gobelin of the 17th century

the coffer-work ceiling of rosewood. Glass doors 20 ft high and 6 ft wide (on the left) lead to the colonnade in front, on the garden side. Opposite the desk of the Führer a broad fireplace of marble is let into the wall. Above, the wall is decorated with a portrait of Bismarck by Lenbach

Germany's first defeat was suffered in the Battle of Britain. For that reason *Signal* hardly covered it, and instead stepped up its propaganda campaign against Britain and subsequently the United States. The Vichy régime of Marshal Philippe Pétain was publicised in flattering colours, but the realities of life in occupied Europe can be read between the lines of *Signal* editorial policy. Gasoline was scarce and so was bread. The Strength Through Joy movement, providing holidays which offered the masses pleasures once reserved for the rich, was in retreat. Most Germans who travelled to Mediterranean waters in 1941 did so as part of the forces invading Greece and Crete. Although Italy joined her Axis partner on June 10, 1940 in order to participate in the partition of France, where, incidentally, she played an extremely ineffective and inglorious role, Mussolini decided to attack Greece on his own later in 1940 and suffered serious and unexpected reverses. In the spring of 1941 Hitler sent the Wehrmacht into the Balkans and Greece, and *Signal* sought to bolster the image of Il Duce and his régime on the propaganda front while Hitler's armies pulled Italian irons out of the fire in Greece. The Balkan blitzkrieg of 1941 was another spectacular success for Germany, but the problem of an unconquered Britain still loomed large in Nazi minds. Anti-British propaganda accelerated, and Anglo-American deals, such as the exchange of 50 American destroyers for 99-year leaseholds on British bases in the Western Hemisphere, rankled. So did the successes of convoys in the Battle of the Atlantic.

In the light of the possibility of America's joining the Allies in the near future, with American ships in the Atlantic adopting a belligerent policy toward German subs and surface craft, closer co-operation between Germany and Japan became an ever-greater necessity. The Berlin-Tokyo Axis was more of a propaganda tool than a reality. Foreign Minister Matsuoka's state visit to Berlin in early 1941 was fruitless from Japan's point of view, since Hitler did not bother to tell his ally that he was planning to attack the Soviet Union later in the year. As a result Matsuoka negotiated a non-aggression pact with Stalin on his way back to Tokyo. Hitler attacked Russia two months later.

Anti-American propaganda filled the pages of *Signal* from 1941 on. After Pearl Harbor American culture was degraded more intensively as the American impact upon the war in Europe and North Africa became more tangible. The Nazi successes in the Desert War in 1942 were stressed until Alamein. For months thereafter a long silence on North Africa ensued, only to be lifted briefly when the Afrika Korps made a last stand in Tunisia. The story of the American pilot captured in Tunisia is quite spurious. Once Tunis was taken in May 1943 and the Italian campaign launched, *Signal* decided to concentrate on the futility of the Allied bomber offensive, a theme which alternated with the inhumanity of the Allies in bombing civilian populations. By 1944 *Signal* tried to portray the Americans as frivolous jitterbuggers who were preparing a scorched earth policy, analogous with Sherman's march to the sea in the American Civil War, if and when they and the British actually invaded France. At the same time *Signal* showed that Organisation Todt, the Nazi labour group, and the Wehrmacht were shoring up the defences of Fortress Europe along the Atlantic Wall in preparation for the invasion.

Much of this propaganda effort must have fallen on stony soil. Circulation began to drop in 1943 for *Signal,* and the inconsistencies of their arguments, fairly transparent in its first years of publication, were all too obvious. Germany was worried that she was losing the war in 1943 and 1944, and *Signal* mirrored that concern. *Signal* would lose more of its readership in 1944 for quite another reason. The readers, the peoples

The statesman

Patient and calm, he awaits the opportune moment for action, and with a passionate devotion to the welfare of his people, the Duce conducts the affairs of his country with the sure hand of a genius

Colour photograph
by Elsbeth Heddenhausen

Geneva, May 1931. The European Committee of the League of Nations condemned the Austrian-German Customs Union. *This was one of the most momentous mistakes of the Committee which then ranked as the chief embodiment of the Pan-European idea. Our picture shows the Session in the temporary glass hall of the League of Nations in Geneva under the Presidency of the French Ambassador, M. François-Poncet (arrow). Further to the left are the German Foreign Minister, Herr Curtius and the Austrian Minister, Herr Schober. On the right is M. Aristide Briand*

The false path of Pan-Europe

Count R.H. Coudenhove-Kalergi
author of "Pan-Europa" which was published in 1913 and which became the foundation of the Pan-European Movement

In the year of damnation, 1923, appeared the book, "Pan-Europa". It was dedicated to the Youth of Europe and bore on the cover "the sign under which Pan-Europeans of all the States will be united, the Sun-Cross, the symbol of humanity and reason".

He who, in the middle of the Austrian and German inflation and in the face of the helplessness and disintegration of the Reich, could call in the German tongue for unity in Europe, must be characterised as either extremely foolhardy or completely ignorant of the world. The author, R. H. Coudenhove-Kalergi, was an unknown young man from Vienna. It soon became known that this Viennese Count was neither a German nor a member of the nobility of the vanished Dual Monarchy, but a strange international apparition, —a European with a Japanese blood strain. Was he possibly a pioneer who foresaw the pressing necessity of things to come? Did he belong to the new Europe which is now on the march? No, in spite of his youthful bearing, Coudenhove was completely in the toils of the old Europe which had sealed its fate in the suburban treaties of Paris. "The political leadership of the world to-day lies in Washington, London, Moscow, Tokyo and Paris. Here are the centres of the international fields of power. The plans for the future World Empire are indicated there." We can read this on the map which we have reproduced where Coudenhove delineates his programme for the new alignments and division of the world. In another place he says: "If Napoleon had won at Leipzig, the United States of Europe would now be in existence, either under a Bonaparte or a Republican régime," and "The sixth Europe reaches as far eastwards as the democratic system". That was Coudenhove's chief article of faith. In like manner he saw his Pan-Europe of the future as a perpetuation of the Versailles frontiers—"for, whoever touches these frontiers, meddles with the peace of Europe"—with Paris as the centre of power, and "Germany affiliated to the western Powers", all with the final purpose of taking the side of England in world policy against Russia. The surprising paradox with

Coudenhove is that on the one hand he states that "Europe binds herself to ward off every foreign attack against the English motherland", (e g. a possible air attack on London by Russia), while on the other hand, England's service in return is to consist solely in the protection of the French and Dutch East Indies and he says that "In the event of a Russian-European war, England could remain neutral".

This was written and published in 1923. Not till seven years later did France evacuate the Rhineland. In the meantime the Treaty of Locarno, 1925 and the Berlin German-Russian Treaty of 1926 were concluded as a sort of re-insurance for Germany's entry into the League of Nations. The German crisis was on the point of breaking out again, this time as part of the World-Crisis which also shook the American economic structure, to its very foundations. It was then that the official realization of Coudenhove's Pan-Europe was established thanks to the initiative of the old French statesman, Aristide Briand who, after the retirement of Austen Chamberlain and the death of Stresemann, remained alone on the scene at Geneva. But it was not more than a diplomatic recognition on paper.

"Monsieur Briand gave a lunch which was attended by the Foreign Ministers of the 27 European nations participating in the X. Assembly of the League of Nations. At the conclusion of this gathering, Monsieur Briand developed his ideas concerning the organisation of Europe. After a dis-

cussion, the delegates present declared unanimously that they took cognisance of the initiative of the French premier in inaugurating a bond of solidarity between the European Governments and welcomed it sympathetically. All those present undertook to engage the attention of their respective Governments with this question." Thus runs the official press communiqué of September, 1929, in the typical Geneva style of the League of Nations Secretariat. Eight months later, eleven years after Versailles, the French Government, on May 17, 1930, with the coming into effect of the Young Plan, gave the final order for the evacuation of the Rhineland and solemnly handed to the 26 other European Governments, including Great Britain, a seven-folio paged Memorandum concerning the organisation of a European Federation.

The perusal of this Memorandum to-day has a stimulating effect that is almost spectral. The proverb "Wash my fur and don't make me wet" is exemplified in long drawn-out sentences. After we have been profusely assured that the projected Federation of Europe is in no sense in opposition to the League of Nations, to the Hague Court nor to "any ethnical group which, in other parts of the world or in Europe, exists outside the League of Nations", comes the passage which later on, when the first attempt at an establishment the new European order was made, resolved itself into nothing less than the cloven hoof of the entire scheme. "This Pan-European policy which must

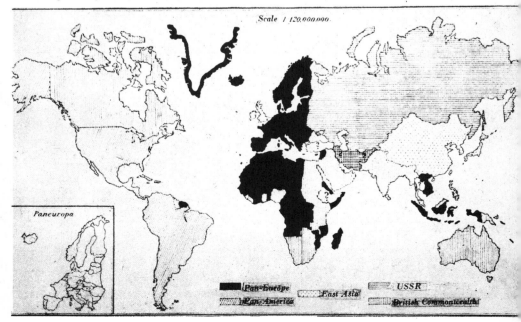

Scale 1 120,000,000.

Paneuropa

■ Pan-Europe   East Asia   USSR
Pan-America   British Commonwealth

be the goal in our endeavour to forge the first links of solidarity between the individual Governments, contains in itself a conception which is the exact opposite of that which formerly determined the formation of customs unions in Europe, by virtue of which—while inland customs were abolished—, those on the common frontiers were raised which, in actual fact, were weapons against all nations not included in that particular customs union."

With this twisted argument, the modest project of an Austro-German Customs Union was laid low in May, 1931, and—, ironically enough, was buried in that self-same so-called European Committee which had been formed at Geneva on the basis of the French Memorandum. The Chair was taken by M. François-Poncet, later, French Ambassador to Berlin, who accused the representatives of the Reich Government and the Austrian Federal Government in sharp terms of high treason to Europe, for having dared, in some measure to mend the tatters of Central European industrial disintegration in at least one place. Next to him, tired and weary, sat old Briand with his grey lion's mane and the eternal cigarette in the corner of his mouth. He had hoped to become President of the Republic during those weeks but had been rejected by his many enemies, not least because he was reproached for having favoured the much feared "Anschluss". That was Geneva's Pan-European Policy in practice!

We will, however, take a look at the replies of the Governments to the French proposals. The Paris Memorandum suggested the calling of a European Conference and—in traditional Geneva style—the setting-up of a select European committee. "As a safeguard against one-sided influences on the part of any single power", it was suggested "that the Chair should be taken in turn". The Chair was naturally taken at first by France, with the result as above! The Memorandum further dealt chiefly with the self-evident priority of politics over economy and carefully avoided all allusion to the problem of the Revision of the Treaties of 1919. Consequently, the answer of the Reich Government of July 11, 1930, had, of course, to contain the reservation: "All attempts to better the political situation in Europe will be dependent on whether the principles of equality, of equal security, and of the peaceful adjustment of the vital and natural needs of the nations are applied. When existing conditions violate these principles, effective means must be found to change them. It is impossible to try to build a new Europe on a foundation incompatible with the vital laws of human progress."

And what had the Government of Great Britain to say to the proposals submitted by her French ally? The answer of July 16, 1930 was in no way encouraging. His Majesty's Government deferred a final decision pending relative conversations with the Dominion Governments, stating, moreover, that "they were not convinced, on further and mature examination, that the institution of new and independent international organisations were either needed or desirable".

Pan-Europe as a buffer State for Great Britain and Great Britain's public refusal to participate in any such weak and fanciful plans concerning the community of the European States, form the actual history of this mistaken Pan-European idea. The European problem is being solved centrally today by the self-same Central Powers which in those days were the helpless objects of one-sided and lifeless political schemes.

Max Clauss

Europe as the jig-saw puzzle of England

"The only policy which can guarantee England's security is the creation of a peaceful and friendly system of States in Europe which will act so to speak as a buffer against Russia and prevent her further penetration into British waters." That is how Coudenhove saw Europe as quoted from his book, from which we have also taken the accompanying map. In reality, however, the position was much worse. The European map was a jig-saw puzzle, the pieces of which were moved about continually by England. Our draftsman had a vision (right)—the pieces of the game,—the European States, thus sorted out by the English players, are arranged in a peculiar order . . . they form part of England's plan. England certainly understood how to prevent European unity to her own advantage

VICHY

Pictures

from a quiet residence

The room where the Marshal of France works *is in the Hôtel du Parc at the corner of the Rue du Maréchal Pétain and the Rue Petit. The French art of debating has been changed under him to the laconic method of the soldier. The devotion with which Marshal Pétain dedicates himself to his task keeps his ministries, which have also established their headquarters and conference chambers in hotels, continually working under high pressure*

Awaiting the Marshal. *The French Head of State, Marshal Pétain, is seen only on rare occasions. On official occasions, however, and at the rallies of the "Chantiers de la Jeunesse" the upright figure of the man is seen who conducts the work of the "Gouvernement Français" with dignity and authority*

The changing of the guard in front of the Hôtel du Parc *In front of the other ministries, too, the guard is changed every hour. These men are chosen regular soldiers and this small military ceremony always attracts interested spectators, for it is the only ceremonial reflecting the activity of the Government in Vichy*

"France ! The Family ! Work !" With these words the Marshal exhorts the French to put forth every effort that France may live. These words and his portrait are found everywhere. It seems to watch with ironical eye all those who come to Vichy for a few days to intrigue, to spy and to whisper... These people are the émigrés who are not in possession of the permission to reside in Vichy and who now carry on their banking transactions in back rooms in Lyons and in Clermont-Ferrand, all those who are still unable to grasp the fact that their heyday is past

A striking personality: the Cadi Bentaied Mohamed Ben Kaddour, a legionary who has fought for 18 years in the French colonial service, brought the Marshal the loyal greetings of his tribe. The Cadi was accompanied by one of his sons

This is the Vichy of the visitors taking a cure. When they received permission to enter Vichy, thanks to their ailing livers, they had imagined that everything would be so interesting. The avenue surrounding the park does lead past all the large hotels and, in consequence, past the ministries, it is true, but how soon this stroll is over and how interminable is the day!

PARIS ON WHEELS

Smart — even on a bicycle

Although they invented the bicycle, the Germans, curiously enough, make less use of it than other nations. In Denmark, Holland, and France the bicycle is far more common than in Germany. The Dutch practically grow up on bicycles. In Germany only people who must, ride bicycles, whereas in other countries people obviously cycle for

The Parisienne of 1941 goes shopping by bicycle. Often the cycle has the queerest contraptions attached to it to accommodate the shopping basket, the dog, and even the baby

The Parisienne keeps her reputation for smartness even on the bicycle. She is a sportswoman from top to toe, and yet she only needs to take off her coat and gaiters to appear ready dressed for town

pleasure. There are of course economic reasons: tram fares, especially in Holland, are extremely high, and when one asks people why they are such enthusiastic cyclists, they very often reply that it is the cheapest method of getting from one place to another. Then the shortage of petrol must have brought as many cycles on to the road as cars were taken off. But these are only secondary reasons. The fact is that Danes, Dutch, and French cycle because they enjoy it.

Those who have travelled widely in France must remember the afternoons when it seemed as if all the young French girls had gone cycling. At a certain hour of the day something seems to impel the French girl to jump on to her bicycle and to go somewhere.

One is astonished when one meets a couple of Dutch lovers on bicycles. They look like centaurs in love; they ride along with their arms around one another and seem to be part of their machines. They move so gracefully and with such assurance that the observer soon forgets his anxiety and only wonders why the children

The cycle-car is the normal week-end conveyance of many Parisians. It looks like a car but that is all!

of such people should trouble to learn to walk. They ought to be taught cycling from the very beginning. Even the poorest of the poor can afford to buy cycles in Holland. In the markets there are stalls which deal in second-hand parts; for a few pence one can buy these parts and make a bicycle out of them.

At the last Olympic Games the people of Berlin were astonished to learn that there is an Olympic contest that they had entirely forgotten—tandem cycling. In Germany the tandem is rather comic,

The original form of the cycle-car is the old tandem— a perfect symbol of marriage. for the husband steers and the wife helps him—at any rate she seems to

The cycle combination, with supports and reinforcements on the front wheel, converts the simple cycle into a universal conveyance which can transport heavy loads or oneself quickly and pleasantly

The motor-cycle side-car is often combined nowadays with ordinary cycles because of the shortage of petrol. In Holland and France there are even cycle-taxis. The Dutch in their enthusiasm for cycling even use them as wedding coaches

whereas in France and Holland it is quite a commonplace. The cycle-car, the modern brother of the tandem, is only known as a toy in Germany whereas in France it is the poor man's motor. In France there are as many tandems and cycle-cars as there are canoes in Germany. The German likes to spend his week-ends on the water: the Frenchman prefers the road, and no wonder, for in France the beautiful roads run up hill and down dale and along the loveliest rivers, besides, France is the home of the classic cycle race, the "Tour de France".

According to the decrees of fashion a woman is elegant when she is suitably dressed, and for the cyclist to be smart her costume must be such that is does not hinder her while cycling and yet does not make her appear masculine. When she cycles, the suitably dressed woman wears a combination of sports and street costume. The Parisienne in her cycling costume is graceful and pleasing to the eye. The light short sports coat prevents her from looking like a caricature of a sports girl.

A cycling professor. This practical construction is easier to propel than an ordinary cycle, but one needs a certain amount of nonchalance in order to appear with it on the street

Maurice Chevalier

singing

"'Y a de la joie"

to the prisoners of war in a camp which was formerly "his"

"'Y a de la joie," the famous song hit, recently gave great pleasure to prisoners of war in a camp in Germany. And it was 'sung by Maurice Chevalier himself! Accompanied by a medical officer, who is a prisoner of war, Chevalier sang after a lapse of 24 years at the spot where he lay during the Great War as a wounded prisoner

PK. photographs: Front Correspondent Kind

Enthusiastically cheered, the artiste leaves the circle of his French comrades. He not only sang, but also spoke to them of home and of the patience he had to show when he suffered the same fate

A new song sung in the camp for the first time was the big surprise which Maurice had prepared for his countrymen. The gestures with which he accompanied it and which our photographer has succeeded in catching, show that Chevalier can act as well as he sings

25 years later

"War-bread"—as baked after a quarter of a century

"War-bread" is a word which awakens unpleasant memories in the minds of all who had to eat it in 1917. Why is our "war-bread" so incomparably better today? The expert replies: "The secret is in the bakery"

1 **Three quarters rye and one quarter barley** *are the chief ingredients of our modern war bread. To these are added a small percentage of potato flour*

For centuries bread has been the staple food of every nation. We might expect, therefore, that in the course of time people would have learnt to bake appetizing, easily digestible and nutritious bread. But man's apprenticeship days are never over for the circumstances under which he lives continue to develop and change and not under the stress of war and its exigencies alone.

The present war, like the last World War, has profoundly affected the food situation of Europe. During the last war, however, the British hunger blockade forced people to resort to a substitute and flour was stretched with maize and lupin-seed, with inferior ingredients and roughage lacking any food value. Some malicious people even declare that the old "war-bread" contained sawdust and tree bark.

Today people do not look for substitutes but for ingredients which can compensate for a possible loss. We know that there is a shortage of albumen in the food of Europe. We know too that bran contains grains of aleuron; these cristalline grains in their natural state are indigestible and must be broken up. Rye flour contains 14 % of this albumen-like ingredient which it is well worth while utilizing. Flour for bread is therefore made of a mixture of three quarters of this valuable rye flour, one quarter of barley flour and a small percentage of potato flour. This wholemeal bread is baked twice as long as bread made of wheat and rye, that is an hour and a half to two hours instead of forty-five minutes and at a higher temperature. In this way the grains of aleuron are broken up and the bread is given a firm crust and a finely grained structure which prevents it from becoming dry and stale. More care and application are now demanded of the baker. He must see that the dough is thoroughly leavened and that the bread is well baked so that is that it does not remain moist.

Though in the beginning, the bread had several shortcomings and did not agree with some delicate stomachs, the bakers quickly adjusted themselves and the bread-eaters too. Even the eye has grown reconciled to the fact that good wholesome bread is black.

It is quite possible that this type of bread will outlive the war and that people will forget that when it first made its appearance it was looked upon and eaten with mistrust. But it is the good things that last...

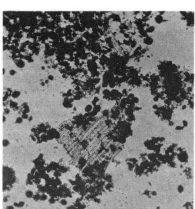
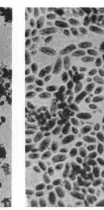
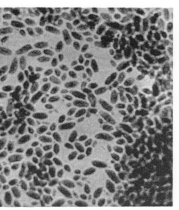

Dough under the microscope

2 *The 800-fold enlargement reveals the composition of the flour: the dark spots are grains of starch, the shaded portions are bran rich in vitamins*

3 *These bacteria in the leaven make the bread easily digestible. They cause the dough to rise so that the heat can penetrate the entire mass*

The wild waves

4 *are the fermentation going on in the yeast as seen by the camera. It is caused by the carbonic acid produced by the yeast and lactic acid bacteria*

The mixing

5 *of the fermented leaven with the new dough is an important process familiar to us from cake-baking. It is responsible for the pores in the bread*

Our daily bread after one and a half hours in the oven: interior and exterior

6 *A glance into the loaf. The dough has lost part of the water content, the albumen has coagulated and the ferments have been killed so that the bread can keep*

7 *A glance at the loaf. The delicate network of lines on the crust is produced by the dextrin. It results from the bursting of the grains of starch in the flour and has a faint sweetish taste*

8 **The real secret of all bread-baking:** *the correct temperature. At a temperature of 280 degrees Celsius dropping to 160 degrees the baking-time required for a loaf is one and a half hours. The process can, however, take as long as 22 hours as in the case of certain types of black bread*

Thermopylæ

During the hard fighting in the Greek mountains, heavy German artillery continually had to be employed in order to force a breakthrough by the Germans. Above the flash of the guns and the smoke, the white peaks of Olympus rise in eternal peace

The main resistance of the enemy has been broken at Thermopylæ. Mechanized columns follow the rapid advance of the tanks. Enemy fire is still occasionally directed against the line of advance. The crew leap from the lorry and take cover. But the advance can no longer be held up

After days of fighting and marching: the warm springs of Thermopylæ! Uniforms are stripped off in a moment, and the marching troops have soon become a jolly group of bathers
Photographs:
P.K. Müller

This is how the German troops were greeted in most places in Greece

At the head of the population, the Greek Orthodox Archbishop and the Mayor of a small town greet the commander of the troops just marching in

A memorable sight:
The flag of the young and victorious German Army waves above the centuries old pillars of the Acropolis

To the Führer of the German people

The entry of the German troops has once more brought law and order to Greece. A letter addressed to the Führer by the People's Commission of Alexandropolis (formerly Dedeagach), the capital of the Greek district of Ebros, provides especial confirmation of this fact:

"The population of Alexandropolis, who for three days have now lived in the territory occupied by the glorious German troops, have today voluntarily gathered together in order to express their heartfelt thanks to Your Excellency as Supreme Commander of the glorious German army. They promise always to give testimony to their unalterable gratitude for the great civility and true chivalry shown by the courageous troops of occupation to the population. Life, honour, property as well as customs and national tradition have remained untouched. This is already demonstrated by the fact that life is continuing just as before along the same paths."

Alexandropolis, 10th April 1941
The People's Commission of Alexandropolis wishes to convey to your Excellency its gratitude and admiration.

Bishop	President
Pataron Heletios	Anas. Pentzos

Members
Nic. Stiropoulos   Konst. Saridis
General Secretary Manganaris

The capitulation
The agreements are signed. Left: General Jodl from the Führer's Headquarters; behind (standing): The Chief of Staff of the South-East Army, General Greiffenberg; in the middle (seated): The representative of the Greek Army, General Tsolacoglu who later formed the new Greek Government
Photograph: Schlickum (P. Com.)

Above the Acropolis

The engines hum as the German machines sweep across the deep blue skies of Greece. Below them in the landscape they see the red-brown earth, the cypress hedges, the white walls, and the marble stones. classical land greets them with its pillared halls and temples. A new epic is sounding over the

…ortal Athens of Pericles. The buildings he created in spite …he Peloponnesian War and which still today are a testi-…y to the superior spirit that animated the Greek ideal of beauty, are witnesses of the glorious events of our time. The engines hum — and far below the unforgettable pano-rama unfolds and fades away once more for an iron will is driving them on. But the dazzling fame that clings to their wings and the victory that accompanies them are lasting things.

Photograph: Röder (P. Com.)

Here
BRITAIN was repulsed

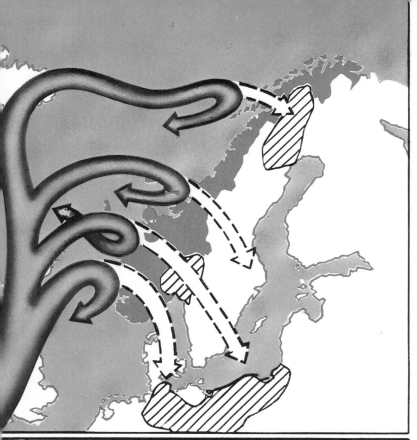

April 1940

A Northern Front against Germany—

was Britain's first idea, when the Eastern Front collapsed after a campaign lasting only 18 days and Germany's strong fortifications in the West made an attack seem inadvisable. In April 1940 London prepared an attack on the Scandinavian states with the object of seizing the Swedish ore mines and preparing the advance against the North of Germany. But Germany anticipated the British by occupying Norway and Denmark ten hours before. — Britain was obliged to retire.

May 1940

Belgium and Holland

were then favoured with the British hopes of an offensive. The governments of the two countries were made pliant by propaganda, agreements and economic dependence; the attack on the Ruhr district was prepared by means of discussions between the General Staffs and concrete military measures. Germany once more dealt her blow first and Britain was driven off. The Dutch, Belgian and French armies capitulated in less than six weeks

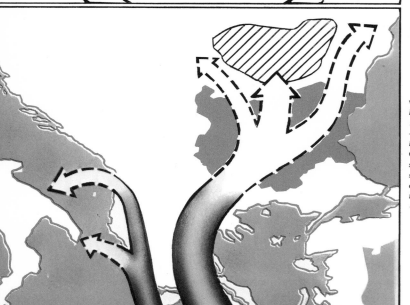

Autumn 1940

And now a Southern Front

was Britain's next slogan. Italy was to be attacked from the Mediterranean —with North Africa as the base—and from Greece, Germany's sources of supply in the Danubian states were to be cut off, the Rumanian oil fields were to be destroyed as had been the case during the Great War and Rumania, Bulgaria and, if possible, Yugoslavia also, were to be used as a base for an advance by a Balkan army against the Axis powers

Mr Eden—a traveller with but little success

In December 1939 : Between lunch and dinner a magnanimous handshake for officers of the French army, " Britain's Continental sword," which broke a few months later

In February 1940 : Mr Eden at the Suez Canal, before the gates of Europe, greets Indian troops —which, however, never reached Europe

One year later : Once more Eden has travelled beyond Europe. He arrived in Ankara with Sir John Dill, the Chief of the General Staff, in order to make arrangements for British troops to march through Turkey. From there he flew to Athens. He soon left this spot, however. German troops have marched into Bulgaria

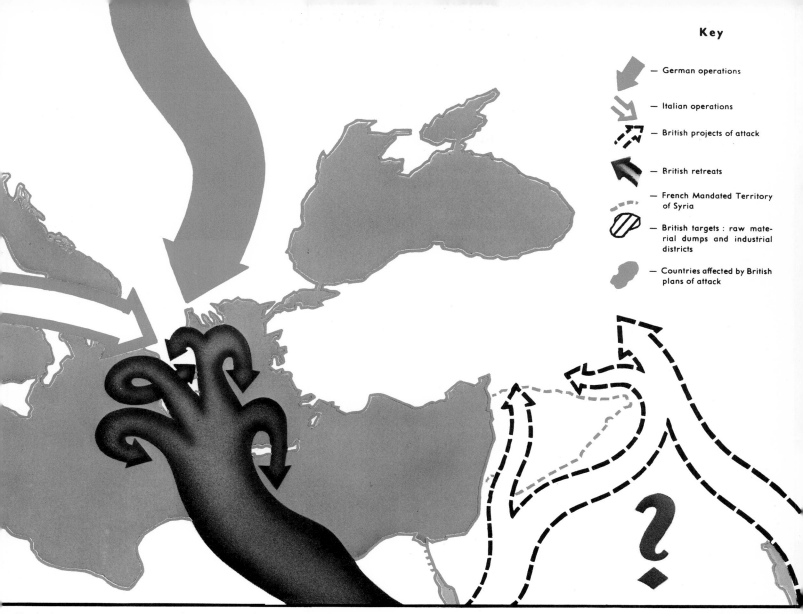

— German operations

— Italian operations

— British projects of attack

— British retreats

— French Mandated Territory of Syria

— British targets : raw material dumps and industrial districts

— Countries affected by British plans of attack

March 1941 : In the Danube lands too British plans have now been frustrated. *Greece and Rumania had received one-sided guarantees from Britain, Turkey had concluded a pact with her, and Bulgaria and Yugoslavia were subjected to strong diplomatic and economic pressure. But only Greece was actually drawn into the war. The British representatives were compelled to leave Rumania and Bulgaria, while German forces took over the defence of the Balkans against London's plans of aggression. Even the final threats and propaganda of the British Foreign Minister were doomed to failure. London cast around for new spheres in which she might sow unrest and began to toy again with the old plan of an attack on Syria and a mustering of her auxiliary troops in the Near East. The world was witness of Britain's defeat in the Balkans. Bulgaria's adherence to the Three-Power Pact was the turning point*

... they did not know where they were going...

By the wire which encloses 15,000 prisoners of war *a lively trade is going on. The 15,000 prisoners of war temporarily housed in these former Greek barracks in the town of Corinth all have considerable sums of money. They are allowed to spend it as they like. They buy food, tobacco and cigarettes. They are also very curious and they all want to know when the war will be over. Our correspondent went into the camp and spoke with many of the prisoners. They told him:*

"Signal's" special correspondent, PK. Grossmann, who is taking part in the campaign in the south-east, has sent us these interviews. During his numerous flights, he arrived one day at Corinth and there found 15,000 prisoners housed in barracks formerly used by the Greek army, partly soldiers and partly people in Britain's pay. He says that never in his life had he seen such a mixture of races as he did here. Grossmann has not given us any information about the spirit of these British "soldiers"... that is sufficiently indicated by the prisoners themselves whom he interviewed.

We swam to Greece ... *Two Indians relate: "We have been in Britain's service for many years. We were still children when we began. We cooked for the officers and cleaned their boots. No, we did not know where we were going. We do not understand English. We travelled for a very long time. When land was in sight, our ship went down. We were below deck and just managed to get out before the boat sank. We are all good swimmers. I think we ran into a mine, or it may have been a bomb. Nobody told us anything. I am", says one of them, who has a white beard, "an old man. I have never had such a good time as I am having now. I am unaccustomed to the food here, but there is nobody ordering us to do this, that and the other, or to go here or go there. We need not do anything."*

Narvik, Dunkirk and now ... *"Yes, I have been in it right from the start. During the last war, I left Australia too late in 1918. But I did see the Rhine. I am sure, it was a very interesting time! Yes, I am a professional soldier and have the rank of captain. In 1940, I was on the spot in time, Norway. In Narvik, it looked as though the Germans had made a mistake. Well, better too early than too late. We managed to get on to the ships, because the French and Poles took over our positions. Then came Dunkirk. We already knew from Narvik what it was like to climb on to the ships under a hail of bombs from the dive bombers. Then we went to Greece. Athens was very nice, and then the Germans came back and fired a number of times. That's all. That happened in the middle of April. It was a Sunday. We were sitting at supper and were intending to drive further south during the night. Suddenly a report came that the Germans were also pushing in from the east. We did not worry any more about supper and immediately got into our cars. We drove for exactly two hours and then it was all over. The Germans had caught us up on other roads. Why should we do any shooting? We got out of our cars and continued our supper ..."*

"In Palestine I suffered from hunger..." *"In 1939 just when H was marching into Prague, I emigrated to Palestine. I am a Jew shoemaker from Darmstadt. At first I had a very bad time, un found employment on an orange plantation. Then the war broke In the autumn of 1940 I was suddenly marched off by British soldi I was given very good food and a uniform. We were paid more mo than we had ever earned. At the beginning of 1940 we were embar on a ship. Nobody knew where we were going. I have not once ta part in an engagement, and concerning my capture I can o say that all the British had suddenly disappeared from the ca I think it was at Lamia that the British officers gave their men o order to drive off on transport lorries. The British officers rema for a few hours before they followed in fast cars. Be doing so, however, they attempted with drawn revolvers to up the retreating Greek soldiers. But the Greeks saw all the British soldiers had already fled. They did not a themselves to be intimidated."*

He fled from London . . . "*Before the war I was a policeman in London. But the duty during the hundreds of nights when we had raids was nothing for me. I could not sleep any more. I volunteered for police service in the army for a period of 12 years. I have not been in any large scale engagements. We all thought that in Greece the R. A. F. was much stronger than the German Air Force. That is what we had been told in England. The Germans are fine fellows. We thought they were barbarians; that is what we had read in the papers. But my pals and I agree that we are treated here in the camp better than we had been by our own officers. Above all, the German officers are friendly towards us. I only hope that the war will soon be over, so that I can return to my wife who lives on the Isle of Wight.*"

"I wanted to earn more money . . ." "*I used to work on the railway in Khartoum. But I got tired of it and I got a job as a stoker on board a ship. I ran away in Jaffa. I became an orange packer on a farm. An Englishman arrived who told us that we could earn a lot of money. I went on board a ship and did not have to work. Then, dressed in a fine uniform, I worked in Egypt in a dock. Then the man came again and asked if we wanted to earn still more money. We naturally wanted to. We were taken to a country where it was cold and there I worked in a harbour with lots of British soldiers. One day the British ran away and told us that we were to shoot when the Germans came. But we did not want to. I am better off now than I have ever been. We have no need to work at all. Have you a cigarette, sir?*"

were not asked . . . "*I come from the island Cyprus, from Famagusta. I was a miner there. the outbreak of war, the British administration d down the mines for two months. Then the h put up posters saying that anybody in Cyprus wanted to work for Britain, would be paid shillings a day. As we were unemployed and arning anything, we naturally accepted the shillings. One morning the gates were closed. lorries were drawn up in front of the mines we were transported in them to the harbour. were embarked just as we were and did not mbark again until we reached Egypt. We not asked. We have never borne arms and not seen a German until we were captured. But e we were in Greece, we scarcely slept at or the German aeroplanes left us no peace.*"

Machinist on a troop transport . . . "*I shall never in my life forget how the three German planes hurtled down towards us with their sirens howling. At first I did not see them. But when our machine guns suddenly began firing, I saw them in the sky. At first they were quite small, but the noise announcing them was terrible. I could see the bombs dropping quite clearly. But I had not even the courage to jump into the water. When I saw the bomb whistling down quite near, I took cover behind an iron door. All I remember is that I was hurled into the air together with the iron door. I suppose I lost consciousness. But I came to myself again in the water. I found a beam from the wheel-house, which had been demolished, and I clung to that. There was nothing more to be seen of our ship. It had sunk in a few seconds. It must have exploded like a barrel of gunpowder.*"

"We are all from Melbourne . . ." My comrades and I, from the very first day of the war here in Greece, said that it was impossible to beat the Germans. They had too many planes and they were very good in the way they used them. Only rarely did we see British planes fighting against Germans, and when we did, it was always the Germans who won. I am a farmer, in fact most of us are from the land. We all joined up, because we considered it the right thing to do. At school we were taught that we must help when Britain is in need. Please don't ask me what we think of this war. I am married and should like to get home soon — I won't say any more."

The booty from 250 wars...

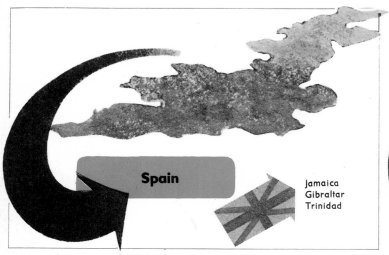

Spain

Jamaica
Gibraltar
Trinidad

The first slogan: Down with Spain! *Britain deprived Spain, the leading world power in the Middle Ages, of Jamaica in 1655 and of Gibraltar in 1704. She subsequently drove the Spaniards out of their possessions in Florida. During the Napoleonic wars the British stole Trinidad and in the years following they supported the South American States in their efforts at secession*

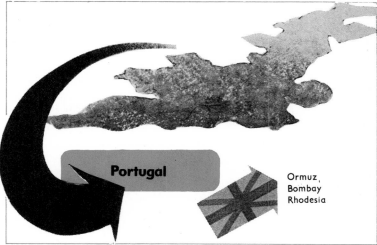

Portugal

Ormuz
Bombay
Rhodesia

The second slogan: Take over the legacy of Portugal! *Round about 1600 the British took advantage of conflicts regarding the succession to the throne in Portugal in order to seize Portugal's most important possessions on the western coast of India as far as Ormuz. They occupied Bombay in 1661 and Rhodesia towards the end of the 19th century. As early as 1820 the British had dealt a blow at the Portuguese Empire by supporting Brazil's efforts to attain independence*

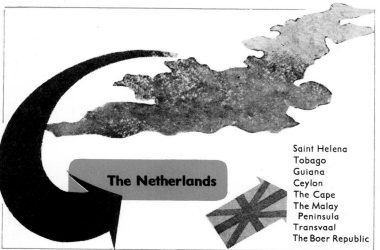

The Netherlands

Saint Helena
Tobago
Guiana
Ceylon
The Cape
The Malay
  Peninsula
Transvaal
The Boer Republic

The third slogan: Rob the Netherlands! *In the middle of the 17th century Britain seized the Dutch settlement of New Amsterdam in North America and renamed it New York. A few years later the British occupied Saint Helena and a century afterwards the island of Tobago in the West Indies. The richest booty fell into their hands during the Napoleonic wars: Guiana, Ceylon, Cape Colony and somewhat later the Malay Peninsula. In 1877 and 1902 the British conquered the Dutch settlements in South Africa: the Transvaal and the Boer Republics*

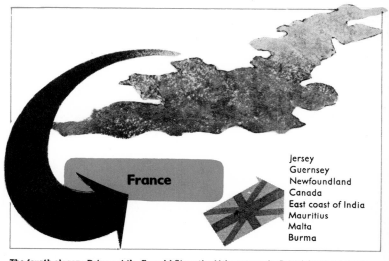

France

Jersey
Guernsey
Newfoundland
Canada
East coast of India
Mauritius
Malta
Burma

The fourth slogan: Drive out the French! *Since the 11th century the British had held the Channel Islands of Jersey and Guernsey as the last pledge from their centuries of war against France. In 1713 they seized Newfoundland and Acadia from the French and in 1763 Canada and the most important possessions in the East Indies. During the Napoleonic wars they stole the Seychelle Islands, Mauritius and Malta, during the 18th century they drove the French out of Burma and a hundred years later at Fashoda frustrated the hopes France had set on the Sudan*

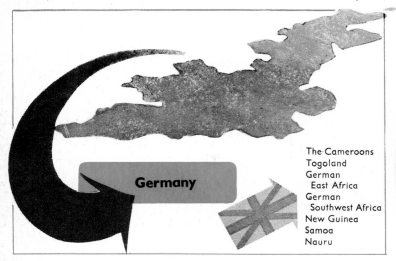

Germany

The Cameroons
Togoland
German
  East Africa
German
  Southwest Africa
New Guinea
Samoa
Nauru

The fifth slogan: Keep Germany small! *In 1914 Britain asserted that she was not fighting to increase her colonial possessions, but after 1918 she gladly collected as booty the main part of the German colonies, parts of the Cameroons and Togoland, German East Africa, German Southwest Africa, New Guinea, Samoa and the Pacific island of Nauru*

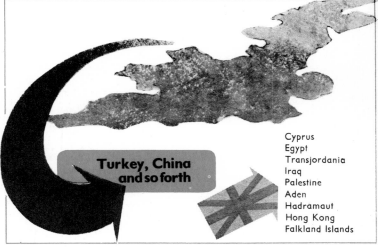

Turkey, China and so forth

Cyprus
Egypt
Transjordania
Iraq
Palestine
Aden
Hadramaut
Hong Kong
Falkland Islands

The eternal British slogan: Take...! *In the 19th and 20th centuries the British took from the Turks Cyprus, Egypt, Transjordania, Iraq, Palestine and the regions of Arab influence Aden and Hadramaut, from the Chinese they took Hong Kong, from the Argentinians the Falkland Islands, from the Thais a number of provinces in 1909 in order to round off their own possessions*

...and then: PAX BRITANNICA

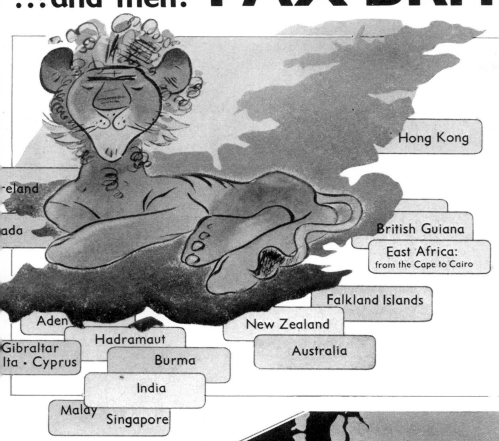

Hong Kong

Ireland

ada

British Guiana

East Africa:
from the Cape to Cairo

Falkland Islands

Aden

New Zealand

Gibraltar
Ita · Cyprus

Hadramaut

Australia

Burma

India

Malay

Singapore

The Empire has had enough of it!

Eleven people work for every Britisher; this simple way of expressing it most clearly demonstrates the importance of the Empire for Great Britain. 45 million people inhabit the British Isles, whilst about 500 million people (of a total of 2 milliards) were embraced by the Empire at the time when it was most extensive after 1918. 15,600,000 square miles of a total of 54 million square miles over the whole earth were ruled by London, the proportion of the area of Great Britain to that of the Empire was more than 1 : 150. The indirect but not less effective influence of the British on numerous independent states enabled them to control more than half the world. 250 wars in approximately as many years were necessary in order to found this power. But in the world the destruction of the natural order cannot be maintained for ever, the first signs are already there:

The Empire is crumbling

A new slogan makes its appearance: Away from Britain! The secession of the U.S.A. was the first blow dealt at the Empire policy of the British. The real dissolution did not become obvious, however, until 1939. Britain first lost Jersey and Guernsey. Then the U.S.A. leased bases on Newfoundland, the Bermudas, the Bahamas, Trinidad, British Guiana, Jamaica, Antigua, Santa Lucia and for all practical purposes took over these regions. Canada and Australia drew very close to the U.S.A. In India, Egypt and South Africa the efforts to achieve liberty increased, Ireland remained outside the British war—and Japan conquered Hong Kong, the Malay Peninsula, Singapore, Borneo, Burma and New Guinea

Happy Interlude
in Wartime

A true little story in pictures,
photographed by Hanns Hubmann

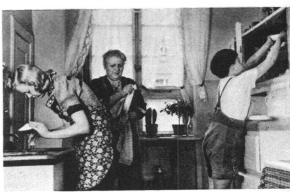

1. Hanns Hubmann, our Berlin photographer, attends a dress rehearsal in a Berlin cabaret, for the purpose of collecting a few good pictures. One of the dancers takes his eye — she looks very familiar to me, he thinks, and speaks to her. Sure enough, it is Gerda Kurz . . .

2. Gerda Kurz, for four years "second from the left"
in the chorus of the Metropol Theater in Berlin. She is no longer "second from the left" in the chorus. Although she was not at all badly off there—she earned 250 marks a month— she was ambitious and wanted to get ahead; Hans Hubmann decided to picturize her story

3. HIS picture occupied the place of honor before her mirror in the dressing-room
"How did you manage it all, anyway?" asked Hubmann. Said Gerda, "Hard work. Sometimes very hard work, but we wanted to get married and Peter's earnings stopped of course when he was called to service, at the very beginning of the war. (He's in a town on the border, you know.) We'll be needing so many things when we marry that I decided something had to be done about it"

4.
Gerda went on with her story:
"I prepared myself for every possible development.
I took vocal lessons twice a week. I went in hard for acrobatics and sports. Training is everything in our profession . . . Of course all this cost a lot of money, but . . ."

5. I was lucky in being able to live at home with my parents
I helped wherever I could, lent a hand in the kitchen and kept a watchful eye on the kid brother's school work . . .

6. "Fetching rations" was also part of my job!

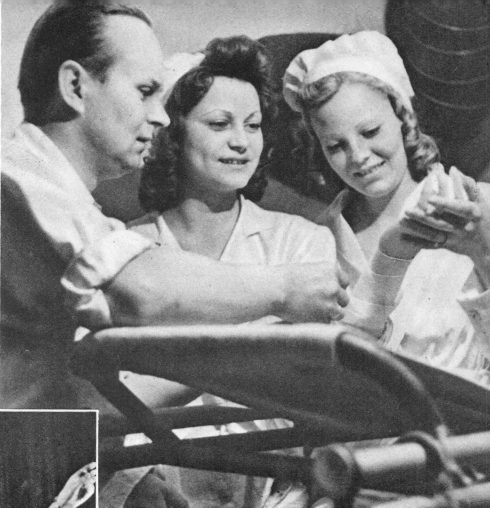

7. "When I thought I was ready to take the jump, I went to the Reich Theatrical Chamber. They at once sent me here to the Kabarett der Komiker (Comedians' Cabaret), under Willi Schaeffer's direction. They said Mr. Schaeffer needed new talent. Competition was hard but I made the grade. Now I'm . . ."

9. Hanns Hubmann photographed her there, and not only on the stage Gerda is doing her bit on the Home Front. She is a nurse in her theater's air protection organization. She has learned all about bandaging and the treatment of poison gas victims

10. A few weeks later . . . Hanns Hubmann is best man — and official reporter — at a proxy marriage. Peter thought the German victory offered a good opportunity to slip into the matrimonial yoke. As his troop is expected to go into action soon, he applied to his company commander for permission to marry. Hanns Hubmann had him send a picture of the "wedding without a bride".(Above) At the "wedding without a groom" Hubmann was present himself, as best man. (Right) Gerda Kurz says "yes" and signs her name in the registrar's office of her district in Berlin . . . A happy little interlude in times of war

8. " . . . solo dancer at the Comedians Cabaret."

STRIKING THE BALANCE

The losses of the British Navy

The following considerations are merely an intermediate balance referring only to warships the sinking of which could not be denied by the British Admiralty

The race. *According to British admissions twice as many British warships are sunk as can be replaced by new launchings. The illustration in which the original number of warships is marked in black and the new launchings red shows the unavoidable and constant decrease of the British Navy during this race between ships sunk and launched*

"Whoever rules the seas rules the trade of the world and the riches of the world, that is the world itself."

In logical application of this principle little by little Britain destroyed all the great seapowers in the world: the Spaniards, the Portuguese, the Dutch, the French and the smaller powers, too, as the "confiscation" of the Danish Fleet at Copenhagen in 1807 proves. Since Nelson's victory at Trafalgar over the combined French and Spanish squadrons in 1805 British domination at sea has been uncontested. Even the first World War 1914-1918 dealt it no decisive blow. With the exception of the Baltic and parts of the North Sea and the Adriatic the Union Jack and the flags of her allies continued to rule the waves even though submarines and merchant warfare caused the British Supreme Command much anxiety.

In 1940, however, the position was radically changed after the defeat of France when Germany won the Atlantic coast from the North Cape to the Bay of Biscay and when Italy entered the war. The ever-increasing activity of the German Navy and Air Force stationed in the newly won bases puts Britain in a very serious position. The losses suffered by the Navy and the mercantile marine are on the increase and the island finds itself facing a mortal danger. In the third year of the war the Empire had to shoulder an additional burden when war began in the Pacific and South Eastern Asia.

This third year of the war is the most difficult within human memory for the British Navy Between September 1941 and August 1942 the fleet flying the Union Jack lost according to British admissions approximately 30% of all big warships in existence at the outbreak of hostilities: 3 battleships, 1 monitor, 5 aircraft carriers including auxili-

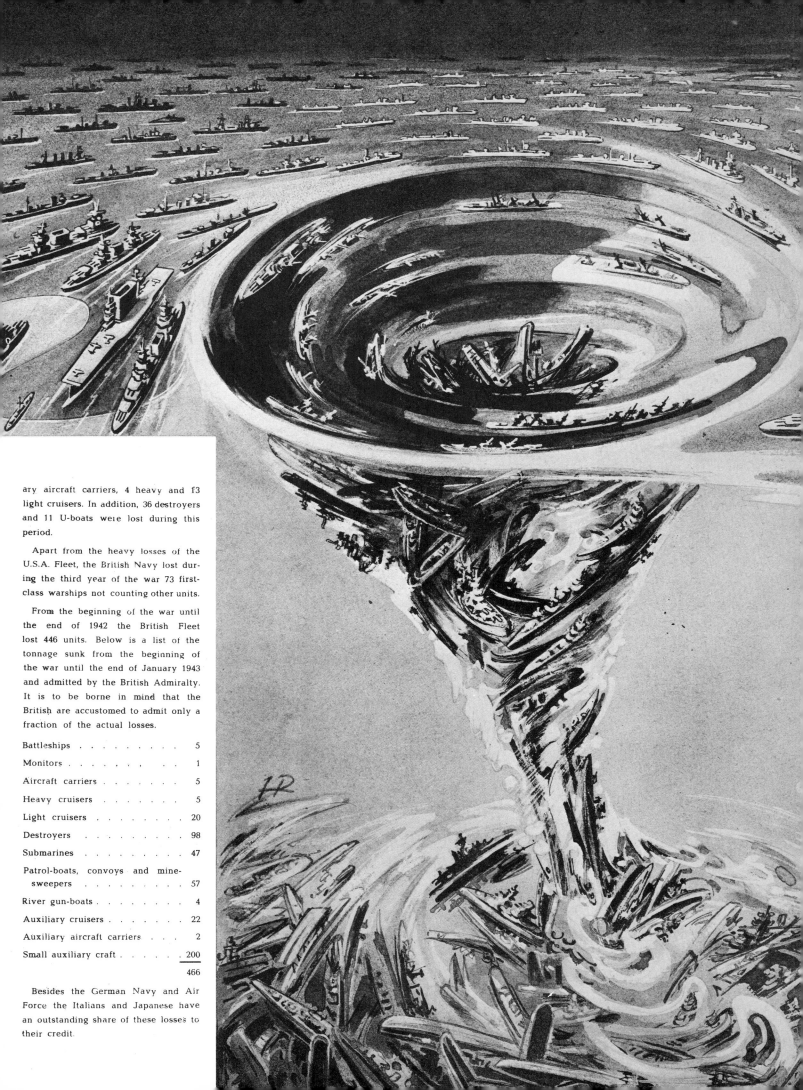

ary aircraft carriers, 4 heavy and 13 light cruisers. In addition, 36 destroyers and 11 U-boats were lost during this period.

Apart from the heavy losses of the U.S.A. Fleet, the British Navy lost during the third year of the war 73 first-class warships not counting other units.

From the beginning of the war until the end of 1942 the British Fleet lost 446 units. Below is a list of the tonnage sunk from the beginning of the war until the end of January 1943 and admitted by the British Admiralty. It is to be borne in mind that the British are accustomed to admit only a fraction of the actual losses.

Battleships	5
Monitors	1
Aircraft carriers	5
Heavy cruisers	5
Light cruisers	20
Destroyers	98
Submarines	47
Patrol-boats, convoys and mine-sweepers	57
River gun-boats	4
Auxiliary cruisers	22
Auxiliary aircraft carriers	2
Small auxiliary craft	200
	466

Besides the German Navy and Air Force the Italians and Japanese have an outstanding share of these losses to their credit.

The fear of death gives him courage. *Whilst this British destroyer is sinking, one of the crew who is a non-swimmer remains in his dangerous position until he is rescued*

On the right: **A wounded giant.** *The bow of the sinking ship towers above the water. The crew of the German U-boat watches the English ship sink to the bottom*

The Battle of the Atlantic

WILHELMPLATZ 8/9

AT THE HEADQUARTERS OF REICH MINISTER Dr GOEBBELS

In the middle of the night: an adjutant brings the Minister important telegrams and reports

In the ante-room: the telephone table with a hundred important connexions which can be obtained immediately

Berlin on a Sunday morning: a city waking up late, recovering from a seventy-hour week. Deserted streets, half-empty trams, infrequent passers-by in their Sunday best, an occasional group of Hitler Youths marching along on a Sunday route march. The boys' faces are fresh and ruddy, the hollow echo of their marching song resounds in the empty streets. They are marching out of the town which is filled today with a refreshing or dismal quietness, according to one's point of view, when compared with the noise and activity of its busy weekdays.

Only in the Government quarter, in the vicinity of the deserted banking houses and fashionable shops in the centre of the town, can one feel quite plainly that workaday life is still going on. It is a long time since there have been any Sundays in the Wilhelmplatz. "A good three years," sighs an attendant in a brown tailcoat. There every day is the same as the next. To some it seems mere chance, to others, in a spasm of excessive fatigue, it seems sometimes perhaps a mockery, that today's date is marked red on the calender.

But everybody here knows perfectly well that the world does not stand still every seventh day. On this day it even uninterruptedly receives certain stimuli. The rotary machines are also working, and transmitters are broadcasting news to every corner of the globe. At the front, the dive-bombers are howling as usual, on the Atlantic, torpedoes are ready to be fired and sharp eyes are scanning the horizon. The daily intellectual struggle continues ceaselessly in the same way. Perhaps even a new round will be begun today!

If he were to disregard the long row of small and somewhat old-fashioned cars of all makes and colours parked there on this early Sunday morning, the unconcerned stranger looking at the handsome white palace at 8-9 Wilhelmplatz would never realize the high pressure activity, the rhythm of work

At 9.30 on Sunday mornings in the Wilhelmplatz

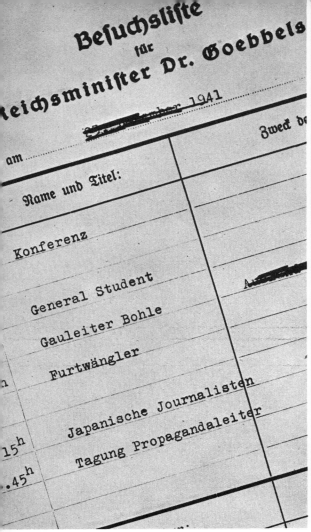

Besuchsliste für Reichsminister Dr. Goebbels

...ember 1941

am .... Zweck de...

Name und Titel:

Konferenz

General Student

Gauleiter Bohle

Furtwängler

15ʰ   Japanische Journalisten

.45ʰ   Tagung Propagandaleiter

The time-table between 11 a.m. and 2 p.m.

The touch of a lever suffices and with the aid of this up-to-date technical installation Dr Goebbels can immediately switch off the programme of the broadcasting stations in Greater Germany and himself speak through this microphone to all listeners ↓

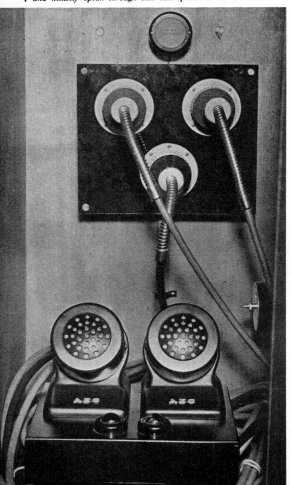

The servant in the brown tailcoat, who used to receive official visits, is now working in a munition factory

Photographs:
Boesig (Atlantic)

Even when Dr Goebbels is away from Berlin on official business, he continually keeps in touch with his Ministry. Documents and papers are sent to him by special courier

like particularly to take a peep behind the veil, when they crowd the Wilhelmplatz every day and look up reverently or filled with curiosity to the windows of the Führer's apartments or the Propaganda Ministry, in order thereby to experience something of the spirit of mystery which always surrounds this square. When the Führer is at his Headquarters or withdraws to the Berghof at times of apparent rest, the curiosity of the daily visitors to the Wilhelmplatz—usually soldiers passing through Berlin or on leave—is concentrated on the Ministry of Propaganda. There are then always certain signs—at least, so a foreign journalist recently asserted—from which it can even be deduced what the political and military situation is when the newspapers, as is sometimes necessary, receive instructions to publish no news. On the eve of political or military events, the Wilhelmplatz has a politically exciting atmosphere all its own. One then has the impression that the thundery sultriness during the last few hours before the lightning begins to flash has become so intense that the secrets in the safes and the rooms of the Ministers, Secretaries of State and high officials no longer have sufficient space.

They apparently begin to take refuge on the square in front of their windows where curious people stand hoping to be able to learn them gradually. It was like that during the last days of August in 1939, it was the same on 5th April 1941, when the storm broke out in the Balkans, and on many other occasions. A traffic policeman in his white coat, tall and blond like one of the heroes of the Germanic sagas, has been a feature of the Wilhelmplatz for years. Siegfried is the most popular policeman in the capital of the Reich. He knows personally all the Ministers and leading personalities in the State and Army. He is known by journalists and diplomats, important and unimportant officials, and they all ask him questions. He knows a great deal, probably because he continually sees the ceaseless comings and goings in the Government quarter. But he is also fully aware of the importance of his post and only speaks when it appears necessary to him to do so. He is a propagandist who at least fits in well with the Wilhelmplatz.

A kiosk on the Wilhelmplatz, which sells postcards and souvenirs of Berlin, introduces the visitor to the private atmosphere of the Government quarter. Edda, Göring's little daughter, can be bought on a variety of postcards, either playing with a baby lion or riding on the shoulders of her beaming father. Dr Goebbels can be seen in his family circle. With seven children this family is, apart from that of the Minister of

going on within its walls, introduced by the master of the house when he took up his quarters there on 13th March 1933.

The sleepy-looking little palace—one of the most beautiful pieces of architecture in the capital of the Reich—has become, under Dr Goebbels, one of the most up-to-date ministries in the world. Many efforts made in other countries to imitate this house and the influence it exercises all over the world, have remained, with few exceptions, only attempts of no importance.

Here, however, at every minute of the day and night, the heart of the political world can be heard beating. Even in peacetime, particularly clever people were able to observe from "unmistakable" signs whether thunder clouds were looming up on the political horizon and now during wartime, the many people out for a stroll would

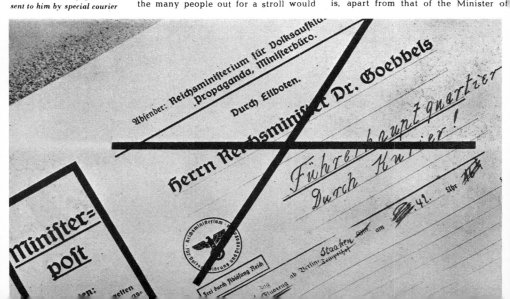

A writing-desk without piles of papers on it

Finance, Graf Schwerin von Krosigk, who has eight children, the largest belonging to a Minister in a régime which advocates large numbers of children as a national necessity and a national virtue.

Although Dr Goebbels drives up the slope in front of his Ministry in his small car punctually at 9 o'clock every morning, the externally visible full pressure activity only begins shortly before eleven. Persistant petitioners intercept the Minister as soon as he arrives and although the day's time-table is drawn up exactly to the minute. Dr Goebbels often spares the time to listen to the cares of some unknown person who thinks he has been unjustly treated on some occasion or other.

The series of conferences, meetings and discussions now begins and does not finish before the afternoon. A stream of prominent visitors, deputations, Ministers, Generals, artists and newspaper men, mostly in uniform, but also sometimes in civilian clothes, now passes, almost according to a programme drawn up to the minute, through the main entrance which is decorated by a large National Socialist

emblem in iron. An attendant in a velvet collar and a brown tailcoat receives the visitors. He is able to greet foreign guests in all the most important languages in the world. In general, the visitors to the house pass a strict control on entering. The experienced attendant, however, knows hundreds of personalities in public life, both Germans and foreigners, whose names have often figured during the last few years in the visiting book of the Minister of Propaganda.

During the course of the years, the Ministry of Propaganda has become a gigantic institute in the form of a political control extending to all spheres of public life and, fortunately for the person concerned, also of private life.

The numerous offices can no longer be accommodated at the Wilhelmplatz. They are situated all over the town and are even strewn as far as the most distant suburbs. This becomes easy to understand when it is taken into consideration, for example, that the Reich Chamber of Culture, the principal organ of all the cultural life in the Reich, with its 800,000 members,

requires an extensive apparatus which all ultimately leads to the Propaganda Ministry. In spite of all the accumulation of work, however, the principle has held sway, ever since the establishment of the Ministry, of consigning all avoidable bureaucratic habits to oblivion and using as little paper as possible.

The up-to-dateness of this house also finds expression in the fact that it gets rid of everything antiquated and employs every refinement of the technical aids the 20th century can offer us. Files of papers are not so important in this house as the telephone, the tele-writer and the radio. For speed is the first commandment in a Ministry whose task it is to care for and guide the nation along its political, mental and spiritual path. Its most important instruments in doing so are the press and the radio.

That is why, at about 11 o'clock every morning, the number of cars increases bringing officers, officials and political leaders to the Ministerial Conference from the Government Ministries, the offices of the Party and the Army. The big Mercedes and

Horch cars of peacetime have disappeared. The small "popular car" fills the picture. Couriers on motorcycles wearing long grey rubber coats drive up, elderly Government messengers, schoolboys and women of various ages bring sealed portfolios. The small crowd of interested people, which can always be found in the Wilhelmplatz, closely follows this "Government business." Officers with the red stripe denoting the General Staff are just hurrying through the main entrance and now a car with the pendant of the "Radio of the Greater German Reich" has just pulled up on the slope.

Dr Goebbels personally presides over the Ministerial Conference every day. Hundreds of telegrams from abroad, press reports and the radio lies of the enemy, reports on the situation from the Reich and the occupied territories, proposals for laws, suggestions and wishes from other Ministries and messages stating the situation on the various fronts provide the very varied material on which the Minister bases the daily political and propagandistic plan of operations from which proceed the parole for the day.

From
Newfoundland
to
Cape Horn

The British sales in the
Western Hemisphere

In exchange for 50 obsolete destroyers, the United States has received from England the right to establish naval and air bases in Newfoundland, the Bermudas, the Bahamas, Jamaica, Santa Lucia, Antigua, Trinidad and British Guiana, situated on the South American mainland—that is to say, on South American soil. The U. S. A. has by this simple procedure brought about a change in the belt of islands and archipelagos lying off the American coast and within the American sphere of political influence which, although at first not proclaimed, has nevertheless finally been openly propagated as the aim of American policy on the Atlantic side. In future ages it will appear noteworthy to historians that the collapse of the British Empire began, as it were, within view of the same continent which dealt the first blows resulting in the destruction of the first British transatlantic colonial Empire. That was approximately 170 years ago. England's expansion since that time has been so concentrated on India and the safeguarding of all routes leading there that the world at large had almost completely forgotten the fact that Britain possessed the strategically important islands off the coast of the American continent. This was not true of the American nations, above all it was not true of the United States. A further advance into the Atlantic always remained for America a goal towards which she strove by the most varied means, soon after the first consolidation of her position as a state. As early as 1823, the Monroe Doctrine was proclaimed, in opposition to any new colonial acquisition in America by European powers. The primary intention was to prevent England from extending her position in the Caribbean Sea, which the North Americans when the first plans for a Panama Canal came under discussion, regarded as within their sphere of influence. By the Clayton-Bulwer agreement of 1850, the two Powers bound themselves to refrain from extending their power in Central America. The U. S. A., however, took little notice of this agreement when Great Britain at the turn of the century, first during the Boer War and later in the Great War, was occupied elsewhere. American policy aimed at encircling the Caribbean Sea, at compensating for every British position by an American one and at gradually breaking down the British barrier in the region of the Panama Canal.

"A source of continual anxiety"

After the Great War, the American horizon was visibly extended. As early as 1923 Senator Reed has made a proposal which suggested that the entire British and, moreover, also the French possessions in the West Indies should be employed to cancel war debts. In September 1929, when the British Prime Minister, MacDonald, visited President Hoover, the *Chicago Daily Tribune* spoke of the demilitarisation or the cession of the West Indian possessions and added literally: "These and the British naval base in Bermuda are sources of continual anxiety for some Americans..." England last year attempted to prepare a counter-move by propagating the idea of a West Indian Dominion after the Australian model. The United States, therefore, by the new treaty has achieved an ambitious aim and England has initiated a sale on the pattern of the 99-year leases, which she has always so willingly employed. This she has done, moreover, on the very spot which is regarded as the cradle of the British Empire.

The conditions prevailing on these islands today are a testimony of an extraordinary kind to British methods of colonisation—different in their results, but always having the same cause, wherever they are applied.

Newfoundland — a step back

The British have always maintained of Newfoundland that an Englishman, to wit John Cabot of Bristol, had appeared there as early as June 24th, 1497 and had planted the British flag. It did, however, not become a possesion of the crown until almost a century later and the rich fishing banks were an object of ceaseless quarrels with the French until the first Entente Cordiale. But it was just on account of its long existence as a British colony, that made Newfoundland worthy of being accepted among the ranks of the Dominions with Home Rule. In the meantime, however, the one-sided tendency of British policy towards India was bound to lead to a decline in the other members. The mother country was no longer able to fill the world-wide spaces with sufficient new blood. Newfoundland was consequently obliged, after appealing in 1933 to London for help, to take a step back. Parliament and Home Rule once more disappeared and a British Government Commission took over the country. Even this Commission, however, was unable to achieve anything in this country, the mineral deposits of which are estimated at 20 milliards gold dollars. A year ago, Newfoundland was faced with the following situation: 70,000 people—a quarter of the population—lived on public relief. Innumerable women and children had to remain indoors during the winter, for they had nothing to wear. School was not compulsory. Every fifteenth person suffered from pulmonary consumption, and there is only one sanatorium in the whole of Newfoundland! Public relief was granted in the form of food, the value of which for adults was 20 cents per day and for children below the age of five 3 cents. Many of the children have never in their lives seen a coin—in a former dominion of what was until now the greatest Empire in the world.

Mr Tucker crosses human races

England's rule over the Bermudas dates back to about the same period. Anybody looking beneath the surface of conditions in those islands—outwardly so prosperous through rich American tourist traffic —will come upon a pitiful product of British colonisation. When George Somers began colonising the Bermudas at the beginning of the 17th century, he introduced black slaves. Daniel Tucker, second governor of these islands, indulged for his private amusement in the crossing of plants, animals and human beings. He crossed an Indian with a negress and advised his followers to pursue the experiment with the resulting offspring. Thirty years later a Mr Forster recalled this recommendation and had sixty Irishmen sent over who had been banished by Cromwell and continued crossing with them. Negroes with blue eyes and red hair, Indians with frizzy hair and similar types which are today ashamed even to visit the neighbouring islands, are found here as the result of several hundred years of British rule, and experimental human breeding.

Liberated negro slaves and their descendants also inhabit the Bahamas, a household word when the ex-King of England, the present Duke of Windsor, was appointed Governor ... because, as it was announced this post just happened to be vacant!

Poverty and destitution
in a World Empire

Jamaica has for long been one of the most important British bases in the central American sphere. Even after the U. S. A. had become independent and even after the first mention of the earliest plans for a canal joining the Atlantic and the Pacific, England reinforced her position on Jamaica by annexing British Honduras, a territory bordering on the Republic of Guatemala.

Establishment of an American base on Jamaica now also involves a political change of power here.

According to the new Anglo-American Treaty, these areas officially remain British colonies. The conditions on the island of Jamaica consequently also merit special attention: this island, so richly blessed by Nature has been called "a home of wretchedness in a world empire" and "a foul blot on British colonial rule." Jamaica, as many other territories was torn from the Spaniards by British

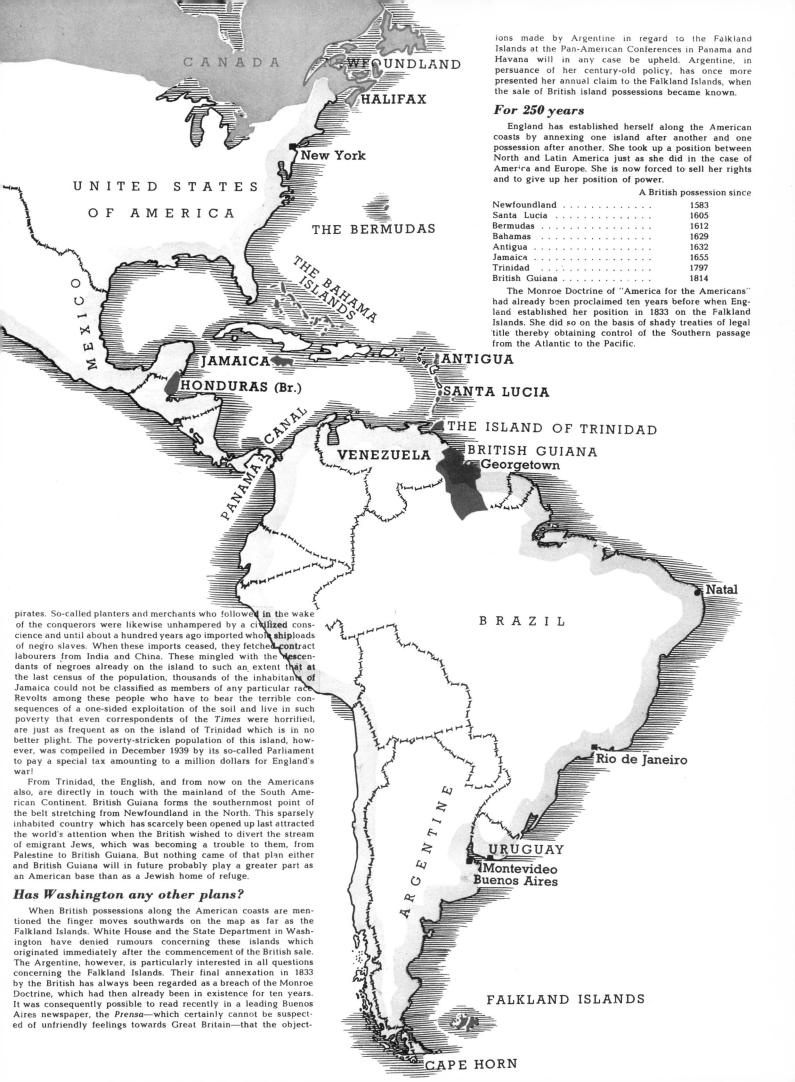

ions made by Argentine in regard to the Falkland Islands at the Pan-American Conferences in Panama and Havana will in any case be upheld. Argentine, in persuance of her century-old policy, has once more presented her annual claim to the Falkland Islands, when the sale of British island possessions became known.

For 250 years

England has established herself along the American coasts by annexing one island after another and one possession after another. She took up a position between North and Latin America just as she did in the case of America and Europe. She is now forced to sell her rights and to give up her position of power.

	A British possession since
Newfoundland	1583
Santa Lucia	1605
Bermudas	1612
Bahamas	1629
Antigua	1632
Jamaica	1655
Trinidad	1797
British Guiana	1814

The Monroe Doctrine of "America for the Americans" had already been proclaimed ten years before when England established her position in 1833 on the Falkland Islands. She did so on the basis of shady treaties of legal title thereby obtaining control of the Southern passage from the Atlantic to the Pacific.

pirates. So-called planters and merchants who followed in the wake of the conquerors were likewise unhampered by a civilized conscience and until about a hundred years ago imported whole shiploads of negro slaves. When these imports ceased, they fetched contract labourers from India and China. These mingled with the descendants of negroes already on the island to such an extent that at the last census of the population, thousands of the inhabitants of Jamaica could not be classified as members of any particular race. Revolts among these people who have to bear the terrible consequences of a one-sided exploitation of the soil and live in such poverty that even correspondents of the *Times* were horrified, are just as frequent as on the island of Trinidad which is in no better plight. The poverty-stricken population of this island, however, was compelled in December 1939 by its so-called Parliament to pay a special tax amounting to a million dollars for England's war!

From Trinidad, the English, and from now on the Americans also, are directly in touch with the mainland of the South American Continent. British Guiana forms the southernmost point of the belt stretching from Newfoundland in the North. This sparsely inhabited country which has scarcely been opened up last attracted the world's attention when the British wished to divert the stream of emigrant Jews, which was becoming a trouble to them, from Palestine to British Guiana. But nothing came of that plan either and British Guiana will in future probably play a greater part as an American base than as a Jewish home of refuge.

Has Washington any other plans?

When British possessions along the American coasts are mentioned the finger moves southwards on the map as far as the Falkland Islands. White House and the State Department in Washington have denied rumours concerning these islands which originated immediately after the commencement of the British sale. The Argentine, however, is particularly interested in all questions concerning the Falkland Islands. Their final annexation in 1833 by the British has always been regarded as a breach of the Monroe Doctrine, which had then already been in existence for ten years. It was consequently possible to read recently in a leading Buenos Aires newspaper, the *Prensa*—which certainly cannot be suspected of unfriendly feelings towards Great Britain—that the object-

"Wenn ein junger Mann kommt" from the Ufa film "Frauen sind doch bessere Diplomaten"

"I very seldom compose at the piano," admitted Theo Mackeben. "It is a delusion of the layman that the composer is continually strumming on the keys. He doesn't strum at all. In the same way, the popular song is not the main thing. The importance of the popular song in the film is almost negligible from the musical point of view. It is an inspiration, the fruit of two minutes—or no inspiration at all. It is quite a different thing if a chanson has to play a dramatic rôle, as in "Bel ami" when the aim was to explain the leitmotiv of the film. The text was to be a clear indication of the hero's character."

"Often enough night is turned into day," says Harald Böhmelt. "But that is what I need: everything must be quiet round about. Over and over again I have to work with the stop watch in my hand, for on one occasion they need music for 30 metres of film and on another occasion the music may only last 58 seconds. And then the transitions! The honourable audience once it has left the cinema, rarely has any recollection of the "incidental music" and this incidental music is just as difficult if not more difficult to compose than the so-called 'hits.'"

"How is it that both the Zarah Leander song 'Es wird einmal ein Wunder geschehen?' and my 'Seemann' became famous so quickly?" asks Michael Jary. "I can't tell you. Perhaps the word 'sailor' calls up a special picture. It is a fact that the song became popular much more quickly along the German coast than anywhere inland. But then… I could almost sing another song about what used to happen in the beginning wherever I appeared when there was a musical instrument within reach!"

"I swear by my sound projector," says Werner Bochmann. "I have a copy of the sound film made for me and then I play it through again so that I can do better next time. I am passionately interested in the technics of sound films. So much depends on the grouping of the musicians in front of the microphone. You often hear of an 'unfortunate mixture' of music and dialogue in films. And people complain that the simultaneous projection often results in the dialogue being indistinct. There are certain facts that one must know: a star's voice is recorded on a certain frequency and you must know this if the music is not to encroach. If this is taken into consideration and if instrumentation and composition are separated as far as possible from the frequency zone of the human voice then the simultaneous projection of music and dialogue cannot have a disturbing effect."

"A popular song cannot be composed to order," says Franz Grothe. "It is not a matter of thought. The easier and more effortlessly the musical inspiration comes, the greater is the prospect of success. And then chance, how the song is put over in the film or in the theatre for the first time, all plays an important part. In the cinema it is already clear whether the song has really got home or not. The wireless sometimes gives a finishing touch."

"Heimat, deine Sterne" from the Terra film "Quax, der Bruchpilot"

Werner Bochmann. He inherited his serene smile from his native Meerane where he was born at the turn of the century. While studying chemistry, he went in for music as a sideline. When he finally chose music for his profession, he recognized that here, too, he had to earn a living. He made this discovery while sitting in a café where an Argentinian band was playing. The band needed a temporary pianist, so Bochmann slipped on the gaucho's costume. In his spare time he composed and sat about in the waiting-rooms of film agencies. One day… He was especially interested in the technical side of the film and developed into a specialist on sound projection. His songs have since gone round the world, for example, "Heimat, Deine Sterne", "Abends in der Taverne" and "Gute Nacht, Mutter!"

Franz Grothe. The fact that his father was agent for a well-known piano factory is said to have had only an indirect influence on his talent for composing. That of his mother, a singer, was considerably greater. This hundred per cent Berliner, Franz Grothe, was lucky enough to be able to devote himself entirely to the study of music. His activity as conductor and regulator for a gramophone record factory was excellent practice. After that he made rapid progress, and when one has the help of a beautiful woman … The composer's wife is the film star Kirsten Heiberg, who is a particularly good interpreter of his song hits. The experience gathered while working with orchestras fitted him for the position of co-founder of the "Deutschen Tanz- und Unterhaltungsorchester" of the German Radio which has since become world famous. As a composer, Grothe has a special talent for songs so that his popular hits have a permanent appeal

MELODIES FOR EUROPE

"War" in U.S.A. but no enemy. *Soldiers of the American Army in heroic pose on guard before a factory making aeroplane parts in New Jersey*

Photographs: PK. Meinhold, A. P., PK. Hochscheidt

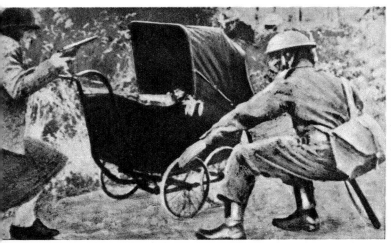

Roosevelt, "the father of war", *at the daily conference during breakfast in bed. Seated on the right is his adviser Hopkins, on the extreme left his family doctor, and in the centre a wise-cracker*

Home Guards *practising the defence of London against the "Fifth Column" and parachutists. A "nursemaid" belonging to the Fifth Column" surprises a sentry*

The last. *Bolshevist "graves" in a "cemetery" in the Soviet Union*

A soldiers' song conquers the air and the hearts of all
...with you, Lili Marleen!

About four years ago in a Berlin café a certain song was sung for the first time. The audience liked it, but it did not make a very lasting impression. Lale Andersen, the cabaret singer, however, recorded it for the gramophone. In spite of all, it was just another song among millions. It was called "Lili Marleen." The words were taken from the volume of poetry "The little harbour organ" by the Hamburg poet Hans Leip, the music is by Norbert Schultze.

Three years later, in summer 1941, the German soldiers' radio station Belgrade was put on the air. Everything happened rather suddenly: among the hastily assembled equipment was a case of more or less (chiefly less) up-to-date records including "Lili Mar-

Lale Andersen emphazises with her hands the rhythm of the opening bars of "The Lamp-post Serenade"

The first bars of the most popular soldiers' song

By permission of the Apollo Verlag Paul Lincke, Berlin SW 68   Photographs: Hedda Walther

leen." The song was broadcast. After a few days dozens of letters came from soldiers asking for the "song with something about a lamp-post in it." Then came a regular deluge of field-post letters from France, Norway, Crete and the Ukraine: "Broadcast 'Lili Marleen'." Now for many months, at 10 p. m. every evening, the Belgrade station has been broadcasting to all fronts the "Sentry Serenade" or the "Lamp-post Serenade", to quote two of the many names by which the song is known, and hundreds of thousands of German soldiers are never tired of hearing it. All over Europe people are whistling it and humming it and Lale Andersen has to sing it at least twice wherever she appears:

„Vor der Kaserne, vor dem grossen Tor
stand eine Laterne, und steht sie noch
davor,
so woll'n wir uns da wiedersehn,
bei der Laterne woll'n wir steh'n
wie einst,
Lili Marleen!"

Literal translation of the above verse:

In front of the barracks, in front of the big gates stood a lamp-post and it is still standing there. Let us meet there again, let us stand by the lamp-post as we used to, Lili Marleen.

What is the secret of its success? Lale Andersen's voice? But she has sung many other songs. The song itself? It had been known for years before it became famous.

Only Lili Marleen could tell us its secret, Lili Marleen whom no one ever saw. . . .

The last verse . . . . „Ont of the silent past, Out of the land of my dreams, your loving lips call to me . . ."

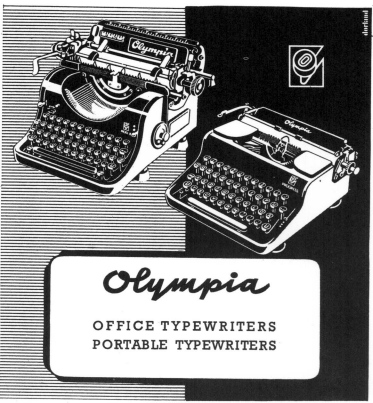

"Du hast Glück bei den Frauen, bel ami," from the Tobis film "Bel ami"

Theo Mackeben. "Film music should be an integral part of the action. The less the spectators can remember of the music in a film, the better it was!" It was Theo Mackeben who uttered this sarcastic pronouncement. Born in Preussisch-Stargard in 1897, he began to play the piano at the early age of five and at fifteen he had made enough progress to perform in concerts. Then the World War broke out. Mackeben was called up and served in a regimental band. Later on, he realized that it was his mission not to interpret but to create. After working for the wireless and the theatre, he began to compose for the cinema. "Bel ami," "Pygmalion," "Heimat," "Das Herz der Königin" are milestones in his film career. His name is linked up with many of Zarah Leander's successes. His operetta "Der goldene Käfig" has just been put on the stage in the Admiralstheater and now the Ufa is enticing him to collaborate

MELODIES

eht sich alles nur im Leben um die Liebe," from the Ufa film "Liebe und die erste Eisenbahn"

"Es wird einmal ein Wunder geschehen," from the Ufa film "Die grosse Liebe"

rald Böhmelt. A glimpse of Harald Böhmelt's home immediately reveals him as an art ⎤ector. He has a special weakness for Eastern Asia which could easily explain the ⎤sticism in his music. Born in Halle, he studied the history of art and philosophy in ⎤ native city. Then, however, his musical talent took the upper hand and sent him from ⎤rdhausen to Halberstadt and back to Halle where he acted as conductor at the municipal ⎤atres. He became known in Berlin as the conductor of the concerts in Monbijou Palace. ⎤n he received offers from the wireless and later from the films. The cinema world ap⎤ciates above all in Böhmelt his folk music, works full of a tender, captivating charm. At ⎤, his film career with all its intrigues and international tendencies was not always ⎤y. But "Was man vergessen kann, lohnt keine Tränen," as he says in one of his songs

Michael Jary. That this former monastery pupil conducted a church choir while still a schoolboy is not a fact which would appear immediately obvious. But bearing this fact in mind, it is difficult to believe that Michael Jary is the composer of "Davon geht die Welt nicht unter" and "Ich weiss, es wird einmal ein Wunder geschehn," the two biggest hits ever scored by Zarah Leander in the whole of her career. This musician's path has taken many a turn, from the municipal theatre in Beuthen through many night clubs in Berlin, until at last his "day's work" was crowned with a scholarship awarded to him by the city of Berlin. This gave him the opportunity to compose "serious pieces." Decisive for Jary's film career was the sailor's song which the Rühmann-Sieber-Brausewetter trio sang with such gusto. Since then he has been a made man

OR EUROPE

Even in wartime German popular music is diffused throughout the world by the cinema and the wireless. SIGNAL selects a few outstanding examples

Aircraft carrier Italy

Italy requires no aircraft carriers. The whole of the Apennine Peninsula is the natural taking-off ground for a strong air force such as Italy has developed. Numerous bases on the islands in the eastern and western Mediterranean make it possible to carry out air attacks even on the enemy's most distant positions. The straits between Sicily and Tunis, Crete and Cyrenaica (in the middle of our picture) and also the waters round Gibraltar (front) which are more than 930 miles from Rome, and the vicinity of the Suez Canal (right, in the background) are daily and nightly the scene of conflicts in which the Italian Air Force, thanks to the central position of its base, plays a decisive part

PK. drawing:
Front Correspondent Hans Liska

On the balcony of the Palazzo Vecchio in Florence

The appearance on the balcony of the Führer and the Duce is preceded by a fanfare of trumpets. The crowd greets these two men, the founders of a new and happier Europe, with tempestuous enthusiasm

A dream becomes reality:

A journey to Italy! Who was formally able to travel to Italy? There were only a few who were privileged to satisfy this longing. It is now possible to travel to foreign countries with the "Strength through Joy" organisation, to spend one's vacation on the Riviera or on even more distant shores

Recreation every evening for thousands:

The world of variety! Two decorative and boldly stylicized programmes of the Berlin variety theatre "The Plaza". Instead of cheap printed programmes in two colours, the best is just good enough for the audience. (Above and right). Not a few keep and collect these programmes in memory of happy hours

Yachting — an exclusive sport?

This is no longer the case in Germany. Anybody is able to take up yachting in the same way as he can indulge in riding, tennis, hockey etc.

The Japanese state visit to Berlin

Matsuoka in conversation with the Chief of the Reich Press, Dr. Dietrich

The Japanese Foreign Minister with representatives of the press: reception of Matsuoka for German reporters and correspondents of those states which have signed the Tripartite Pact

In the Foreign Press Club:

The Japanese Minister for Foreign Affairs conversed with German and foreign journalists

On the way to the first meeting
with the Führer in the new German Chancellery. Matsuoka is conducted to the Führer's study by Herr Meissner, Minister of State. Left, Group Leader Schaub

Lunch at the Führer's residence
Reich Marshal Göring greeting the Japanese guest. Right, the Führer. Between Göring and Matsuoka, Gesandter Schmidt

JAPAN'S LONG ARM

Revolutionary air strategy in the Pacific

The Pacific Ocean, on which Japan is fighting out her great struggle for the new order of Eastern Asia against the United States of America and Great Britain, is the largest theatre of war ever known in the history of the world. This great expanse with its extensive archipelagos imposes its own peculiar laws upon the conduct of the war, particularly upon war in the air. Japan long ago realized the particular features of this great expanse and in every way adapted her armaments to suit them. In this connexion, Japan's particularly zealous development of the air arm of the navy is characteristic. Special attention was paid to aircraft carriers and aircraft depot ships. These weapons are able to operate at very great distances and are therefore the obvious instruments of war in large spaces.

The encirclement which failed

Japan's strategical position on the outbreak of war in Eastern Asia was at first by no means particularly favourable. The encirclement of Japan aimed at by the United States had to a certain extent been achieved by the development of a number of groups of islands under American rule, some of them even being situated inside the Japanese living space, to form modern naval and air bases. In addition, Great Britain had also definitely directed her predominance in the China Seas against Japan.

From the purely military standpoint, the situation before the outbreak of war, bearing in mind the relative strengths at that time, was approximately as follows.

The American Pacific Fleet, with its bases on Hawaii, the Philippines and other advanced outposts, in conjunction with the available air forces, was able to guarantee with relative certainty the protection of the west coast of America including the Panama Canal. Danger from the air threatened at most the advanced American bases in the Pacific but scarcely the American Continent itself. The distances from the nearest Japanese base in the Pacific to the western coast of America were too great for this to be the case. It seemed impossible for aircraft carriers to penetrate very far into the American sphere of power as long as the fleet of the United States remained intact.

The situation was very similar in the south-western Pacific, that is to say, in the British sphere of interest which extends from India via the Malay States to Australia and New Zealand. Here, too, the possibility of a direct menace from Japan appeared to be only small, especially as it was considered that her air and sea power were held in check by the United States.

On the other hand, a threat to the Japanese Empire coming from Hongkong, the Philippines, or Guam, was by no means out of the question. The flying distances from these points to Japan are very great, it is true, so that air attacks on a large scale were not very probable, but the possibility that a strong British and American naval force could blockade and hamper Japan could not be lightly dismissed.

These conditions have been decisively changed during the first few weeks of the conflict with the United States and Great Britain by the action of the Japanese forces. The capture of the American bases Guam, Wake and the Philippines as well as the rapid occupation of the British fortification of Hongkong removed the most important enemy bases in the Japanese living space and, more particularly, placed the war in the air on a different footing. The reactions caused by the newly created situation are so great that they also affect the European theatre of war.

The hunting ground of the aircraft carriers

The great distances in the Pacific, which according to European standards make war in the air impossible, have not become smaller as a result of Japan's successes. But the considerable weakening of the American Pacific Fleet in the battle of Hawaii and the annihilation of the heart of British sea power in Eastern Asia by the sinking of the battleships "Prince of Wales" and "Repulse," which occurred simultaneously, have given the Japanese Navy its liberty of movement and consequently every opportunity to carry out offensive operations. The Japanese aircraft carrier fleet is now in a position to carry air warfare to the extreme coasts of the Pacific Ocean. Who could today seriously make an attempt to prevent the fast Japanese aircraft carriers from suddenly appearing, for example, on the west coast of America and there attacking the numerous military objectives? The effectiveness of the aircraft carrier resulting from the present relative strength in the Pacific must not be underestimated. The Japanese Navy has a considerable number of aircraft carriers of high speed at its disposal as well as several aircraft depot ships from which seaplanes can carry out their attacks. This fleet of aircraft carriers is supported by a considerable battle fleet which is today perfectly well able to deal in the Pacific with the united British and American naval forces. This battle fleet is therefore able to protect the passage of the aircraft carrier fleet to the most distant coasts of the Pacific Ocean.

Japan has already shown on several occasions to what use she puts her aircraft carriers. The Japanese Navy has passed beyond the old points of view that the aircraft carrier is to a certain extent the eye of the fleet, that is to say, that it carries out reconnaissance duty, or that it merely undertakes the air defence of naval units. Rather does it regard the aircraft carrier as a potent weapon of offence and uses it as such. The Japanese successes have sufficiently demonstrated what possibilities are made available to a fleet by these revolutionary tactics. Japanese aircraft carriers played a decisive part not only at Hawaii, where bombers and torpedo bombers starting from aircraft carriers smashed the American battle fleet, but also during various landing operations.

The aircraft carrier fleet makes the air arm of the Japanese Navy a very mobile, far-reaching weapon particularly suitable for use over long distances. Its mobility is all the more

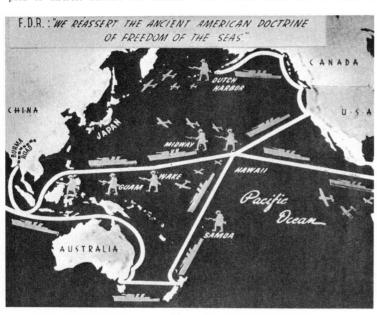

Franklin Delano Roosevelt: "We reassert the ancient American doctrine of freedom of the seas." (From the "United States News" of 6. 6. 1941). This freedom meant in reality the complete tyrannization of Japan by bayonets, air and sea power

Bands linking major U. S. and British bases indicate how an American-British Navy dominates the seas. In the Pacific Japan is outweighed almost three to two

HOW THE U.S. NAVY WILL FIGHT THE AXIS

"How the U. S. Navy will fight the Axis." (From the "United States News" of 8. 8. 1941). The black line between the American and British bases was meant to show how Japan can be blockaded and overcome by the superior joint American-British Fleet

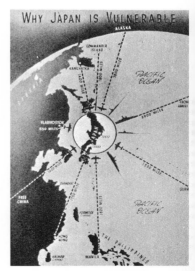

"Why Japan is vulnerable." (From the American periodical "Look" of 1. 7. 1941). A picture of the total encirclement. The military and economic strangulation of Japan was considered easy

dangerous for the enemy as the Pacific is for Japan a theatre of war offering the advantages of a struggle on the interior line in

Japan can send her large fleet of aircraft carriers in any direction she chooses

Regions in danger from the air with a 300 mile defensive zone

Everything has turned out differently: Japan tore the meshes which strangled her. Whilst Japan is operating on the interior line, her enemies are conducting a difficult defence which splits up their strength along the tremendously wide circle of the exterior line

nothing less than classical form. It enables offensive operations at any point on the extreme edge of the Pacific to be effectively supported by concentration in the air, whilst the enemy can move his air defence forces only to a restricted extent and never sufficiently quickly on account of the tremendous distances. Thus, for example, mutual support of the American and British air forces in order to ward off surprise attacks by Japanese aircraft carriers appear completely impossible, and even on the eastern or south-western sectors of the Anglo-American exterior line the distances are so great that the air defence is in an extremely difficult position.

Both of Japan's enemies, the United States and Great Britain, have tremendously long stretches of coastline to defend against air attacks starting from aircraft carriers. As they had scarcely reckoned with this eventuality in consequence of the over-estimation of their own power, their air defence, which was established before the war, is completely inadequate today under the altered strategical circumstances in the air.

Forced to adopt the defensive

What it means, however, for the United States to oppose an effective air defence against the air arm of the Japanese Navy along their west coast becomes clear when it is realized that the American air forces must also undertake the defence of Canada. About 30 degrees of latitude separate Alaska from California and the coastline has a length of approximately 2,500 miles. In addition, the region in the neighbourhood of the Panama Canal must also be defended.

Thousands of planes, fighters and bombers, with which nobody in America had previously reckoned, will be necessary in order to provide the west coast of America even with the most scanty defence, planes which were originally intended for Great Britain, as well as thousands of A.A.-guns, searchlights, etc. And many thousands of men who could otherwise have been used elsewhere or have been employed in the American armament industry, will have to keep watch. The same is true of the British sector in the south-western Pacific. Even if the Malay States, as already appears the case, are abandoned by the British, a huge region nevertheless remains for which an air defence must be created at all costs. The fighting in Malay and elsewhere has already sufficiently shown how small the preparations here were and how difficult it will be for Great Britain to send planes and equipment to the East. The available air units were much too weak to be able to cope with the Japanese Air Force and reinforcements were not available.

Precisely what was most unpleasant for the United States and Great Britain has occurred. The Pacific has become a theatre of air war, although not in the same sense as is the case in Europe. A few hundred Japanese planes borne on aircraft carriers make it essential to develop a gigantic air defence system calling for the employment of large numbers of planes. All these forces are for practical purposes lying fallow, for they cannot be used in an offensive operation against Japan because they are prevented from doing so by the great distances in this area.

The effect which this situation has upon the European theatres of war is obvious. What Great Britain and the United States have hoped to achieve in the next few years, namely to confront Germany at some time with a superior air force, has by this time receded far into the distance. —*lz*

Records
of political decisions
of world importance

SIGNAL here reproduces the first photographs, other than those transmitted by wireless, from the theatres of war of the Japanese partner in the Three-Power Pact. They reached Europe by devious routes and as rare and imperishable photographic records, they supplement the official Japanese reports on the onward rush of a nation which since the second week of December of last year has caused the world to hold its breath

The announcer of the Japanese victories: Colonel Hideo Ohira. *He is in charge of the information department of the Imperial Headquarters. It was from his lips that the victories at Hawaii and Hong Kong, Singapore and Java, in Burma and off the Solomon Islands reached the world. Terseness, clarity and reliability are the features of his announcements*

Pearl Harbour becomes the grave of the U.S. Pacific Fleet. *In the early morning hours of 8th December 1941 Japanese bombers and torpedo bombers plunged down from the overcast sky over Hawaii towards the American battleships anchored off Ford Island. At the same time Japanese submarines broke through the mine barrages and attacked the warships. High fountains of water spurt into the air, the first signs of a work of destruction unprecedented in naval history* ↓

"Surprise—attack—success" *was the message transmitted by the commander of the Japanese aeroplane squadron to his aircraft carrier half an hour after the opening of the attack. Justifiably as this photographic record shows: the leading battleship of the Oklahoma class (above), struck by torpedoes, is already sinking, and bombs are hailing down on the two next ships as the explosions show. The two battleships lying to the side already have a list and their oil is gushing out . . . On the quayside a petrol tank is exploding. And the Japanese continue to attack . . .* →

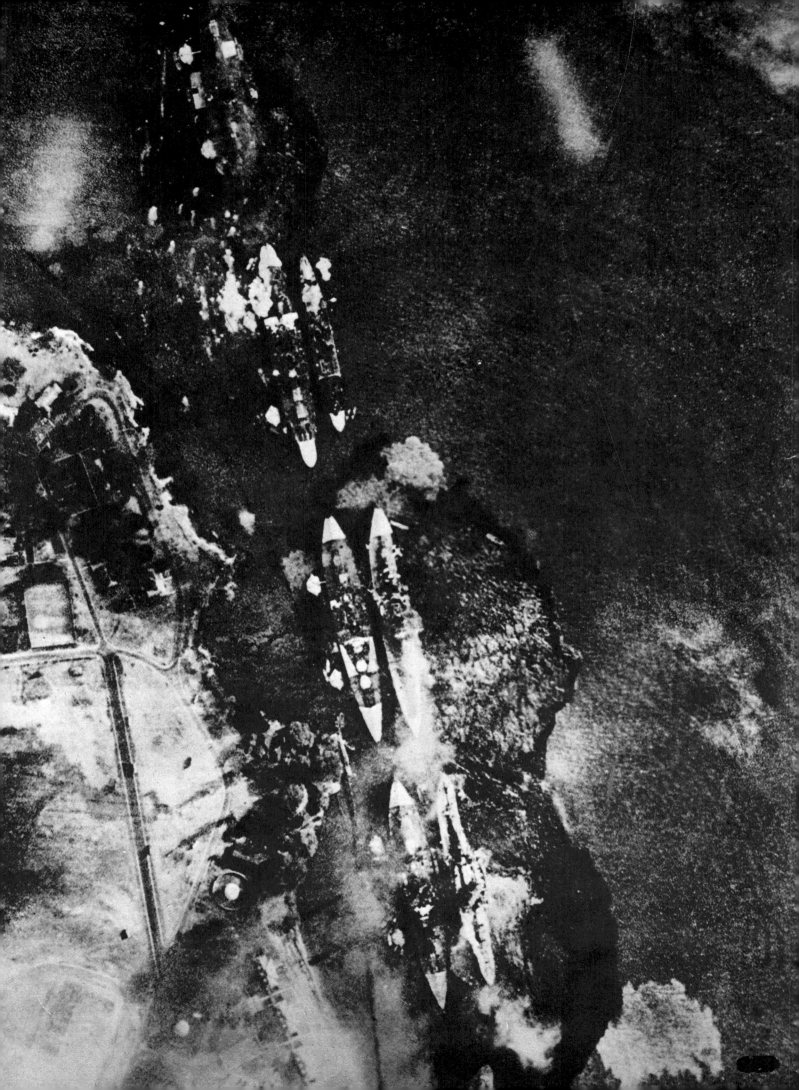

ROOSEVELT–
Emperor of the World?

In this number "Signal" is beginning a series of articles on Roosevelt's policy. The first article that we are publishing today shows how the tentacles of dollar imperialism are reaching out over the whole world. A second article will show how Roosevelt's plans to stir up the American people's enthusiasm for war succeeded. The third article will answer the question: "Are the U.S.A. capable of ruling the world?"

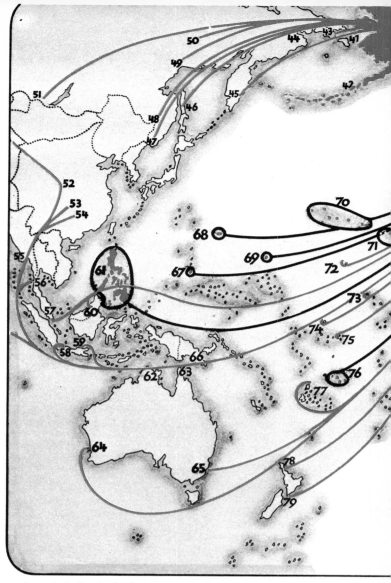

Recently "Current History," perhaps the best political periodical published in the U.S.A., contained an article on "America's Destiny" by Basil C. Walker. "Current History" belongs to the publishers of the "New York Times" and has at its disposal all the home and foreign news services of this widely distributed newspaper whose close connections with leading political and economic circles in America are well known.

"Our day has come"

In his article Walker writes that it is the task of the Americans to master the present situation with bold decision and to force events into a path which leads to a world such as they wish. The only kind of peace in which they are interested is a "pax americana" similar to the one-time "pax romana" and "pax britannica." By helping Britain, he goes on, they are wearing out the arch-enemy. America's history has prepared her for the rôle she has to play. Present day developments in the world point to America as the only nation fitted for the position of leader —not to save Europe or the European system, but to make America the leader of all free people in the whole world in the American epoch that is dawning. The longer they hesitate, the harder and bloodier will be the task. A quick decision is the cleverest. Their day has come, he says. They must advance without delay.

At last, in these few sentences, the leading political monthly of the U.S.A. has made Roosevelt's real aim as clear to us as we could wish: it is not the defence of the democracies or of the western hemisphere, not even defence against the "aggressors," but purely and simply world domination, the economic and political conquest of the world. For "pax americana" means nothing other than the conquest of the world by Washington, just as "pax britannica" is nothing other than the pseudonym of that system which has subjected to the interests of London vast expanses of the earth which were not allowed to develop their own.

What Basil C. Walker reveals in his article is the programme for a campaign of aggression not only against Germany but against the whole of Europe and the great complementary territory of Africa, not only against

Japan but against the whole of Asia and the South Sea countries. The fact that the South American States are treated as mere political vassals by their big brother in the north interests Germany particularly because many of them are united to her by ancient ties of friendship. As for the rest, Europe, England excepted, has always respected the Monroe Doctrine. We have always left the states in the two Americas to settle their own affairs among themselves. We do not interfere.

All the more urgently, in consequence, do Europe and Eastern Asia demand respect for their own "Monroe Doctrine." It is up to Amernica to do as much as she will for the defence of the western hemisphere, but even a child cannot be persuaded that this hemisphere must be protected in Central Africa, in Batavia, or in the Urals. Roosevelt wants to make himself the Emperor of the World. He would like to play the rôle of a modern Louis XIV for whom the whole world offers just enough scope for the realization of his imperialistic ambitions.

Two world powers fade into nothingness

Roosevelt has already to his credit two big successes in which nobody would have believed two or even one year ago. The two greatest powers of modern times, the British Empire and the Soviet Union, have resigned their leading positions in favour of the U.S.A. and from day to day are becoming more and more dependent on Washington. Today these two powers are begging America for help and are ready to surrender in return their most valuable possessions, even their independence, if one were to believe what many Britons say. They know that without this help they cannot stand out alone against Europe which is defending herself with supreme energy. For this small Europe is fighting stubbornly, tenaciously—and victoriously against the hideous danger of Bolshevism. And at the far end of the Euro-Asiatic continent is Japan watching, silent and patient, and prepared to reply to each move with a counter-move. But both are occupied. One is busy with the war against the Soviets, the other with the war against Chungking. They are, therefore, not in a position to defend themselves as efficiently as if they

were free. And Roosevelt is taking advantage of this situation to encircle Europe and Japan, to place around their necks the rope with which he intends to strangle them. He is even prepared to make an alliance with Moscow if it will facilitate a landing in the Asiatic continent from where he can launch an attack on Japan.

America is trying to establish herself in every corner of the world which offers a starting point for attacks on Europe and Eastern Asia. She is prepared to use any means to further her aims: economic pressure, military power, political intrigues, cultural propaganda. A tour around the world will be sufficient to prove it.

Stepping-stones across the Atlantic

As the "New York Times" reports, the U.S.A. wants to induce Brazil to take over the protectorate of the Azores. Portugal's firm attitude in the face of the only too clearly manifested "interest" of the U.S.A. in the islands off the west coast of North Africa has made Washington cautious.

Perhaps—they are saying in the U.S.A.—the Portuguese will be less hostile to the occupation of the Azores if it is done by Brazil and not by the U.S.A., for Portuguese is spoken in Brazil too. Perhaps this proposal will succeed in sowing discord and mistrust between Portugal, the little mother country in Europe and Brazil, the big daughter in South America. Every attempt to upset the relations between

Europe and South America is welcome. Portugal has, however, consistently reinforced the garrisons of the Azores, of the Cape Verde Islands, and of the Madeira group. Washington does not yet dare to use force, for using force against the tiny country of Portugal would serve to reveal its clear intentions only too clearly, and therefore Brazil is pushed forward.

The occupation of these islands to which the Spanish Canaries also belong, would do more than protect South America from the "aggression" of the totalitarian states. More important is the fact that if she controlled these, America could control the sea routes between Europe and Africa south of the Sahara. Washington knows well enough that South America is threatened neither by Germany nor Italy—it wants to gain control of the stepping-stones across the Atlantic from where it would be able not only to attack South-Western Europe but also to extend its influence far into Africa. This is what the Americans have in mind. They want to build themselves a bridge-head in West Africa against Europe.

Why Wavell had to go

As the "Washington Times" reported in the middle of July, the difference between Churchill and Wavell which led to the recall of the latter from the post of Commander-in-Chief of the Eastern Mediterranean were due to the fact that Wavell, like the Americans, was of the opinion that Britain's posi-

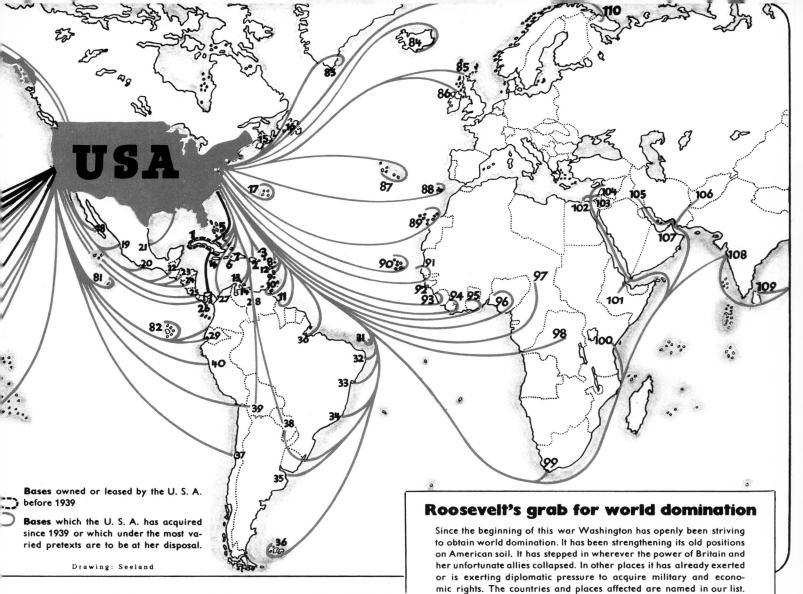

USA

Bases owned or leased by the U. S. A. before 1939

Bases which the U. S. A. has acquired since 1939 or which under the most varied pretexts are to be at her disposal.

Drawing: Seeland

---

tion in the Eastern Mediterranean was untenable in the long run. The front should be moved back to a line running south of the Sahara across Africa. This would mean that the hard pressed British Mediterranean Fleet would be free for action in the Atlantic. The Americans and the British could then concentrate their energy on West Africa. Wavell had a good press in the U.S.A., but he was not able to put his plans into action. Instead he was transferred to India. The attack on Dakar has not been repeated up to now.

The encirclement of Europe

To accomplish this, comparatively unimportant harbours on the African coast were garrisoned with American consuls, regular air lines were opened up and the steamship companies put on more steamers. In 1940 as compared with 1939 the U.S.A.'s foreign trade with Africa increased approximately 40 %. Since 1939 America has been exporting to Africa important armaments and articles for the equipment of troops. This fact is explained if one recalls that the southernmost part of the French Empire in Africa, French Equatorial Africa. has split away from the Vichy Government and is under the control of people who have joined forces with de Gaulle. From French Equatorial Africa across Belgian Congo which is likewise hostile to Europe, to Anglo-Egyptian Sudan and across Kenya to the eastern projection of Africa an American cordon which is to be prolonged across Egypt northwards

to Palestine, Transjordania and the territories of Syria and Iraq that have been forcibly suppressed.

In the Persian Gulf the tentacles radiating eastwards from America over the whole of Europe meet those reaching out across the Pacific and the Indian Ocean to strangle East Asia. For in the petroleum fields in the Behrein Islands American capital supplies oil to the British troops and ships in the Indian Ocean and the Red Sea. From the Persian Gulf the encirclement of Europe is extended to include India. Here the intermediate links, Turkey and Iran, are missing. Although these states desire nothing more passionately than to preserve their neutrality, from day to day it becomes more and more apparent that the Anglo-Americans will display just as little respect for the sovereignty of Iran as they previously did for that of Iraq and Syria. As usual the "intrigues of German citizens in Iran against Britain" must furnish the pretext although the Iran Government officially announced that the behaviour of the 650 Germans in Iran is correct in all respects and a threat is out of the question. Under the most varied pretexts the Americans and the British are trying to induce Afghanistan to join the front against Europe.

Europe, an American economic colony?

If one bears in mind also that the Union of South Africa, with its gold

Continued on Page 33

Roosevelt's grab for world domination

Since the beginning of this war Washington has openly been striving to obtain world domination. It has been strengthening its old positions on American soil. It has stepped in wherever the power of Britain and her unfortunate allies collapsed. In other places it has already exerted or is exerting diplomatic pressure to acquire military and economic rights. The countries and places affected are named in our list.

West Indies
1 Guantanamo (Cuba)
2 Puerto Rico
3 Virgin Islands
4 Jamaica
5 The Bahamas
6 Haiti
7 San Domingo
8 Antigua
9 Santa Lucia
10 Trinidad
11 British Guiana
12 Martinique
13 Aruba
14 Curaçao

Canada and the Bermudas
15 Halifax
16 Placentia Harbour
17 The Bermudas

Central and Southern America
  MEXICO
18 Santa Margarita
19 Acapulco
20 Salina Cruz
21 Vera Cruz
22 GUATEMALA
23 FONSECA BAY
24 NICARAGUA
25 COSTA RICA
26 PANAMA
27 COLUMBIA
28 VENEZUELA
29 ECUADOR
  BRAZIL
30 Marajo (mouth of the Amazon)
31 Fernando de Noronha
32 Pernambuco
33 Bahia
34 Rio Grande do Sul
  ARGENTINE
35 La Plata

36 FALKLAND ISLANDS
  CHILE
37 Valparaiso
38 PARAGUAY
39 BOLIVIA
40 PERU

Alaska
41 Nome
42 Dutch Harbour

Siberia
43 Providentia
44 Anadyr
45 Petropavlovsk
46 Alexandrovsk
47 Vladivostok
48 Chabarovsk
49 Ochotsk
50 Verchne-Kolymsk
51 Irkutsk

South Eastern Asia
52 Lanchu
53 Chungtu
54 Chungking
55 Rangoon
56 Thailand
57 Singapore
58 Batavia
59 Surabaya
60 Brunei (British Borneo)
61 Manila

Australia
62 Port Darwin
63 Thursday Islands
64 Fremantle
65 Sydney
66 PORT MORESBY
  (British New Guinea)

South Seas
67 Guam
68 Marcus Island
69 Wake Island
70 Midway
71 Hawaii
72 Johnston

73 Palmyra
74 Howland
75 Enderbury (Phoenix Islands)
76 Tutuila (Samoa)
77 Fiji Islands
78 Auckland (New Zealand)
79 Wellington
80 Tahiti
81 Clipperton
82 Galapagos

The Atlantic
83 Greenland
85 Iceland
85 Northern Scotland
86 Northern Ireland
87 The Azores
88 Madeira
89 Canary Islands
90 Cape Verde Islands

Africa
91 Dakar
92 Bathurst
93 Freetown
94 Liberia
95 The Gold Coast
96 Nigeria
97 French Equatorial Africa
98 Belgian Congo
99 Cape Town
100 Kenya
101 Abessynia
102 Egypt

The Near East
103 Palestine, Transjordan
104 Syria
105 Iraq
106 Afghanistan
107 The Bahrein Islands

India
108 Bombay
109 Trincomali

Arctic Ocean
110 Murmansk

Roosevelt — Emperor of the world?

production as the deciding factor, is almost entirely dependent on the U.S.A.'s willingness to purchase—for the agricultural products of the Union are practically unmarketable today—and that that part of Africa which lies south of the Sahara urgently needs the U.S.A. who are the only customers on whom it can reckon, one can clearly recognize the U.S.A.'s intention of making the whole of Africa dependent on her good will and finally of bringing the continent not only under her economic but also under her military and political control.

When one hears that American engineers, technicians, and trained workmen are building aerodromes, landing-grounds and living quarters on African soil (British Gambia south of Dakar), that intervention in Liberia has already been announced, that the occupation of Greenland and Iceland are already accomplished facts, and that American experts are developing air bases in Northern Ireland, one realises beyond a shadow of a doubt that America desires to subdue not only Germany and Italy but also the whole of Europe, England included. She hopes to be able to prove that Europe depends on America's good will for her food supplies and that at the same time the U.S.A. can even mete out military chastisement. Europe, including England, is to be transformed into an economic colony that owes obedience to America, and the difference between the indivi-

dual European states is to disappear.

Finally, when one observes the unconditional support given by the U.S.A. to the Soviets whose designs on Europe have been established facts for some time—if they had succeeded Europe as a cultural conception would have been destroyed—the whole body of the European states reveal themselves as a community facing a common fate and with common rights to live which must be defended against the threats of a common enemy.

The tentacles reaching out for Asia

With the same consistent ruthlessness as in the case of the Atlantic the U.S.A. are reaching out to seize Asia. Here it is Japan and powers allied or friendly to her, Manchukuo. Nanking-China, French Indo-China, and Thailand, that are exposed to the ever increasing pressure exerted by America. Here, too, Roosevelt is trying to tighten his grasp. Using all the strength and means at her disposal, whether military, political, or economic, America is proceeding with the encirclement of Japan, the leading power in Eastern Asia.

Since Bolshevism, hard pressed by the fighting forces of Europe, is taking refuge in a vassal relationship to the U.S.A. as has already been done by the British Empire, it has been possible for Roosevelt to approach Japan from the north, a move which had had

up to now only very imperfect success. Alaska, the western point of which is only a few miles distant from the extreme eastern point of North-East Siberia, and which combined with the long chain of Aleutian Islands provides a kind of bridge to the northeast of Asia, was already a long time ago developed into an important American air and naval base. The naval port Dutch Harbour on Unalaska, one of the large islands of the Aleutian group, was built up into a northern counterpart of Pearl Harbour on Oahu, the most important of the Hawaiian Islands. Hawaii was the heavily fortified key position of the American naval forces concentrated in the Pacific.

In the north no real progress was made because frequent storms and dense fog lessen the strategic value of the Aleutian Islands and the south coast of Alaska. Now the Americans, who do not grant help to the Soviets for nothing, want the Bolshevists to make over to them bases in North-Eastern Siberia. As they have already promised support to the Soviets in a formal agreement, one can safely assume that they have already landed or are about to land soon in Kamchatka, on the coast of the Ochotski Sea, at the mouth of the Amur, perhaps even in Vladivostok. They could send formations of the Air Force there by this route across the Asiatic continent without even touching Japanese spheres of influence. By so doing they would be within easy reach of the heart of Japan. It must be mentioned here that the northern part of the long island Sachalin that lies at the mouth

of the Amur belongs to the Soviet and the south to Japan.

In the central Pacific, America's striving for supremacy has been becoming more and more apparent. The bridge from Hawaii to the Philippines, to whom the U.S.A. have promised a mock-freedom dating from 1946, and which today extends on to Thailand, Singapore, the Dutch East Indies and British India, was systematically improved. The bases on Johnston and Palmyra— south-west and south of Hawaii—were completed on the 15th of August. Farther to the south-west work is in progress on the islands of Howland and Enderbury in the Phoenix group. The American naval and air base Tutuila in the Samoa Islands is already old, having been completed some time ago; with the British Fiji Islands it completes the bridge to New Zealand and Australia. Farther to the north, in the direction of the Philippines, Midway, Wake, Marcus, and Guam are being developed.

The U.S.A. is working at high pressure on the further development of Corregidor and Cavite in Manila Bay in the Philippines. American bombers flew to Java, for the Dutch East Indies have long since degenerated into a mere tool of American politics. In Borneo aerodromes are being built which will serve to protect Singapore from the flank in the southern Chinese Ocean. Singapore itself, in a case of emergency, could perhaps be defended only with the help of American naval and air forces.

The existence of a military alliance between the U.S.A., England, British India and the Dutch East India, Chung-

king China, Australia, and New Zealand is an open secret in the Far East. In connexion with this co-operation which is under the guidance of the U.S.A., America has set aside 40 million dollars for aerodromes in the south-west of China. The U.S.A. and England wish to prepare 600 machines for service in Kweiyang and in other places in South-Western China, and to detail 200 pilots there. In addition Hopkins, Roosevelt's Extraordinary Ambassador in Moscow, has prepared the conclusion of a military alliance between the Soviet Union and Chungking. Further, Moscow is to undertake to complete with Anglo-American help the branch of the railway running eastwards from Turksib to Central Asia as far as Lantschau in Kansu straight across Hsingkiang.

Along the Thailand, Indo-China, and China frontiers of Burma, petrol dumps, hangars, and living quarters are being erected by American engineers with the help of American money. The reinforcement of the British garrisons in Singapore, the Malay States, and in Burma point at the unmistakable fact that an Anglo-American action is being prepared against Thailand which would be offering similar violence to a small state as was offered to Iraq and as British policy has been offering to India and Egypt for many years. By making a timely agreement with the Japanese and by calling upon them to protect both of their interests the French Government has saved Indo-China from Anglo-American intervention. Thailand too, as her last actions prove, is inclining to the Japanese side.

It is a matter of course that there is something behind the granting of transport planes and the recent additional loans (10 million pounds sterling and 50 million dollars) to Chang Kai Chek, the tenacious defender of the rest of China He is the Anglo-American's continental dagger which is threatening the Japanese position in South-Eastern Asia and which under no circumstances must be withdrawn. For the Americans the important thing is to open up the gigantic possibilities of the Chinese market for exploitation by their economic imperialism. If the American plans succeed, Chang could retire after doing his duty. Just as Britain by her clever policy of the balance of power kept Europe powerless by always supporting the weaker side against a stronger adversary, so the U.S.A. today are acting in the gamble for Asia. They are supporting the weakened Soviet Union and Chang Kai Chek who has been driven back to the remotest provinces in the south-west in order to overcome Japan who has earned the leadership in the Far East by her achievements and her strength.

And why? Escape from her own problems!

Just as in Europe, the U.S.A. wish to prevent by all the means in their power that the states of the Far East should arrive at a suitable solution of their justifiable demands. If this were to happen America's attention would be directed to her own problems. In Roosevelt's own country all the questions and tasks which cannot be solved in the old-fashioned way are waiting for solution; it is easier to interfere everywhere and to make the world into the battlefield of American imperialism of the Roosevelt stamp.

Even though the countries belonging to the British Empire voluntarily content themselves with the position of vassals of Washington, it is no reason why the old homes of culture, Europe and Eastern Asia, should bow before that class of Americans whose standard of values is the dollar and for whom the films of Hollywood are cultural achievements of the highest grade.

JU 88

JUNKERS FLUGZEUG- UND -MOTORENWERKE A.-G. DESSAU

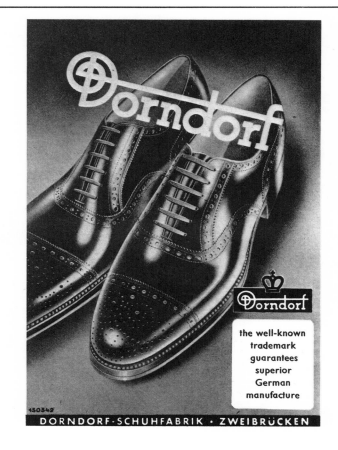

The desert sand flies up...
A German fighter breaks its journey at an Italian aerodrome at the front in Africa

Desert sand and palm-trees...

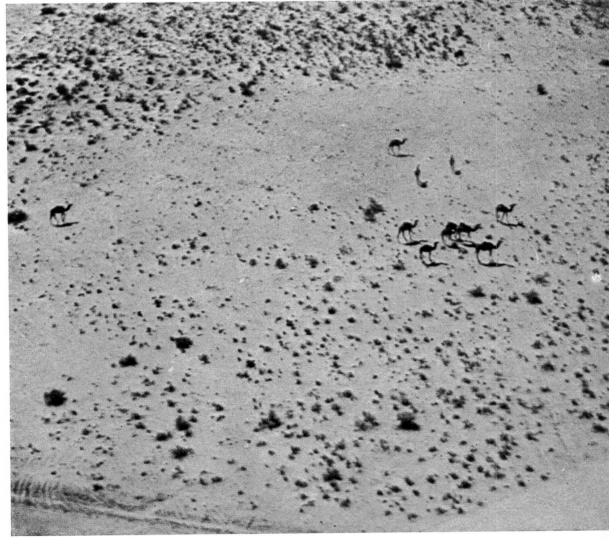

A picture brought back from a reconnaissance flight . . .
The camels belong to a British convoy, the movements of which it was the duty of the German machine to observe

A battle-plane setting out from Sicily on an air raid in the direction of Malta

THE
AIR FORCE EMBLEM
on the Southern Front

Shot down by German anti-aircraft guns

The wreckage of a British plane which attacked on aerodrome in Sicily. On the right: Battle-planes on an aerodrome in Sicily

The watch in the desert

It has stood the test on all fronts. *This A.A. gun was in Poland, accompanied the advance through Belgium and France and is now in one of the advance bases in Africa on the Halfaya Pass. It has travelled more than 6,000 miles and has experienced snow, rain and heat. Shell after shell has gone through the barrel. The last examination showed, however, that no measurable wear and tear could be found at any spot. Both barrel and gun carriage are still in the best of health and the sureness of aim of this old warrior is as good as it was on the very first day*

Between Libya and Egypt

A stretch of country about 625 miles wide, without roads or tracks, the Libyan desert, separa[tes] the chief centres of Libya from those of Egypt. Only at two places, at the oases of S[i] Jarabub and 125 miles north, at Sollum on the Mediterranean coast, does the terrain al[low] military operations of any size to be carried out. Sollum and the bay which stretches as [far] as the desolate sand and granite hills in the desert had been converted by the Bri[tish] into a strong fortress to which they attached the importance of a miniature Gibra[ltar].

The victor "without experience of the tropics" General Rommel, the Commander-in-Chief of the German Africa Corps, together with officers of his staff, visits the scene of the Battle of Sollum. British military experts had predicted a rapid victory for the British Commander-in-Chief, General Wavell, whom Churchill has since transferred in disgrace to India, because General Rommel had had no experience of the tropics

A cool bathe after a hard ba[ttle]
The counter-attacks of the German t[roops] during the Battle of Sollum, during w[hich] such heavy losses were inflicted on [the] British, were carried out with the ther[mo]meter at more than 120 degrees Fahren[heit]. After the enemy's retreat the crews of the [Ger]man tank refresh themselves in the wate[rs of] the Mediterranean *Photographs: PK. Moosr*

The Germans in Tripoli

German sentry in the harbour of Tripoli. *It was here that the German troops landed on African soil for the first time*

Parade beneath the palms. *One of the German tanks which soon afterwards were victorious in their first engagement with British troops in the desert*

Wearing pith helmets in the streets of Tripoli. *Dense crowds of Italians and natives line the streets of Tripoli through which the German troops are marching for the first time*

The commander of the German forces in Africa inspecting the troops

Photographs: H. Schneider, PK

His first flight in Africa

An American airman tells his story

PK. Photographs: War Correspondens Friedrich, Wagner

① A German war correspondent in Africa photographs an American bomber as it crashes some distance away on the horizon. The cloud caused by the impact becomes visible first and then ...

② ... there is an explosion followed by a dense black cloud which rises steeply into the air and—picture below—slowly disperses. Another front correspondent, however, spots the American pilot descending by parachute

③

④

Dragging his parachute along behind him, the shot down American flying officer approaches with his hands raised in surrender. He is eager to talk, a natural reaction after the mental strain of the air engagement and being shot down. The American lieutenant says that he is 24 years of age, a native of Philadelphia and had volunteered for service in Africa. The journey had been deuced unpleasant. His ship had made long detours and had finally sailed close in along the coast of Africa being menaced all the time by U-boats. At long last he had reached the front but had been brought down on his very first flight ...

⑤ A little later the American met his vanquisher, a sergeant-major who has been awarded the Knight's Insignia to the Iron Cross. Their encounter took place at an altitude of 18,000 feet. The American lieutenant admits that he was extremely surprised to find himself suddenly attacked by a German machine in spite of the security provided him by the large bomber unit in which he was flying. He had then tried all the usual tricks in order to shake of his antagonist who had nevertheless forced him to go down to 3,000 feet and scored many direct hits on his plane so that finally he had no other alternative but to bale out ... The American was quite obviously pleased to have escaped so lightly. His machine (picture below) is a complete wreck

⑥

A reconnaissance party returns. *At dawn the party had left the advance position on the Halfaya Pass and marched towards the British lines, eight miles there and eight miles back. They penetrated behind the British outposts and made important sketches of the positions. They are now returning along the shore of the Mediterranean from their dangerous enterprise*

Seven men return to their quarters. *They are passing through apparently untouched desert empty of human beings*

The desert sand has now swallowed up four of them. *This photograph was taken a few seconds later from the same spot*

Refreshment after a sixteen mile march. *A cool drink and a piece of good wholesome bread*

An M.G. nest in the very front line. *Only the mouth of the barrel peeps above the ground. The hand grenades are lying ready for use on the protecting sandbags. Since June of this year when the British were defeated at the battle of Capuzzo, they have avoided this invisible position and not attempted another attack*

Camouflage and deception

On the left: **The last one disappears here.** *The whole country is cut by trenches miles long and spreading to a depth of several hundred yards. These positions are so well situated and camouflaged that they cannot be recognized even only a few yards off*

On the right: **What the reconnaissance party discovered.** *The salt lake between the German and British positions described by a previous patrol has again been seen today and a photograph has even been taken of it. It does not, however, actually exist. The reconnaissance party marched through it. It consisted of sand like everything else all around and was only a mirage*

Photographs: PK. Kenneweg (7)

The four plagues of the desert

PK. Kenneweg, "Signal's" reporter who is at present with the German and Italian troops fighting in North Africa writes to us: "I don't know which of the plagues is the worst. Like misfortunes, they seldom come singly. Dripping with perspiration, tortured by thirst and flies, and almost suffocated by dust, we curse every desert on the face of the earth"

Sand *Our faces are caked with dust. We a driving along the 40-mile road that ru through the desert round Tobruk. The car can or do 5 miles an hour here. It rocks like a ship in storm, jolts along the uneven road surface, and ru up against boulders. The sand rises, smothering both and man. It fills our eyes, our mouths, our nostr our sleeves, and our caps, and trickles down backs. The journey lasts eight hours. When we arr at our destination, we are all entirely beyond cognition. There are many such roads in Afri*

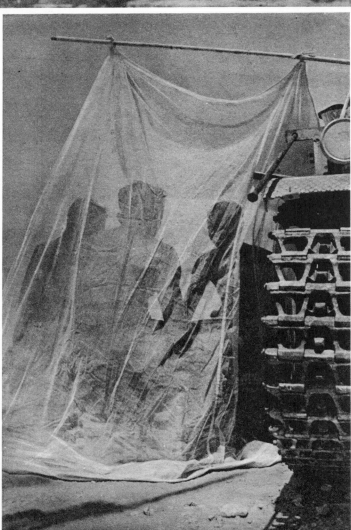

Mosquitoes *Thank heaven we are equipped with efficient mosquito nets! They are easy to set up, and when we make a halt or in our quarters, they afford good protection. The rest of the time the mosquitoes reign supreme. We have given up trying to fight against them. We have abandoned our hands, arms and faces to them and only beat them off when we want to take a bite. Now and then one of us jumps up and dances about cursing. A cloud of flies rises, but it helps only for a few seconds*

Thirst *We have to get accustomed to the water here. It has a salt content of 5 to 13 per thousand We use the least salty for making tea. The water cans are all marked, and woe to the ma who uses good water for washing on a journey through the desert. As long as the tea is hot, the sa taste is unnoticeable; cold tea, on the other hand, is very salty. But whether hot or cold, it is a bad thirs quencher; it might even be said to aggravate it. In the evening in sheer desperation we swallow the cor tents of our mineral water bottles in a few gulps. "Do you remember the water we had at Derna?" th soldiers exclaim almost lyrically. "That was real water, wasn't it?" The water in every well her differs. The company that is lucky enough to have sweet water within reach is the envy of the whole fro*

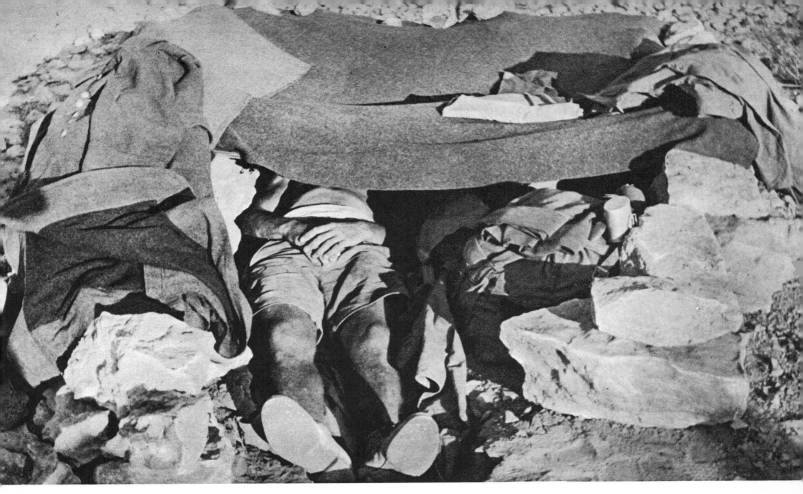

Heat

"How hot is it there really?" people often ask me in letters. Soldiers have a habit of exaggerating, for they are not too particular about a matter of ten degrees or so. Here are the facts: On the coast at midday the thermometer measures 104 to 122 degrees F., inland it is 9 degrees hotter. And in the shade? There is no shade. A soldier can make himself a kind of tent with stones and blankets and so enjoy a little shade, but it is not advisable to lie in it for long during the daytime. It gets hotter and hotter there, so that it is like lying in a Turkish bath. One could also spread a tent-cover as a kind of roof and sit under it, but a soldier has not much time to spare for lounging around. The best solution is to get accustomed to going about in a bathing costume and a topee and to take advantage of the breaths of wind that come in from the sea now and then. At night it is considerably cooler, sometimes the thermometer sinks 36 degrees, so that one can sleep quite soundly. If one is lucky, one may find one of the old water holes in one's sector. (Picture below) They are 5 to 6 yards deep: the cover, pierced with a little hole, is about one yard thick. They are deliciously cool, free from mosquitoes, and sand-proof. These are the only places where, enjoying a cool drink, one is free from the four greatest plagues of the desert Photographs: PK. Kenneweg

TUNIS: PERSONAGES AND COMBATS

By the mere invasion of French Morocco and Algeria the United Nations had expected to gain control over North Africa and thus secure a convenient base for an incursion into the European defensive front. They had counted upon the fact that France and her colonies were weakened and disrupted by incapable politicians and treasonable generals, calculating that victories and conquests, of which they were so urgently in need, could easily be obtained. The Axis Powers, however, succeeded by their resolute counteraction in establishing a bridgehead in Tunis. Thereby they not only brought confusion into General Eisenhower's plans of advance and operation, but at the same time they formed an advance bastion for the protection of the entire northern coast of the Mediterranean. It is of great importance that all of Europe should recognize the significance of the fierce combats raging in the North African desert under a blazing sun or in the inaccessible mountains of Western Tunis. PK. War Correspondent B. Wundshammer, who spent several weeks on the Tunisian front, relates his impressions at this newest theatre of war in a series of articles

The officer commanding the Axis forces in Tunisia. Colonel General von Arnim (on the left) at the officers' observation post of a German division in Central Tunisia. On the right the division commander

The Leadership

When in the middle of November 1942 German parachutists and airborne troops occupied the harbours and bays of Bizerta, Tunis, Sousse, Sfax and Gabès, the Anglo-American tank forces were almost at the gates of those towns. Masterly leadership most effectively employed the small but powerfully equipped Axis units and within a few days shattered the enemy's hopes. At Tebourba, a few miles west of Tunis, an attack carried out by a few German tanks under the personal command of General Fischer, a wearer of the Oak Leaves, who was killed on the Tunisian front on 1st February 1943, placed the initiative to a considerable extent in the hands of the Germans. Dive-bomber units, fast bombers and dashing fighter squadrons effectively supported the operations of the ground troops. Reinforcements flowed into the country across the Straits of Tunis. The system of employing small units with high firing power distributed apparently at random, which the enemy did not discover until too late, successfully made up for the enemy's superiority in numbers and material.

The armoured wireless car of Colonel General von Arnim during a operations

His Royal Highness Sidi Mohammed El Moncef Pasha, Bey of Tunis, thanks the people from the window of his palace for their ovations upon the occasion of the festival Aid el Kebir

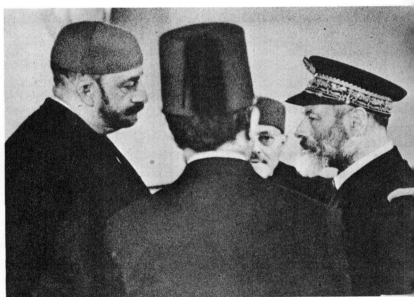

↑ *The French Resident-General, Admiral Estava, extends to His Royal Highness the sincere wishes of Marshal Pétain for the welfare of the Tunisian people*

Colonel General von Arnim, Commander-in-Chief of the Axis forces in Tunisia, is most heartily welcomed by His Royal Highness, the Bey ↓

In front of the palace of the Bey of Tunis: The representatives of the Axis Powers are received with cheers and clapping of hands in front of the palace in Hammam-Lif

Reception in the Palace of His Royal Highness

Upon the occasion of the great Arab Festival Aid el Kebir, His Royal Highness Sidi Mohammed El Moncef Pasha, Bey of Tunis, gave a reception to the representatives of the Axis Powers in his winter palace at Hamman Lif. The Commander-in-Chief of the Axis forces in Tunis, Colonel General von Arnim, was welcomed upon his arrival by the Arab population with cheers. The Bey of Tunis as well as the Commander-in-Chief manifested most heartily their determination to intensify the collaboration of the Axis Powers and the Tunisian population. We quote from the speech of His Royal Highness the following sentences: "... I express my gratitude for the protection extended by Germany and Italy to the population of Tunisia against the Anglo-American aggression. All Tunisia is firmly convinced that the Axis Powers will soon succeed in restoring order and peace throughout the country. I gratefully acknowledge the exemplary and disciplined conduct of the German-Italian troops who have won the full sympathy and admiration of the Tunisian people. Our hearts, as well as the hearts of the entire Arab world are with your brave soldiers in this struggle."

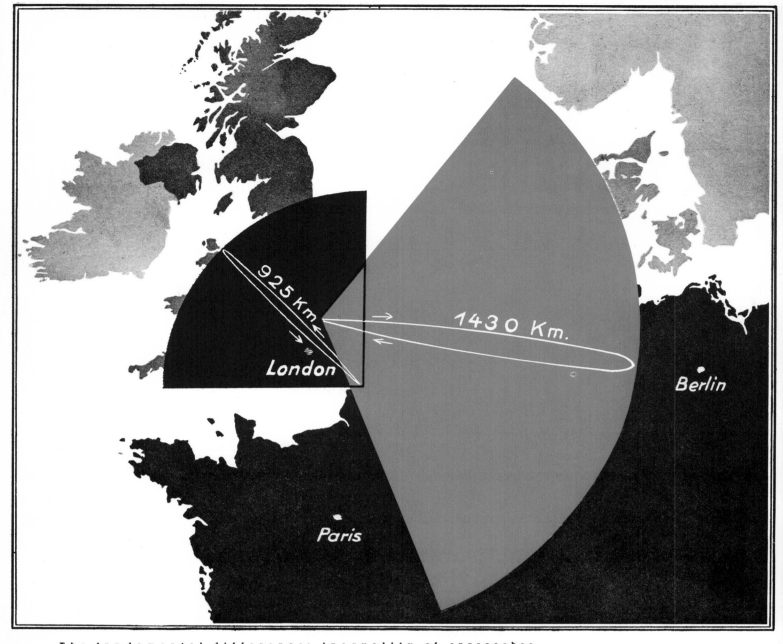

925 Km.

London

1430 Km.

Berlin

Paris

The fundamental difference: inequality of approaches

In order to fly to their objectives in Britain and return to their bases, the planes of the German Air Force have to fly an average distance of 575 miles. The Royal Air Force, on the other hand, in order to carry out attacks on Germany and to return to England must cover on an average a distance of 900 miles. The greatest advantages resulting from this difference in the R.A.F.'s range of action are clearly demonstrated by our map which is drawn exact to scale. "Signal" here shows the dire consequences which this presents for British air warfare and for British air armaments as a whole

Two kinds
of
air parity

The great mistake

in the British plans

for air warfare

One of the favourite themes of British ministerial speeches is the assertion that Great Britain will soon catch up the superiority of the German Air Force, a fact fully guaranteed by America's help. As soon as an equal number of fighters has been arrived at or perhaps superiority in the air has been achieved, the R. A. F., they state, will soon have destroyed Germany's armament industry and thus have annihilated the German "war machine."

To catch up Germany's air armament would be no easy task even for the united efforts of Great Britain and America, for steps were taken at an early date to ensure that the production strength of the German aeroplane industry should not lose its superiority. But even in the case of numerical parity the R. A. F. would enjoy only an apparent air parity and would by no means have achieved the same actual fighting power. To deny this would be to overlook the unequal con-

ditions under which the war in the air between Germany and Great Britain is being fought out in consequence of the present geographical situation.

Since the victorious campaign in the west, the German Air Force has directly faced the British Isles. In front of it, at a distance of only between 60 and 200 miles, lie the industrial regions and harbours of Southern England; the Midlands, so important to the armament industry, can be reached after a flight of about 250 miles and even the Scottish ports are not more than between 450 and 480 miles away.

Corresponding objectives in Germany are, on the other hand, very much further removed for the R. A. F., for the industrial areas in the occupied territories of Northern France, Belgium and Holland which are in close proximity to Great Britain do not, as far as Germany is concerned, play any important part in the armament industry. The objective which can most easily be reached by British aeroplanes is

western Germany which, however, lies not less than 325 miles from south-eastern England. British bombers in order to reach north-western Germany have to fly 400 miles and to reach central Germany not less than 490 miles.

The difference in the distances which have to be covered by the German Air Force and the R. A. F. in order to reach the regions where their main objectives lie, naturally varies according to the areas compared. The general situation is, however, shown pretty accurately by comparing the distances between northern France and the Midlands on the one hand and south-eastern England and north-western Germany on the other. In the first instance, the return flight plus 10 % for deviation from the course and searching for the objective is 575 miles, and in the second instance 900 miles.

Assuming that both the R. A. F. and the German Air Force possess planes which are in all respects identical, of

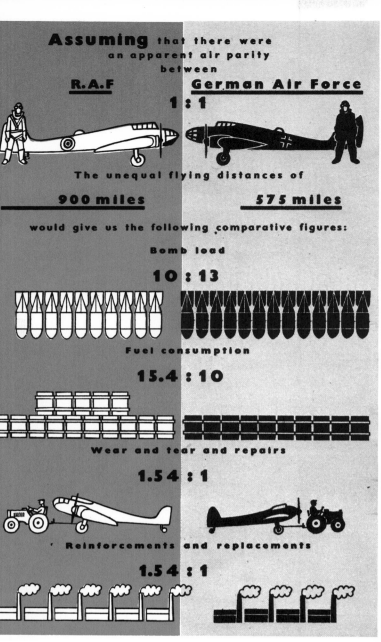

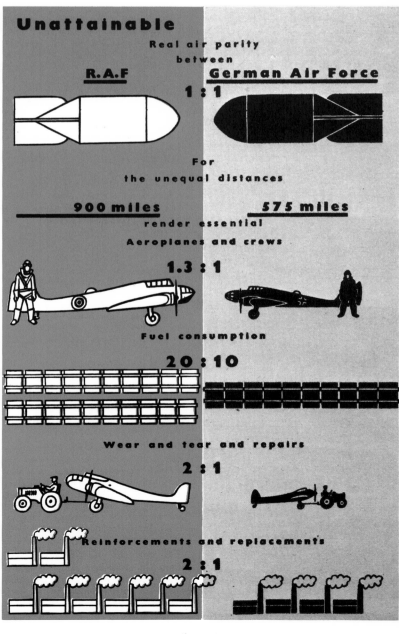

Assuming that there were an apparent air parity between

R.A.F   German Air Force

1 : 1

The unequal flying distances of

900 miles   **575 miles**

would give us the following comparative figures:

Bomb load

10 : 13

Fuel consumption

15.4 : 10

Wear and tear and repairs

1.54 : 1

Reinforcements and replacements

1.54 : 1

Unattainable

Real air parity between

R.A.F   German Air Force

1 : 1

For the unequal distances

900 miles   **575 miles**

render essential

Aeroplanes and crews

1.3 : 1

Fuel consumption

20 : 10

Wear and tear and repairs

2 : 1

Reinforcements and replacements

2 : 1

---

greater than that of the German plane with a shorter flight. But as it takes 130 British planes to carry the same load of bombs as is carried by 100 German planes, the greater consumption of fuel on the British side actually amounts to 100%! For Great Britain this means a very considerable increased demand for oil tankers.

In the same way, the wear and tear of each plane, and especially of its engine, is 55% greater on every flight on the British side. This results not only in the necessity for a correspondingly more extensive repair organization, but also in a very considerable extra number of auxiliary planes and engines. The general reserves of aircraft material, assuming that the aeroplanes on both sides have the same "life", must be twice as large on the British side as on the German, without taking into consideration the reinforcements made necessary by enemy action!

We have thus made clear the conditions necessary to enable Great Britain to catch up the German superiority in air warfare and achieve real air parity. It will be necessary for her fighter squadrons to be numerically stronger than Germany's by one third, and the general reinforcements in aircraft would have to be double as great as the corresponding reinforcements on the German side. Not until then could the R. A. F. drop as many bombs as the German Air Force. The problem thus facing British air armament, even including American help, offers no prospect of a solution. The difficulties, which finally consist in the necessity for Great Britain and the states supplying her producing twice as much aircraft material as Germany, in order to achieve and maintain mere parity with the German Air Force, could only be equalised by an extraordinary superiority in engineering technique. But especially in this connection, the prospects of success, in view of the extraordinary highly developed German industry, are exceedingly small. The disadvantages resulting from the differences in distance explained at the commencement of this article cannot be compensated for by the employment of larger planes with increased carrying capacity, for to produce such planes also requires a corresponding increase in working time, materials and industrial equipment.

---

a type of which the characteristics might be, for example, 1,600 H. P. engines, a speed of 235 m. p. h., a load of one ton of bombs, a total range of 1,250 miles, and a fuel consumption of 320 kg. p. h. or 0.89 kg. per kilometre. If the furthest possible range of action is not being completely utilized, every kilometre saved means that 0.89 kg. more bombs may be carried. The comparison of distances just made under these conditions has the following results:

In the case of the German Air Force: a total distance of 575 miles has to be flown. On this flight, 100 planes would carry 195.5 tons of bombs and would use 82.5 tons of fuel.

In the case of the R. A. F.: a total distance of 900 miles has to be flown. On this flight, 100 planes would carry only 151 tons of bombs and would use 127 tons of fuel.

In order to carry 195.5 tons of bombs to the objective, like the German Air Force, 130 planes would have to be used by the R. A. F. with a total fuel consumption of 164 tons. The result of this simple calculation is obvious and its consequences in estimating the actual fighting power of the British bomber squadrons in air warfare between Germany and Great Britain are of fundamental importance.

Great Britain is still far from apparent air parity with Germany, that is to say, she can never oppose the same number of aircraft to the German planes. She can never even hope for real air parity, for that would mean: If the British squadrons wished to carry the same weight of bombs on every flight to Germany as the German squadrons can take to England, they would have to be numerically stronger by 30%! We are here even assuming that the British planes are of the same quality and, above all, have at least the same transport capacity as the planes used by the German Air Force. The large number of planes necessary naturally calls for a corresponding increase in every kind of ground organization as well as the employment of a correspondingly larger personnel.

The longer flight to objectives in Germany makes it necessary for the R. A. F. to fly approximately 55% longer and thus puts a correspondingly greater strain upon the crews. This greater physical exertion must in the course of time have a detrimental effect upon the efficiency of the flying personnel.

The amount of fuel required by every British plane in consequence of the longer flight is approximately 55%

Zoot suiters – jitterbug

Two new American slang terms explained by SIGNAL

There are many Mexicans living in California who have become citizens of the United States. In general they are harmless, good-natured people who simply look for and find a living in the soft, warm climate of the Pacific Coast. Nevertheless, the Mexican problem in the western states is no new one. The internal chaos resulting from the war has suddenly rendered it as acute as the negro problem.

In Los Angeles, as in many other American cities, the adolescents without regular employment form gangs, a kind of murder and burglary clubs, which make the streets of Los Angeles unsafe at night. Robberies have increased in a terrifying manner and from time to time seamen have been found stabbed in the back in deserted streets when they have been paid off after returning from long journeys to Japan.

Like the swing boys in the eastern states, who make themselves conspicuous by their careless dress, these young Mexicans have adopted their own costume consisting of strange trousers wide at the knees and narrow at the ankles, three-quarter length coats and hats like those once worn in Europe by poets and composers. The American slang term invented for this uniform is "zoot suiters," and the zoot suiters of Los Angeles have gradually acquired a questionable fame.

In summer there was a regular explosion in the Pacific port just as violent as the racial disturbances in Detroit, New York and other cities. The Mexican zoot suiters had again stabbed a seaman somewhere, upon which hundreds and thousands of sailors and whites hunted the zoot suiters through the streets of the Mexican quarter, stripped them when they laid hands on them and flogged them. The police took the side of the unruly mobs and arrested only naked Mexicans for creating a public scandal.

For days the city of Los Angeles was shadowed by these disturbances which were the prelude to a general persecution of all the "coloured inhabitants" of the city. In the end not only did the mobbers pull out in handfuls the long hair the zoot suiters wore to their uniform, but they pursued anyone who was looked on as a Mexican.

The American magazine "Time" of 21st June wrote that at the bottom of this unexpected outburst of racial hatred was a much more serious problem, namely that these juveniles have only been American citizens for two generations. Their fathers and mothers are still Mexican at heart. They want to be American but are looked upon askance at home. At the same time, the rest of the Americans refuse to recognize them in any way. In spite of the boom in war production, these young Mexicans find it difficult to obtain regular employment. They are neglected and abandoned like wreckage and drift-wood on the seashore.

"Time" is of the opinion that this is one of the reasons why they wear this strange, romantic costume and why they have taken up the idea of burglary and murder clubs. In fact, however, America has here to do with one of the particularly outstanding characteristics of the complete break-up of discipline and morals in her youth.

In New York, for example, such a hysterical amusement panic has broken out among the young people that some places of entertainment like the Paramount Theatre in Times Square run non-stop day and night shows for the whole 24 hours of the day for the young. The hall resounds with an unbroken stream of jazz tunes, extravagant dances are demonstrated and enthusiastically imitated by the swing boys and swing girls. These exhibitions have nothing to do with high spirits and gaiety but rather are they the latest climax in indecency and degeneracy. These exponents of swing have been given a new name in the States and are called quite simply jitterbugs.

We are not speaking here of unusual or chance eccentricities but of widespread symptoms affecting ever-widening circles. The papers are full of descriptions of this mass hysteria and comparisons are made with the children's crusades. Psychiatrists even publish their diagnoses of it. The unstable foundation of American society has been undermined to an incredible degree by the war. At the moment the American colossus is reaching out farther than ever. Internally, however, it is being attacked by a number of insidious poisons against which the leading politicians have no effective antidote. It is clear for all to see that the big internal problems facing America are only in their initial stadium.

What is a waltz? *It is danced only by old-fashioned Europeans. The jitterbug, the latest in dancing from the U. S. A., is what the couples of all nations have been waiting for . . .*

Wide at the knees and narrow at the ankles.
The coming fashion for men in the opinion of zoot suiters in the U. S. A. What do you think of it?

A sensation? *Only one man was stabbed but now there is a regular manhunt. One of the everyday pictures to be seen in any American magazine*

The dawn after the night of terror. *Smoke is still rising from the burnt-out opera house (on the right) and a large hotel; it hangs over the square where men belonging to a salvage corps are seeking a few minutes' rest on mattresses which have been saved*

A NIGHT OF TERROR...

War Correspondent Hanns Hubmann experienced one of the heavy night raids on a town in the west of Germany. Ten days later, he revisited the same town and its inhabitants. SIGNAL here publishes his report

This town in western Germany has already been the object of a hundred night air raids. Of more than a hundred, but this one was one of the worst. War Correspondent Hanns Hubmann was there and saw the innumerable conflagrations. The opera house and many of the large hotels were destroyed. Reich Minister Speer, with whom Signal's War Correspondent was travelling, helped to salvage mattresses and other things. Hundreds and thousands of people lost their homes. Everybody helped in saving what could be saved. On the morning after the raid, the smoke was still hanging like a pall in the streets, but the people were already hastening to their work again. Yet their faces reflected the terrors of the night. Ten days after this night raid, Hubmann returned to the town. The marks of destruction on the housefronts were naturally still unchanged. But the faces of the people and their whole life clearly showed that they are overcoming the hardships of the nights of terror. How they are doing so is shown by Signal's photographs. Men who take home a bunch of flowers to their wives ten days after such an air raid and women who cannot hide their so disarming anxieties about hats and handbags, people who stream to their work in the early morning after the night of devastation as though nothing had occurred—such people are stronger than their fate.

The dawn after the night of terror. *On their way to work already, they pass ruins and wounded people. They have had no time to shave, because they all want to be at their machines at 6 a. m. as usual. The trams are not running and at most they have a bicycle at their disposal for getting to the factories*

The waitress Kate

The morning after the night of terror, Signal came across her sitting with a colleague on a few stools she had saved together with a number of other things including the cash register from her café (on the left of the picture)

↓ Ten days later, *the reporter happened to see her working as a National Socialist People's Welfare helper distributing food (on the right of the picture)*

Architect and photographer...

"Hallo, where are you taking that pail?" "Up the ladder to the staircase and then to my atelier!" Mrs Hehmke-Winterer, a photographer, lives on the 5th floor. The atelier was not wrecked. Her husband, the architect Konrad Wagner, has built a makeshift hearth out of a few bricks. They fetch water from a pump in the yard. She has a smile on her face for life is still going on as usual.

The dawn after the night of terror. *Wagner and his wife, in front of their house*

Ten days later *the architect Wagner is again at work with his women assistants in a makeshift office in the heavily damaged house*

The dawn after the night of terror. *Their appearance still bears marks of the night of devastation. They have taken off their collars to be able to fight the flames and do salvage work. The alert had brought them together by chance in an air-raid shelter—Schäfer, the municipal inspector, Strathmann, the grocer and Arenswald, the master basket-maker. They had done good work. Ten days later? (See below)*

They have recovered their good spirits . . .

. . . for they still have their Rhineland humour. These three men are a municipal inspector, a grocer and a master basket-maker. Ten days after the heavy air raid things are taking their normal course again—the one is selling sausage, the second is carrying on his office work between makeshift walls and the third is again making neat baskets.

"This is my office now. Don't you agree, cupboards take the place of a wall nicely?"

"Would you like some real Brunswick tongue sausage again? It has just come in fresh!"

"I've just finished making these baskets. And there is a new pane in my shop window, too"

THE ANACONDA SYSTEM

A consideration of military science by Walter Kiaulehn

Ulysses S. Grant is responsible for the war morality introduced by the United States. His system, known as "Grantism," is America's contribution to the conduct of war

William T. Sherman, the inventor of the "locust strategy." He openly waged war on a whole people and betrayed his honour as a soldier for "victory"

Philipp H. Sheridan wanted to be even more cruel than Sherman from whom his favourite quotation was: "Even the crows have to bring their own food with them." The war against civilians was the ideal

Robert E. Lee, the "defeated" General of the Southern States. "There are things a gentleman does not do." It was this belief which brought about Lee's ruin. He capitulated to criminals not to soldiers

The world is today witnessing the ghastly fact that war not only does not spare women and children but in part even aims directly at their destruction. The author, who is well known to SIGNAL's readers from his many studies and inquiries, has investigated the origin of this "strategy"

"Our method of warfare is different from that in Europe. We are not fighting against enemy armies but against an enemy people; both young and old, rich and poor must feel the iron hand of war in the same way as the organized armies. In this respect my march through Georgia was a wonderful success."

General Sherman to General Grant. (End of January 1865)

Both the date and the author of this letter must appear extraordinary to every European. How could an American general write such a monstrous thing just at that particular time? The most noble minds and hearts in Europe were then making every effort to humanize warfare as far as possible.

On the other hand, a 45-year-old man in Ohio, America, the son of a lawyer of Puritan descent, General William Tecumseh Sherman, had invented a new warfare that was directed against the enemy people, against the civilian population. Sherman was the inventor of locust strategy. His doctrine was: Where I have been, the war has ceased, because all forms of life no longer exist. It involves nothing more nor less than the suppression of humane warfare.

The cruelties of the Marquis de Sade and the atrocities perpetrated by Jack the Ripper have never led to mass suggestion. Sherman's strategy, however, has been acclaimed as classical. After carrying out his acts of cruelty as a general, Sherman was appointed Commander-in-Chief of the United States of America. His method has become the American ideal. It first infected the Anglo-Saxon world; the great Moltke ominously predicted at the end of last century that in future wars armies would not fight against one another but peoples. During the first World War the Americans did not have the opportunity to apply in Europe the lessons they had learnt from Sherman. Their first appearance in Europe during this war, however, the bombardment from the air of undefended monuments of culture, shows whither this path is intended to lead.

Sherman's strategy is the art of war employed by the unsuccessful. It is necessary to bear this in mind when considering Sherman's methods. He was unsuccessful but by no means untalented. It was his fate always to have to fight against enemies better than himself. He never won a success against an enemy of equal strength. He usually fought against weaker foes and was defeated by their superior art based on European precedents. He owed his greatest military success, the occupation of the town of Atlanta, not to his own skill but to a mistake made by his enemy. (Anybody jumping to conclusions will now say that a mistake made by the enemy is always a part of success. That is not true. The greatest generals have celebrated their triumphs against enemies who did not make mistakes.)

In the order of the day to his troops after the occupation of Atlanta (8th September 1864), Sherman said: "We must admit that the enemy opposed us with skill and endurance. At last he made the long awaited mistake and sent his cavalry to our rear much too far to be able to recall them." The price of his mistake, as we have already said, was Atlanta, the capital of Georgia. The enemy general evacuated the town after realizing his error. Sherman found only wounded men incapable of further fighting. He was ambitious and had grown tired of such wretched successes. He therefore continued the war in accordance with an idea he had already conceived some time before.

Under the pretext of liberating the slaves

We are discussing what is known as the War of Secession. "Secessio" was what the ancient Romans used to call the effort to achieve independence. All previous wars of that nature in Europe were now completely overshadowed by the War of Secession between the Northern and Southern States. Superficially this war was being fought on the question of the abolition of slavery. The North wished to give back their liberty to the negro slaves in the South. The result was that by the end of the war 100,000 Negroes were fighting against the armies of their liberators.

There is no need for us to delve into the events leading up to the war. Temperament and religious fanaticism converted it into one of the bloodiest massacres in history. There were many innovations both on land and at sea. Land mines were employed on a large scale and armoured warships made their first appearance. In his book "Der Krieg ohne Gnade" (War Without Quarter), the Swiss historian Bircher says that force of arms alone could not decide the war. It was not until Sherman employed his locust strategy that the Northern States won the victory.

The end of Atlanta, the beautiful town among the hills of Georgia, was the signal for the commencement of the new era.

On 5th September 1864, Cogswell, the commander of Atlanta appointed by Sherman, ordered the inhabitants to evacuate the town. These instructions were couched in the following terms: "All the families living in Atlanta the male members of which are serving with the Confederates or have gone to the South, are to leave the town within five days. They will be allowed to pass through the lines towards the South. All citizens from the North not belonging to the army or having the permission of Generals Sherman or Thomas are to leave the town within the same period. Anybody found in the town afterwards will be imprisoned."

Nobody at first believed the truth of this order, for nobody apart from Sherman knew what it meant. Who could have suspected that this order was the first step along a path never yet trodden in history.

General Hood, Sherman's opponent, was also informed of this measure by letter. At the same time he was offered an armistice. Hood replied: "General, I have received your letter of yesterday from the hands of citizens Boll and Crew. You say in it: 'It is in the interest of the Union that the people of Atlanta should leave the town. I have no alternative and consequently accept your proposal for a ten days' armistice and will do everything in my power to remove the people of Atlanta to the South. And now allow me to say that this measure, which is without precedent, exceeds in calculated and intentional cruelty anything in the dark history of warfare. I protest in the name of God and humanity against your driving the

women and children of a brave people from their homes and hearths."

The citizens of Atlanta protested together with General Hood.

A document

General Sherman answered them in the same way as he answered General Hood. He wrote to them as follows:

"Gentlemen,

I have received your letter of 11th inst. and the request for the withdrawal of my order. I have read it carefully and believe all the sufferings you mention which will be the consequence of its execution. And yet I do not withdraw it..."

"In order to end the war we must annihilate the army of the rebels who have revolted against the law and the constitution In order to annihilate them, we must push forward to the places where they produce their arms and equipment and store their supplies. Atlanta cannot simultaneously serve military purposes and be a safe place for families. From now on there will be no trade, no industry and no agriculture there, a shortage will soon come about and force the families to move away. Why not rather go now when all preparations have been made and the removal is facilitated instead of waiting until the fire of both armies renews the scenes of the previous month. I cannot communicate to

you my next plans, but you cannot believe that the army will remain here quietly and I can tell you that my plans make necessary your removal which I will now facilitate for you in every way."

There was, however, one man to whom Sherman had communicated his plans. This was Lieutenant-General Grant, the Commander-in-Chief of the Northern States. Sherman had sent a messenger to him bearing a letter with several seals. It was very dangerous to send this letter, but Sherman had to do it if he did not wish to expose himself to utter condemnation. He was looking for somebody to relieve him of the responsibility and Grant accepted it because Sherman promised him victory. Just as Sherman became the instigator of President Lincoln's assassination as the result of what happened, so, too, he prepared the way for his friend and companion, Grant, to occupy the empty presidential chair. Grant became the most popular man in America in consequence of Sherman's "victories."

In his letter Sherman did not write everything, for otherwise Grant, who loved to emphasize his Christianity, would not have consented after all. Sherman told everything only a few weeks later when the new strategy had already proved successful and Grant, intoxicated by victory, could not draw back if he did not wish to relinquish fresh victories.

The great march of the locusts. In 1864—1865, General Sherman marched through Georgia and Carolina with 60,000 men. His intention was not to fight but to destroy the homes and food supplies of the civilian population. He thus carried out the "Anaconda Plan" and the Southern States capitulated to the criminal in the face of his crime. Whole towns such as Atlanta were blown sky-high. About 37,000 square miles of cultivated land were systematically devastated, that is to say an area larger than the whole of Holland and Belgium. (See the map for a comparison)

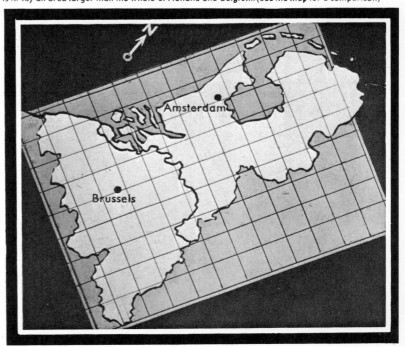

The art of warfare employed by the unsuccessful

Sherman said that it was foolish to continue the war in the manner of a normal campaign as had been the case so far. The way the war was being fought meant that you were continually dependent on the enemy. Whether you advanced or retreated, you always had to reckon with the enemy. The war could only be brought to a close by surprise operations and such surprise operations could only be carried out if the enemy was prevented from

sticking at your heels. Sherman said that it was his intention to disappear without the enemy being in a position to follow him. It was his aim to reappear somewhere else by surprise.

But how would it be possible to shake off the enemy?

It is necessary to destroy his supply base, was Sherman's answer. "I will sow economic ruin throughout the country so that no soldier coming after me will find anything to eat." Georgia

and its capital, Atlanta, had already been very much weakened by the war. Sherman consequently wrote to Grant as follows: "Until we can repopulate Georgia, it is useless to defend it, but the complete destruction of its roads, its buildings, its population and its military resources is essential. The attempt to defend its roads costs us a thousand men every month and brings us no advantages. I can carry out the march and make Georgia howl."

Grant requested Sherman to express himself more precisely and Sherman answered:

"Hood can go to Kentucky and Tennessee, but I believe he will be forced to follow me. Instead of being on the defensive, I shall be on the offensive, instead of guessing at what he intends, I shall compel him to guess

my plans. This makes a difference of 25 % in warfare. (In military language, it is the advantage of the initiative.) I can turn in the direction of Savannah, Charleston or the mouth of the Chattahoochee. I prefer to march through Georgia to the sea destroying everything on my way... Therefore, if you hear that I have set off, order scouts in Morris Island, Ossabaw Sound, Pensacola and Mobile B.

shall turn up again somewhere and, believe me, I can take Macon, Milledgeville, Augusta, Savannah and then appear again behind Charleston so that I can starve it out. This operation is not purely military and strategical, but it will show the South's weakness."

It is necessary to read these two letters carefully in order to understand Sherman's real purpose. They are

be of use to the enemy. The truth is that Sherman wished to act on the offensive but not against the enemy's army. He wished to make the land of Georgia howl, not the army of Georgia of which he was afraid. He was plannin[g] a bold crime and covertly indicated h[is] intention in the words: "This operatio[n] is not purely military and strateg[y]ical..."

The whole of Atlanta was blown sky-high

Sherman had his way. Atlanta was evacuated and razed to the ground according to a carefully thought out plan. Sherman was in command of 60,000 men. This army had supplies for thirty days and consequently did not need to forage. Sherman divided his army up into four corps and two wings and gave them orders to march parallel to one another. Two corps were thus always marching together, the whole in four columns, right across the country, flanked by cavalry and mounted batteries. Their commander was General Kilpatrick. It was he who issued the order that only the ruins of houses should show to coming generations that Kilpatrick's cavalry had passed that way.

By 14th November 1864 every man in Sherman's army was on the march and only the demolition party was left in the deserted city. Sherman sent off a last telegram to Washington saying: "All is well" and then the telegraph station was blown sky-high to be followed by the town of Atlanta. Sherman and his 60,000 men now disappeared even for Washington.

In the middle of December the ghostly army reappeared near Savannah. The 60,000 men had covered the 220 miles from Atlanta to the sea like a whirlwind. Behind them they dragged along an army of starving Negroes whom they could not very well shake off because, after all, they had come as the liberators of the slaves.

This march, however, was only Sherman's apprenticeship. Although he had burnt the cotton and grain everywhere, and the mills and innumerable houses had been reduced to ruins by his hordes, he still continued to maintain the semblance of commanding an army on account of Grant. Plundering was officially forbidden. It was not until they reached Carolina that the last bonds of discipline were shaken off by Sherman's troops and that they lost the name of soldiers.

Yet Sherman already now, after h[is] march through Georgia, wrote the lett[er] to Grant containing the frightful word[s:] "We are not fighting against enem[y] armies but against an enemy peopl[e,] both young and old, rich and po[or] must feel the iron hand of war in th[e] same way as the organized armies. [In] this respect my march through Georg[ia] was a wonderful success."

An American admirer of Sherman, [G.] W. Nichols, has provided some d[ry] figures in his "Story of the Gre[at] March" (published 1865, London). [On] its march Sherman's army confiscate[d] 100 million dollars' worth of grain a[nd] cattle. The troops used 20 milli[on] dollars' worth for themselves and t[he] remainder was destroyed.

This figure includes only the foo[d] supplies; the destroyed houses, roa[ds] and equipment have never been ca[l]culated. This "wonderful succes[s"] stimulated the other generals. She[ri]dan, one of Grant's cavalry general[s,] destroyed 100,000 bushels of whea[t,] 50,000 bushels of maize, 6,200 tons [of] hay and 11,000 head of cattle in Roc[k]ingham County alone.

For years after the conclusion [of] peace, the people in the Southe[rn] States, who had formerly been so ric[h,] were still clad in rags.

Grant was delighted when he hea[rd] the news of Sherman's appearance. [He] immediately sent him a new plan [of] campaign. Sherman was to make h[is] way by the quickest route, that is [to] say, via the sea, to Grant in order [to] support him in his hard struggle agai[nst] the great General Lee of the Southe[rn] States and his wonderful, fearle[ss] cavalry.

But Sherman did not come.

Grant did not yet understand. [He] still believed that Sherman was longi[ng] to fight, but Sherman did not want [to] fight or only when there was no oth[er] alternative.

Sherman had long ago relinquishe[d] all military ambitions and cut himse[lf] off from every conception of soldier[ly]

"War without quarter." These photographs were taken eighty years ago. It was then that the Americans invented "total warfare," the war against civilians and property. The destruction of the railways led to the mass employment of pioneers. Total war showed its terrible aspects for the first time. The modern form of reporting on wars also came into existence. Below is a reproduction of the very first photograph taken of a battery in the field whilst firing. The tremendous explosion caused the photograph to lack clearness

written by one soldier to another soldier in soldier's language. A clever soldier is writing to his not quite so clever superior. Without absolutely telling him lies, he yet conceals his intentions in the technical language with which they are both familiar. On one occasion he pretends that he wishes to adopt the defensive and consequently must destroy Atlanta. He acts as if he wished to prevent his enemy from pursuing him. It has always been thus since the days of

classical antiquity. A retreating army destroys everything that could be of use to the advancing enemy. Sherman proposes this old defensive rule to his superior. In his next letter, however, he writes: "Instead of being on the defensive, I shall be on the offensive, for in military language that is the advantage of the initiative etc." Why, if he wishes to launch an offensive, does he destroy everything as he advances? Only during his retreat would a normal soldier destroy everything that might

honour. He had become a violent criminal who wished to confer victory on his country's politics whatever it cost the enemy. "War," says Clausewitz, "is the continuation of politics by other means." Sherman adapted this axiom and made of it: ". . . is the continuation of politics by every means." There we have Sherman's terrible originality. He had converted war from being an act of violence against an enemy army to an act of violence against an enemy people. He went even further and made of it an act of total violence. Even violence has limits imposed on it by morality. Sherman had intentionally disappeared with his entire army and, far removed from all control and all protest, had led war across the limit set even on violence into the zone of unbridled crime. When he reappeared, Savannah fell and the world regarded this as a sign of Sherman's bravery and of his military genius. What had really happened in Georgia was learnt after the conclusion of peace by only a few people. The world was scarcely interested in it, for in Europe war broke out between France and Germany, and, moreover, American propaganda ensured that the world was fed with touching stories from "Uncle Tom's Cabin."

During the time he spent in Georgia, Sherman enriched the history of tactics by only one feature, but that alone should have sufficed to exclude him for ever from the company of gentlemen.

He had prisoners of war put on to carts which had to drive along in front of his own troops. If they were blown up Sherman knew that a minefield lay ahead. He answered all protests against his cruel treatment of defenceless people with the icy coldness characteristic of all his writings.

Sherman sent a letter, in which he explained his own new plan, to Grant who was still waiting for him in vain. He did not want to cross the sea as Grant had ordered, so as to fight against - Lee, but wished to march through Carolina and devastate it like Georgia, no, not like Georgia, but far more cruelly, far more thoroughly, in fact, totally. He wrote as follows: "Certainly Jefferson Davies (the President of the Southern States) keeps his people well disciplined, but I think that confidence in him has been shattered in Georgia and it soon will be in South Carolina. The whole army, moreover, is eager to be revenged on South Carolina. I tremble when I think of its approaching fate, but I know that it has deserved everything coming to it."

With a trembling heart—never has anybody scorned noble feelings with more blasphemy — Sherman gave his army the order to break camp: The Swiss military historian, Bircher, whom we have already mentioned, wrote in "War Without Quarter": "The instructions were to destroy roads, horses and people which were mentioned in that typical order!"

Once more the army moved off along a wide front marching in four columns. Behind it lay the devastated region of Georgia and before it the prosperous and rich area of Carolina. No revenger could follow Sherman, for how could he have fed himself? Sheridan said cynically: "Even the crows have to bring their food with them."

Gone with the wind . . .

The marauders of General Sherman's army called themselves "bummers." In name they were soldiers, but actually it was 60,000 bandits who marched through Georgia and Carolina stealing more than they could eat themselves. "Roads, horses and people are to be destroyed." Acting in accordance with these orders, they burnt everything they found and even took the poultry away with them. The two pictures, above and alongside, are contemporary illustrations from the book by the American, Nichols, entitled "Story of the Great March" (1865). The horrors of the first total war are here seen with the eyes of an American from the Northern States and not as an accusation levelled by the Southern States. Mitchell's novel "Gone with the wind" is based on such sources. This book was a great literary success in Europe a few years ago. In the Southern States of the U.S.A., where the horrors of 1864 to 1865 were perpetrated and are not forgotten, the novel led to a number of riots

A victim of his countrymen

The actor Booth, who came from the Southern States, murdered Abraham Lincoln, the President of the Northern States, in a box at the theatre. Booth had intended to assassinate the man responsible for the atrocities, but Grant, the man really responsible, remained away from the performance at the last minute

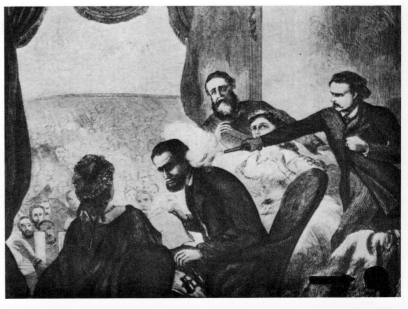

One of three hundred-thousand:
A worker who has been employed for one and a half year on the West Wall. His wife and three children live in a village in central Germany. Every half year he comes home on leave like a soldier, from the "front" . . .

The Men of the OT

Picture series of the work done by the Todt-Organisation in the West Wall fighting zone

A steel helmet for every worker in the fighting zone
Enemy fire can be expected daily. The men then leave their posts and rush through shrapnel-proof trenches to the next dugout or bunkers in the rear

In the "labyrinth" of the fighting zone: the "pilot" takes the lead . . .
Each group of workers is looked after by a soldier who knows the lay of the land and can safely lead the men to their posts through mine-fields and barbed wire entanglements. Additional bunkers and embrasures are being built here. The front workers, who are not soldiers, are instructed by the Todt-Organisation's trained leaders concerning the proper conduct in a fighting zone

Behind protecting trees and screens . . .

Invisible to the enemy the West Wall workers carry on. Between them and the front line soldiers there is an active cameradship. Machine-guns protect them against enemy shock-troops and reconnoitering units. Everything looks quiet behind the barbed wire, but . . .

. . . Things hum in the excavation

The last planks are being applied. Concrete mixers are already on hand. Protected by a front line soldier the German front line worker, works for — the front line soldier

Tunnels eat their way through the hills . . .

Connecting galleries lead from one fortification to the next. The compression hammers are in the hands of miners who have come to the West Wall from all parts of the Reich.

The Eastern Front

Germany made many mistakes in World War II, but undoubtedly the fatal error was in going to war against the Soviet Union while Britain remained unconquered. The Nazi-Soviet alliance was never more than an *ad hoc* arrangement for both sides. Soon after the articles describing the great advantages accruing to Germany from the Russian alliance appeared, the first stages of Operation Barbarossa, the invasion of Russia, were presented in all the lavish style and panache that one had come to expect of *Signal*. Some readers must have been amused by the editor's explanation why a conflict between the Nazis and the Communists was inevitable a few weeks after the attack had begun. And perhaps cynical too, since the horrors of the Ogpu were only a fraction of what the SS perpetrated against Slavs and Jews in the Russian campaign.

For the first time since the spring of 1940 *Signal* photographers had a subject worthy of their attentions. The fight in the East was a monumental struggle, with three German army groups pressing toward the Ukraine, Moscow and Leningrad. The offensives fizzled in the winter of 1941-42. The defences around Leningrad held, and a siege ensued which was to last almost three years. The Wehrmacht was stopped in the suburbs of Moscow, and although German armies captured a good part of the Ukraine, atrocities committed against the Soviet people turned what could have been depicted as a liberation from Stalinism into hard, partisan activities against the Third Reich which *Signal's* propaganda could do little to combat. *Signal* and the Propaganda Ministry portrayed the struggle against Communism as a fight for European civilisation against the Mongol hordes of the East. Hundreds of thousands of volunteers from occupied Europe joined the Waffen-SS in a genuine response to this appeal.

But the realities of Nazi rule could not be disguised. When Reinhard Heydrich 'protector' of Bohemia-Moravia, was assassinated by British and Czech agents in 1942, Hitler ordered the town of Lidice in Czechoslovakia to be razed to the ground. All its male citizens were killed. Whatever panegyrics *Signal* could muster to make a martyr of Heydrich could not have gained much support among those who knew what happened. But that is precisely the point. Communications in Nazi-controlled Europe were strictly censored. Thus, *Signal* could convince many French and Dutch that Heydrich was a martyr, even if the Czechs remained sceptical.

Once it became clear that the Nazis were not to win another lightning victory in the East, *Signal* searched vainly for new propaganda themes to exploit. In the autumn of 1943 it appeared likely to both sides in the struggle that the battle for Stalingrad would be the turning point in the war. *Signal* prepared the ground for the expected triumph with a number of articles describing the horrors of this titanic battle. Some time after the battle had been lost, Dr. Goebbels ordered that this defeat, unlike so many others, must be acknowledged. *Signal* responded with a call for renewed dedication to German military traditions to fight on to preserve Western civilisation against Communism.

The year 1943 was a sad tale of setback after setback for the Wehrmacht. The greatest tank battle in history near Kursk was never reported. Further articles depicting the pan-European nature of the German struggle appeared, including the army of General Vlasov, who commanded a group of anti-Communist Russian forces against the Soviet Union. Soviet inhumanity as expressed in the genocide of Katyn Wood, where thousands of Polish officers were slaughtered by the Communists, was among the few genuine points made by *Signal's* propaganda team.

Toward the end of the war *Signal* could only call upon Europe for renewed efforts in a losing cause. The editor's prediction of a Third World War between Russia and America if Germany lost World War II has a haunting ring about it. *Signal* was not always wrong. The secret of *Signal's* success throughout Europe was its appeal to traditional values in a chaotic period. *Signal* stands as a unique historical document and a monument to the Thousand Year Reich which lasted for only twelve

The leaders of a unit supported by tanks are reconnoitring the snow-covered terrain for enemy movements. Large black patches loom up against the darkness of the wooded horizon—soon the guns will roar

Why Germany and Russia?

Lessons of History

Peter Durnowo, councillor of state
A year before the war, the councillor of state, Peter Durnowo, warned the Czar against a policy directed against Germany

One day in August 1913, a year before the Great War, a memorandum was handed to Tsar Nicholas II, sent by the chamberlain Durnovo. The Tsar read it attentively, and then it wandered into the archives. It was first discovered and published after the Revolution. But nobody took any particular notice of it, as at that time there were too many sensational revelations.

Even so, the contents of this memorandum were extremely remarkable. The prudent chamberlain warned the Tsar of the danger of war with Germany. He not only prophesied the defeat of Russia, but he also reckoned, which is most extraordinary, with the possibility of Britain and France emerging from this conflict victorious, in spite of Russia's defeat. If this were the case, he wrote, the Allies would in no way defend the interests of Russia during peace negotiations. The result would be the end of the reigning dynasty in Russia. Such a risk could only be incurred in the event of there being no solution to the conflict of vital interests as between Germany and Russia. There could be no question, however, of such conflict of interests, and a glance at the history of both empires should be sufficient to prove this.

Even in old Russia there were men who could see clearly and who possessed the talent of political foresight. Had they possessed the qualities of political leadership as well, Russia would have been spared disastrous wars.

Durnovo did not possess these qualities, he was certainly a leader, but only the leader of the ultra-conservative group in the Council of State, called the "Bisons", whose reactionary policy finally led to the Revolution. The greatest statesman who arose during the dynasty of the Tsar towards the end of the 19th century was the minister Witte. He too dreamt of a triple pact between Germany, Russia and the U.S.A. Witte was an exponent of Russian imperialism in the period before the Great War. He had definite goals. He followed them with tenacity and achieved them. "Peaceful penetration"

into Manchuria, the occupation of the Pacific coast, the construction of the East China railway, all these were his work. An active policy in Asia· on the part of Russia was, however, in his opinion only possible so long as Russia continued to be on terms of peace and harmony with Germany. All the essentials for this actually existed. Russian expansion consisted only in· pushing towards the east and southeast. None of Russia's or Germany's important interests could ever clash with one another. Germany s need for colonial expansion caused just as little disturbance to Russia as Russia's expansion in Asia caused Imperial Germany.

Such a train of thought was a mere matter of course to the older generation of Russian statesmen. These politicans had won their political spurs in the 19th century.

Their fathers had fought side by side with Prussian regiments against Napoleon, at a time when the Russian Field Marshal Prince Kutuzov had proclaimed for the peoples of Europe "Liberation from the tyranny of the Corsican" in the joint names of the Russian Tsar and the Prussian King. Such memories live long. There was also a fact not without importance, namely, that Tsar Alexander I and his brother and successor Nicholas I were racially more German than Russian, in addition to being both married to German princesses. It was during that period of "traditional friendship" that Russia under the Tsars was the most powerful and her frontiers extended furthest. Why could not this state of affairs have remained? It did remain, until British diplomacy succeeded in provoking the Crimean War. In 1853, one month after Turkey had declared war on Russia, the Turkish fleet was destroyed by the Russian fleet in the Anatolian harbour of Sinope. A storm of indignation broke out in England. The same Foreign Minister, Palmerston, who had represented the bombardment of Copenhagen without a declaration of war to be a praiseworthy act, now spoke of "a Sinope massacre". The

British Government continued the policy of provocation. The diplomatic conference in Vienna, under Prussia's influence, had worked out conditions for a compromise which would be acceptable to Turkey and was recognized in advance by Tsar Nicholas I. As soon as these proposals for a compromise became known, an Anglo-French fleet appeared in the waters of the Black Sea and turned what had appeared to the whole world to be Russia's voluntary acceptance into an agreement imposed by force.

Here the British had counted on the Tsar's character, on his feudal and chivalrous ideas of honour, justice and prestige, for he declared: "However great the risk may be, I will now never assent to a compromise."

The Treaty of Paris in 1856, which concluded the war, showed what Britain's aims were. Russia was obliged to renounce the fortification of her harbours and her fleet in the Black Sea. Russia did not forget, however, that Prussia had been the only power during the Crimean War to have no direct or indirect connexion with the anti-Russian coalition and had not in any way benefited from Russia's misfortune.

The result of the Crimean War was a political success for British diplomacy, and at the same time a personal triumph for Napoleon III. 42 years previously Tsar Alexander I had defeated the great Napoleon. Now, the nephew of Napoleon I dictated peace terms to the nephew of Alexander I in Paris. The Russian nephew, however, was not long in replying. His answer took the form of a retort on France and at the same time an expression of thanks to Prussia: in 1866 during· the Austro-Prussian War, Alexander II, decided to adopt an attitude of friendly neutrality towards Prussia. In 1870 he went still further: he informed Vienna that if Austria should rise against Prussia, the Russian army would occupy Galicia with 300,000 men.

Was this merely a policy of personal revenge and thanks? No, behind it stood Russia's true inter-

English and French warships in the Black Sea
In 1853 when the compromise proposed to end the Russo-Turkish disagreements was announced a Franco-English squadron appeared in the Black Sea and so changed the voluntary Russian agreement in the eyes of the whole world into a compulsory move.

ests. The Tsar made use of the French defeat to set aside the Treaty of Paris and to build up a new fleet in the Black Sea.

It now appeared as if a new period of "traditional friendship" between Germany and Russia would begin. The gains which the conformity of their foreign policies had achieved were apparent to everyone.

Meanwhile British diplomacy did not remain idle. Twenty years after the Crimean War, when a new war broke out between Russia and Turkey, ending this time in complete victory for Russia, Britain again showed her hand. At the same moment as the Grand Duke Nicholas—father of the Commander-in-Chief in the Great War—was dictating provisional peace terms to Turkey, 19 miles from Constantinople in the little village of San Stefano, the British fleet appeared in the Sea of Marmara and anchored before the Turkish capital.

As usual, "public opinion" in England demanded war "as the Empire had been dealt a heavy blow", although it was not quite certain how or why. At that time "Jingoism" made its appearance in England; in those days in all the London music halls a new popular song was to be heard: "We don't want to fight, but by Jingo if we do, we've got the men, we've got the ships, we've got the money too."

a fourth Russian plenipotentiary. "I behaved in such a way at the Congress that at its conclusion I thought that if I were not already in possession of the highest Russian Order set in diamonds, I would have to receive it now", said Bismarck, amid loud laughter, in his speech to the Reichstag on 6th February 1888. At the critical moment of Anglo-Russian tension, the Reich chancellor presented himself late at night to the British plenipotentiary, Lord Beaconsfield (Disraeli), who was ill in bed, nevertheless obtained his consent to further negotiations. It was only thanks to Bismarck that Russia received at that time the town of Batum on the Black Sea from Turkey.

When Anton von Werner, the painter, was commissioned by the city of Berlin to paint a picture of the Congress in full session, the chancellor insisted that he should be portrayed sitting side by side with the second Russian representative, Count Schuwaloff, whom Bismarck esteemed very highly as a man and a diplomat, in contrast to the first representative, Prince Gorchakov. On the other side, however, Bismarck placed the representative of Austro-Hungary, Count Andrassy, thereby revealing the whole difficulty of his position. Bismarck was really looking for a compromise; he defended Russia everywhere he could, but at the

"Will Your Lordship be so kind as to point out the desired frontier?" said Prince Gorchakov.
finger could not find Kars. Everybody smiled. "The matter is not important enough to waste time on", said Disraeli sharply.

This was his concern for the "vital interests" of Turkey. But his ability in regard to cutting "his pound of flesh" from his friends was shown a few days later. While Disraeli was passionately defending the interests of Turkey in Berlin, The British Ambassador in Constantinople signed a treaty for the cession of Cyprus by Turkey to Britain. This information reached the members of the congress through the newspapers.

To the protests of France's representatives in Berlin, Disraeli answered: "Just take Tunis!" And when the Italians protested, he said to them very confidentially: "Just take Tunis!"

Simultaneously, the British were able to create the impression in St. Petersburg that Bismarck had assisted them against Russia. France was at variance with Italy, Russia with Germany—and Britain had pocketed Cyprus!

Bismarck, in order to check this British manœuvre, should have openly associated himself with the Tsar and abandoned Austria. He was unable to do this. It was not a question of a diplomatic failure,

The Congress of Berlin as represented by Anton von Werner
Bismarck instructed the painter to represent him shaking hands with the Russian delegate. Count Schuwaloff. On the other side he placed Count Andrassy, the delegate of Austro-Hungary. This picture symbolises the difficulty of Bismarck's position: he was looking for a compromise

"By Jingo", an old form of oath such as "the devil take you", now came to stand for "jingoism" and thus became the challenging symbol of British imperialism.

Russia's advance into the Balkans brought another Power on to the scene: namely, the Habsburg monarchy, for which the Balkans represented the sole possibility of political and commercial expansion. The position became critical. Russia began to arm for a new war. But even if Russia's prospects of victory were very small, the dangers which this war held for Austro-Hungary were very great.

Such were the considerations which led Bismarck to take up the difficult rôle of an intermediary, of an "honest broker" in the conflict which threatened to overthrow all existing conditions in Europe. He played this rôle in a masterly fashion. At the Congress of Berlin, he literally "took command" in the truest sense of the word of all the representatives of the Powers gathered there together, wrote a participant, although they represented the élite of European diplomacy.

Bismarck did his utmost to safeguard the interests of Russia at the conference. As he himself later relates, he looked upon his own part as if he were

same time he could not simply sacrifice the interests of the Habsburg monarchy in favour of Russia.

To the Emperor William I, the Chancellor wrote: "Your Majesty knows that on the many occasions when we have been obliged to make a choice between Russia and Austria, I have always, wherever feasible, shown a greater inclination to favour Russia." It was, however, not always and not in every case "feasible", and the Chancellor advised his Emperor to cultivate German relations with Austria with greater assiduity than hitherto.

No; Bismarck, however hard he tried, could not be a "broker" in the real sense of the word. The real broker, the true Shylock of diplomacy during the Congress, was Lord Beaconsfield. His grandfather had not been a merchant of Venice for nothing. He succeeded with inimitable ingenuity in isolating Russia and leaving her, after a victorious war, with possessions of very small value in the Caucasus. And actually, he did not even want to cede these. During a very heated discussion about a piece of land near the Turkish town of Kars, someone asked: "Where is Kars then?"

"Will Your Lordship be so kind as to point out the desired frontier?" said Prince Gorchakov.

but the tragedy of a great man for whom St. Petersburg had just as little comprehension as Berlin. Tsar Alexander said: "Prince Bismarck placed himself at the head of the anti-Russian coalition." Later Emperor William II said: "Prince Bismarck is Russian, always was Russian, will always remain Russian and be at heart a resolute antagonist of Austria." Both statements were absolutely wrong. The political dilettanti could not understand the superhuman objectivity of a man prepared to sacrifice his sentiments and himself to the interests of the State.

It is, however, sometimes very difficult to comprehend this interest. But here it was absolutely apparent. This was the opinion of the chamberlain Durnowo. In a period of two hundred years, the co-ordination of German and Russian foreign policy had always resulted in brilliant successes for both sides; antagonism led to disappointment, even to catastrophe as in the Great War. In history, whenever France went to war against England, or Japan against Russia, one country was always victorious and the other lost. When Germany and Russia clashed in mortal combat, both countries lost. The year 1939 proved that this lesson was not in vain.

Molotoff

On 12th November 1940, at the invitation of the German Government, M. Molotoff, the Chairman of the Council of People's Commissars of the U.S.S.R. and People's Commissar for Foreign Affairs, arrived in Berlin, in

The welcome at the Anhalter Station in Berlin. *Herr von Ribbentrop, the Reich Minister for Foreign Affairs, bade M. Molotoff a hearty welcome on the platform. After the meeting, the distinguished Russian visitor and Herr von Ribbentrop, together with General Field Marshal Keitel, inspected the guard of honour drawn up before the station. The Head of the Russian Government stayed at Bellevue Castle, which the German Government places at the disposal of foreign guests*

The reception in the Hotel Kaiserhof
The Foreign-Minister introduces leading personalities of the State, the Party, and the Armed Forces to M. Molotoff. On the left of the Minister of State Dr Meissner: Herr v. Papen, the German Ambassador

M. Molotoff visits Herm **Göring.** *The Reich Marshal of Greater German Reich, Herm Göring, received M. Molotoff a*

n Berlin

order to continue and to develop, in the spirit of the friendly relations existing between the two countries, the exchange of opinions on current matters by further personal contact.

The reception in the new Reich Chancellery. *The Führer received M. Molotoff, the Chairman of the Council of People's Commissars of the U.S.S.R. and People's Commissar for Foreign Affairs, in the presence of Herr von Ribbentrop, the Reich Minister for Foreign Affairs, for longer discussions in a select circle. M. Molotoff was accompanied by M. Dekanosoff, the Deputy People's Commissar for Foreign Affairs. The historic decision of the Führer and Stalin for friendship between the two great realms, which today have again become neighbours, is one of the most important factors, and one of world-wide significance, for the New Order in Continental Europe*

al residence and had a lengthy rsation with him in keeping the friendly relations between Germany and Russia

During the conversation between Herr von Ribbentrop and M. Molotoff. *In the Minister's antechamber the members of the Russian Delegation wait for the conclusion of the conversation*

Half the world is accessible to Germany

The territories, where Germany's economic connections with the outer world are free from the blockade, extend like a great arc from North Cape to South Libya and Japan in the Far East. In these territories, which are immune from all interferences of the blockade and control, there are stores of material, and granaries which are to be reckoned among the richest in the world. Germany is able to continue without let or hindrance her economic and trade connections with about twenty countries. For the recent months have clearly demonstrated how far the "economic war," which was being planned in London, is really able to harm Germany. Neutral countries have delivered all the more

powerless. Flax, hemp and cotton from Russia and the Baltic States, as also important goods from the Far East, afford further proof that Germany is buying from the Baltic Sea to the Pacific Ocean and Near East, simply because high quality German products of every kind are used from the Baltic Sea to the Pacific Ocean. Ores from Sweden and from Russia, bauxite, copper, antimony, chrome from the south east reach Germany without hindrance. In exchange for these considerable quantities of German coal are delivered in the same way as for timber from the north. Coal has become during the war an important weapon in the carrying on of the economic war. Also in this case

Raw materials pouring in

The raw materials which will render the attempts at blockade by the Western Powers futile are being brought up by train after train in unbroken continuity over the Russisch-Przemysl bridge from the Far East

Readily to a country, which for its part is in a position to fulfil their desires with its deliveries. The attempts on the part of the western powers to buy up articles and force the prices up on the south eastern markets can have no lasting success, for they were not able to prevail upon the south eastern countries to cease delivering their products to Germany or even to cease doing so in an increased degree. For Germany continues its exchange deliveries with the same reliability as before, and remains the same economic partner as before owing to the natural conditions. The western powers however, on the principle of their economic methods in their colonies, made these countries financially dependent by causing them to participate in capital investments, and merely exploited the mineralogical wealth of these countries, in which they themselves were interested, to the prejudice of their whole economic life. As the economic life in Germany is at all times capable of casting this very decisive weight into the scale, she can put to real advantage the fact that half the world is accessible to her. Germany is getting the quantities of oil, which she lacks, from Russia and Rumania, because she can deliver to these countries machines and such other goods as constitute a good investment. For the same reason Germany is receiving from Russia and from the whole south east corn and other agricultural products. In this respect Germany does not restrict herself to purchases, and the taking over of what is delivered, but is further actively co-operating with the separate countries in the work of adapting the, agricultural products of south east Europe to her own growing needs. These consist in long period economic programs against which the activities of the western powers become

Germany is in a stronger position than England, a fact proved by the issue of the Anglo-Italian coal dispute, and the increased export of German coal to neighbouring and neutral countries.

There has thus been formed since the outbreak of the war a net work, which is continually getting finer, of new and intimate economic connections between the continents of the world, in which net work Germany is both buyer and seller. The continually increasing transit traffic to and from Germany is enriching from the shores of the Far East to the basin of the Danube and the Baltic States the countries participating, even when they are neither buyers nor sellers. Enormous demands are in the course of this process being put upon the means of transport of this enormous area, since overseas traffic has been blocked to Germany, which is the chief buyer and seller. All the same the railways will in this war show that they can stand up to the performances of overseas traffic.

Not only have the western powers nothing of equal value to oppose to German war production and economy, to the Four Years Plan and the great concentrated action in the sphere of agricultural products, but they are also not in a position, by means of their economic war and blockade, to cut Germany off from those parts of the world, which have remained accessible to her. Just as the economic leadership of the totalitarian states is showing its superiority to the formal co-operation of interests working at cross purposes, so also will the railway net work in Europe and Asia sustain the struggle with the masters of the seas. Germany's strength is in this war built up upon secure and wide foundations, and it is no longer possible to shake these foundations.

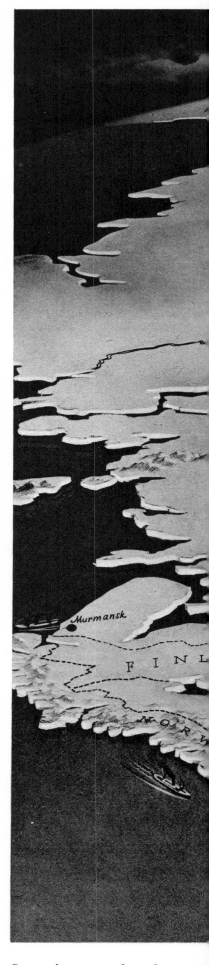

Germany's sources of supply extend from the "West Wall" to the Far East

The economic areas which constitute the basis and guarantee of German war production are about forty-five million square kilometers in extent and amount therefore to about a third of the surface of the continents of the world. Within these areas lies the greater portion of Europe and Asia (the latter not including India) that is to say twenty three states (Italy, Switzerland, Holland, Belgium, Luxemburg, Sweden, Norway, Denmark, Finland, Latvia, Estland, Lithuania, Hungary, Yougoslavia, Rumania, Bulgaria, Greece, Turkey, Russia, Afghanistan, Irac, Japan, Manchoukuo, and China). From these sources Germany obtains all her vital economic necessities

10.00 a. m. :

The German infantry men are lying in their positions among the barbed wire before the citadel of Brest-Litovsk. They are supported by grenade throwers

Infantry and artillery storm the citadel of Brest-Litovsk

Special report by PK. Grimm II and PK. Müller-Waldeck

M. G.'s join in the attack

Light trench mortars of the German infantry do their bit

At 11 a. m. there is a pause in the fighting for the infantry. For the next half-hour the artillery is concentrated on the citadel which is to be stormed. The infantry captain takes advantage of the short interval granted to him and his men to have a refreshing drink

On the morning of 24th June 1941. German artillery and German bombers have prepared Brest-Litovsk for the attack. Our infantry has been lying on the ramparts in front of the fortress for the last three days. It is 10 a. m. — the last act of the drama is about to begin and it is at this point that "Signal's" report commences. In the casemates and barracks, several thousand Soviet troops are fighting desperately against the Germans. The surrounding houses are on fire, and acrid smoke billows over the scene of battle. Soviet snipers fire from the roofs; the Soviet troops show the white flag, but then shoot at the German spokesmen and at ambulance men, and send Russians forward in German uniforms.

11.30 a. m. the German artillery once more intervenes. Fire simultaneously belches from the barrels of guns and howitzers. An extremely heavy cannonade now begins. The infernal din is dominated by the deep roar of a gigantic mortar. Tremendous columns of smoke rise into the air, powder magazines explode. The earth trembles.

"Signal's" correspondents are lying entrenched about 300 yards from the wall of the citadel and watch the terrific effect of the artillery fire from close quarters. One of them describes it as follows: "We continually take cover from the shrapnel, in order not to be within range of that of our heavy guns which is very wide. The explosions tear asunder the earth on the ramparts. The guns suddenly cease firing. After the cannonade which lasted 30 minutes, a complete cessation of firing has been ordered. We are not allowed to fire a shot, not even at the armed enemy, unless fire is first opened on us. The minutes of sudden calm after the infernal din pass in an atmosphere of tense expectancy. A pall of smoke hangs in the air.

There! The first Russians come running over without their weapons. Larger groups are already beginning to appear. The first of them have now reached the ramparts where we are lying. They are searched for arms. Now they are standing with us on the rampart and shout across to their comrades: "Priditje, priditje!" Other groups, with their arms raised, come running across, some of them still without their boots. The terror of the last half hour still shows in their features. They also drag their wounded with them, who are immediately tended by the German ambulance men. Ten minutes later, our flag is flying over the citadel. The Germans have occupied Brest-Litovsk."

11.35 a. m.

The artillery observer lies far in front. It is just five minutes since the German artillery joined in the storming attack. The first powder magazine has been set on fire. A few seconds later it explodes. The citadel's last hour has come. — During the last 25 years the German soldier has fought for Brest-Litovsk three times. This strong fortress surrounded by water, dug-outs, and concrete fortifications has been called the "Verdun of the east." In the Great War, in the Polish campaign and once more in the war against the Soviets, the field-grey of the German uniforms is seething round the walls of this fateful city. And for the third time Brest-Litovsk is stormed

In a race for mercy, *immediately after the artillery had finished the bombardment, the defenders of Brest-Litovsk run towards the German soldiers in the forefield of the citadel*

12.05 a. m.:
The first Soviet soldiers surrend

With their hands up and carrying white cloths *the last Russians leave the citadel. They are not allowed to lower their hands until they have been disarmed in the forefield. This precaution was introduced because Soviet soldiers often waved white cloths — the sign of surrender — but on being allowed to approach nearer they shot at the German soldiers*

The timid behaviour *of this Sov Russian is testimony to the effect Moscow's infamous propaganda. does not believe that the Germa do not fight against defencele prisoners. Meanwhile his comra is beckoning to other Soviet soldie in their hiding-place to surrend*

orming into the citadel. *The smoke the artillery is still hanging over e scene of the fighting when the st German soldier storms into the tadel. Have the Soviet Russians ally abandoned the powerful for-tress?*

2.10 a. m.:

The citadel has fallen

very projecting part of the walls of e riddled fortress, *through which e Bug flows, is carefully guarded. very step forward in the fallen tadel could mean death: the Soviet oops who have been incited against e Germans, take refuge from them the cellars of the barracks*

p. m.: The struggle for Brest-itovsk is over. Through the reets that have been taken y the victorious Germans, the isarmed columns of the Soviet rmy are marching into captivity

The flag of victory
German infantry hoist the Swas-tika on the citadel of Brest-Litovsk. For the third time in 25 years the "Verdun of the east" has been stormed by German soldiers

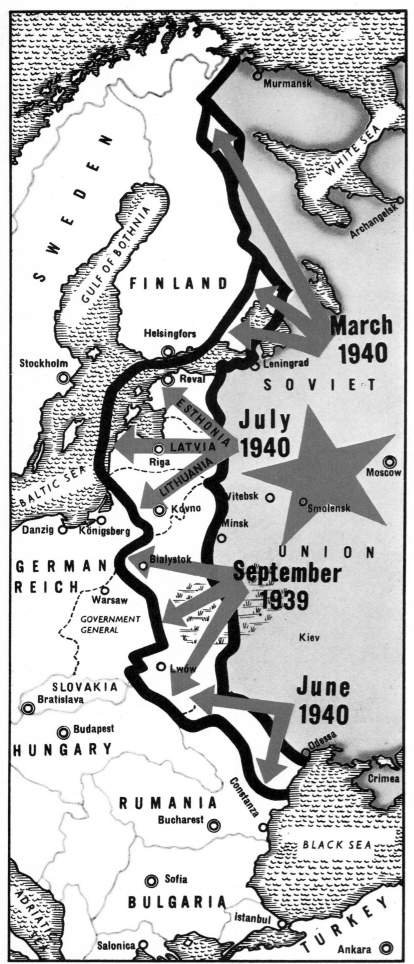

1939/40

Bolshevism takes up new positions of attack

In September 1939 Soviet soldiers marched into Eastern Poland, in March 1940 Finland was compelled to surrender parts of her territory, in June 1940 the Soviet Union forced Rumania to give up Bessarabia and Northern Bukovina, and in July 1940 the three Baltic states were occupied. In this way the Soviet made preparations for military operations against the German Reich and against Europe

The meaning of the struggle

For the freedom and unity of Europe

It was an important hour in the history of the world when Germany decided to take up the struggle against the Soviet Union and Bolshevism. For a quarter of a century the whole of humanity had been oppressed by the menace of Bolshevism. Yes, it seemed that there was no remedy against the preparations which for years were being made in this vast state for a world revolution. And in Moscow the lives and the happiness of millions of people were hazarded in order to be prepared for the day when Communism could commence its campaign of world conquest. The masses, the millions of people in this tremendous state, were deprived of shoes, clothing and all other necessities of life in order to be able to build factories for the manufacture of guns and aeroplanes.

This state of affairs was still unchanged when the new British war broke out in the autumn of 1939. Only for Moscow it commenced too early. Their preparations were as yet not complete and they did not feel strong enough to take part in the big game from the very outset. Stalin concluded a pact of friendship with Germany and waited. On the western frontier of Germany both the French and the Germans had a rampart built of steel and concrete. At that time everybody still believed that such a means of defence would prove impenetrable against any means of attack. Therefore, if a war was to be waged on this frontier, it would last a very long time and this would naturally lead to the exhaustion of both Germany and the Western Powers. In the meantime the Soviet Union could continue to increase its armaments so as to be able, as the last powerful nation, finally to fall upon the other countries now exhausted by the war.

Stalin's calculations were wrong

But it turned out differently. The war in the West lasted only a very short time. It did not even last one year. France was overrun. Stalin's calculations had proved to be wrong. In order nevertheless to reach his old aim he had now to prevent Germany from finishing the war. On account of continued extortions and increasing concentration of troops on the Russian western frontier, through the occupation of positions from which Germany could be more conveniently attacked in the rear, the Reich was prevented from employing its full might against Britain.

It commenced with Russia's attack on Finland. There followed the complete absorption of Lithuania, Latvia and Esthonia. From this example the

world could judge what it would mean for Europe if the Bolshevists had succeeded in overthrowing Germany and in dealing with all the other European states as they had in the case of the Baltic States. The occupation of these states brought the Soviet Union considerably further forward on the Baltic, the Baltic, however, is of the greatest importance for the existence of the German Reich as it is indeed for all the Northern European countries.

Rumania was to take the lead

The Bolshevists' plan became still more evident when they marched into Rumania. In Moscow it was probably hoped that the invasion would cause general confusion in Rumania and would cripple the entire life of the country, so that it would then be an easy matter to carry the Red Revolution into the neighbouring countries. In this case also Germany was to have been dealt a mortal blow. For it was essential for supplying Central Europe with food products and raw materials that peace should reign in the whole of the South-East, on the Danube and in the Balkans, so that land could be cultivated and mines could be worked. They did not succeed in disturbing this peace. On the contrary, Bulgaria, which had always been the favourite aim of Soviet Russian policy, entered into closer relations with Germany. For this, as will be recalled, she was reproached by Russia, although Stalin had undertaken, in the pact with Germany, to observe a certain line of demarcation in regard to Europe, which he had already encroached upon in the case of Rumania. When finally the Yugoslav coup d'état government applied to Moscow, the Soviet Union concluded a treaty with this government, which, having regard to the situation at that time, could mean nothing other than a grave provocation of the Greater German Reich. Probably at this moment it was recognized in Moscow that they had gone too far. They consequently let it appear, outwardly, as if great value were attached to friendly relations with Germany, but it was impossible to deceive the Reich Government any further. On the occasion of the visit of M. Molotow to Berlin at the end of last year, the Bolshevists had already demanded the abandonment of Finland and Bulgaria and also the sacrifice of Turkey. Apart from this, the Reich Government received an increasing number of reports about the activity, which was becoming more intense, of Communist centres and also sabotage and espionage which was being carried on with renewed zeal in Germany and other European countries.

And at the same time they concentrated the main body of their forces on Germany's eastern frontier.

The concentration of the Red Army

The more it became apparent that Germany was likely to defeat Britain, the more energetically did the Soviet Union adopt measures which resulted in the military forces of the Reich being tied up in the East and consequently kept back from the decisive tasks before them. The Union became a true ally of Britain, who for years had been seeking the friendship of the Soviets.

On 1st May, 118 infantry divisions, 20 cavalry divisions and 40 mechanized and tank brigades were concentrated on the eastern frontier of Germany. This represented:

70 % of all infantry divisions,
60 % of all cavalry divisions, and
85 % of all mechanized and tank brigades.

The frontier aerodromes had their full complement of bombers and fighter planes. Parachute formations and innumerable transport planes were ready for immediate action.

The troops stationed in the close vicinity of the frontier were intended purely for attack: — tank units, mechanized infantry, heavy mechanized artillery, parachute troops and bombing squadrons.

Four army groups were formed.

The most northerly, between Memel and Suwalki, directly threatened East Prussia. It consisted of about 70 % infantry and 30 % tank and mechanized units.

South of this, several armies had marched up in the territory around Białystok which forms a salient projecting into Germany. Eastwards, a reserve army was standing by. Of these forces, about 35 % were tank or high-speed mobile troops.

In the area surrounding Lwów, which also projects into Reich territory, there was stationed a further particularly powerful Red Army group. The tank, mechanized and cavalry divisions amounted in this case to about 40 %.

A further army group directly threatened Rumania and the other Balkan States from Bessarabia.

This was no movement of troops for guarding the frontier; it was, on the contrary, a preparatory step in view of a large-scale offensive operation with important objectives. These facts in themselves sufficed to show only too plainly what the plans of the Soviet Union were; actual confirmation was afforded by the discovery of secret Communist instructions and the finding of important documents and maps on which the zones of action and objectives far into German territory are marked. For example, the report of the Yugoslav Military Attaché in Moscow, dated 17th December 1940, contains the following words: "According to statements made in Soviet circles, the arming of the Air Force, the tank arm and the artillery is in full progress according to the experiences of the present war, and in the main will be concluded by August 1941. This is probably the extreme time-limit up to which no perceptible changes in Soviet foreign policy need be anticipated."

The whole of
Europe was suddenly awake

It was evident that this development had been clearly recognized in the whole world and that it was realized what would happen if the attack on Germany succeeded. It was then that the Führer's decision enabled the German Reich to anticipate the attack in the rear which had been prepared In all the countries of the world, even in the broad masses of Britain and America, the news was received with joy that Germany had summoned the strength and the boldness to settle accounts with Europe's ancient enemy in the East before finally dealing with Britain. Germany's Allies, headed by Italy, Rumania, Slovakia and Hungary declared war on Soviet Russia. Finland also fell in with Germany. Sweden allowed the passage of German troops. Volunteer armies were formed everywhere. First in Spain, still suffering from the bleeding wounds received in the struggle against Communism, then in Denmark, Norway and Holland, even in France, who also broke off relations with Moscow. In short, the whole of Europe was suddenly up in arms against Bolshevist Russia. Never since time immemorial had the people of Europe been so united; for upon victory over the Soviet Union depends the destiny of all nations, the fate of the whole world.

But it is not only a matter of destroying Bolshevism for ever, it is also a question of release from that other menace which up to now has only manifested itself from the West, that is to say, where Britain and the United States are trying to cut off the entire European Continent from oversea supplies. In the Great War of 1914 to 1918 the cutting off of the Continent by Britain from the sea would never have led to the desired result, that is to say, to the starving of Europe, if Russia had not at the same time closed the doors against Europe from the East. Centainly it was found possible at that time to defeat Russia, but it was too late, nor was there any way of utilizing the conquered territories for supplying Central Europe. Just as Britain is protected by the surrounding seas, so was Russia protected then and earlier still by her gigantic dimensions which made it impossible for armies to occupy the whole country.

The pincers will break

Today it is different. The battles which have been won up to the present in this war have proved that it is now possible with the aid of mechanization to cover enormous distances with great rapidity. Europe today is in a far better position than the exhausted Germany of 1917 to make the most of such an advantage, not only for itself but also for all those countries which are prevented by Britain and America from receiving necessary supplies from overseas. By reason of the German victories in Russia before which the whole world stands breathless, the cutting off of oversea supplies will remain ineffective in the long run for the whole of Europe. The pincers in which Europe was to be gripped will break. Europe, which on account of over-population was always anxious whether sufficient to eat and sufficient raw materials for industry would be received from overseas, will be freed not only today but also tomorrow and for all time from the tyranny of those who were in a position to curtail vital supplies whenever they thought fit.

Europe will not only be free but will also endeavour to maintain her unity and the co-operation of all the countries within her boundaries which enables her to take preventive measures against the threats from outside. That is the meaning of the struggle which Germany has now undertaken on behalf of the interests of all the people of Europe.

1941:

The gigantic concentration
of Soviet troops against
the German Reich

= approx. 3 infantry divisions

= approx. 3 cavalry divisions

= approx. 3 tank brigades

Drawings: Seeland

An inconceivable sight. *Over the enclosure surrounding the Ogpu prison in Lemberg, the inhabitants of the city are gazing at the corpses of the thousands of defenceless Ukrainians who had been murdered there. In this city alone 2,300 men, women and children fell victims to the terror*

Horror

Lemberg was the first of the many places where, during their advance, the German troops came across the terrible traces of the Ogpu

She still cannot realize *that these fearfully mangled bodies, which she managed to identify by the fragments of clothing, were her relations*

An orphan. *Filled with despair, a girl whose parents were among the victims of the murderous Bolshevist fury, throws herself into the sheltering arms of a friendly neighbour*

A small section of the vast picture of annihilation. *The amount of material of all arms either captured or destroyed in the great encircling battle of Kiev will greatly weaken the enemy. These tremendous losses cannot be made good by deliveries from Great Britain and America. According to the first count, no less than 3,718 guns were captured or destroyed during the battle*

Ruins as far as the eye can see

After the great battle of annihilation east of Kiev

Tanks of all sizes *from the light 15 tonner to the terrific monster weighing 52 tons were employed by the Soviets in the fight against the German units where their fate overtook them. 884 tanks were destroyed or captured*

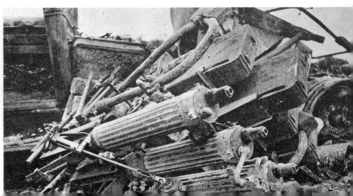

15,000 Soviet vehicles *are lying in chaotic confusion in the ring round Kiev. As a result of the increasingly heavy blows dealt at Soviet industry, this figure represents an important part of the annual production in Soviet Russia*

Inconceivable quantities of important war material *are strewn over the battlefields round Kiev. The Soviet four-barrelled M. G. also succumbed to the superiority of the German weapons*

Tanks break through the Stalin Line

and the infantry follows close behind

The tank general leaves his car *for a few minutes as he drives forward to join the head of his division to give further commands to the officers of some detachments which are waiting to go into action*

The road to victory. *Enveloped in dust, tank after tank rolls on towards the vast expanses of the east. Demolished Soviet giant tanks lie beside the roads along which the German units are advancing*

Street fighting in Schitomir. *With stubborn tenacity, the Soviet troops try to hold their positions in the town. With the help of heavy artillery, street after street and block after block is captured from them*

On the right: **German anti-tank guns** *have brought a Soviet tank to a halt, and have set on fire lorries loaded with petrol*

Photographs: PK. Emil Grimm

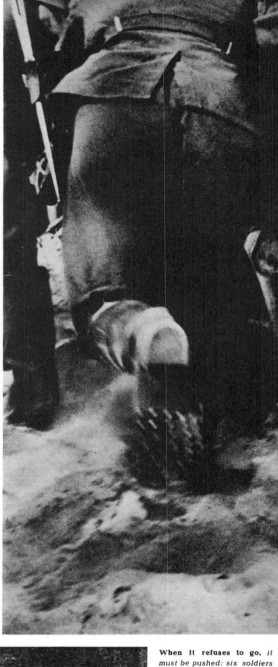

Soviet roads...

What is that? *A German motor-cycle that had almost sunk in one of the bottomless bogs that are called roads in Soviet Russia. The indefatigable motor-cyclist is busy trying to make it recognizable again*

When it refuses to go, *it must be pushed: six soldiers rescue their lorry from the deadly embrace of the sand*

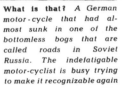

Photographs:
PK. Beissel
SS PK. Zschäkel
PK. Naegele
PK. Wetterau

When the motor-cycle churns *the sand, it is useless to step on the accelerator. Only capable hands can save the situation*

The vehicle sank *half a yard into the deep mud — the driver hopes to get it going again by running the engine all out*

Advance and Rest

"I have done the impossible". The German soldiers on the Eastern Front have been able to write these proud words in their field post letters. Not only in the desperate fighting, but also in overcoming trackless country, they have achieved things that the enemy had thought impossible. They were ready to exert their last ounce of strength at every command, and after every short period of rest they were able to rise refreshed from the deathlike sleep of exhaustion and go forward to the next attack   Photographs: PK. Wanderer PK. Jäger

Seen from a Fieseler-Storch: *endless columns of prisoners on endless roads*

The daily round on the Eastern Front

In the battery position:
21 cm shells have arrived

1100. The partition of Charlemagne's vast empire. Germany was obliged to fight against marauding Hungarians, Wends and Danes. The Normans attacked France and England. Spain defended itself against the Arabs. Hungarian and Arab campaigns against Italy

1100—1300. German Emperors against German Princes. Rivalry with the Pope. Campaigns in Italy. The wars against the Albigenses in France. English campaign against Ireland. Spanish victories over the Arabs. Mongols in Silesia. Normans in Southern Italy

1300—1500. Wars of the Confederacy. The Hansa against Denmark. Teutonic Knights against Poles and Lithuanians. Wars on the Hussites. Peasant revolts in France and England. England against France. Wars in England itself. The Turks in the Balkans

1500—1650. The Turks advanced as far as Vienna. Peasants and knights at war in Germany. French campaigns in Italy and Flanders. The Wars of the Huguenots. Sweden fought in Germany during the 30 Years' War. Cromwell's campaigns in England and Ireland

1650—1780. The War of the Spanish Succession in North France, Belgium, North Italy and the Main region. Turks expelled from Hungary. War in Scandinavia. Prussia against Austria. England and France at war overseas. War between Sweden and Poland

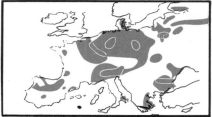

1780—1900. The Napoleonic Wars in Italy, Germany, Belgium, Holland, Spain, Portugal and Russia. Greece fought against the Turks. German and Italian wars of unification. Franco-Prussian and Russo-Turkish wars

What we are fighting for:

For Europe's liberty and the end of its continual fratricidal warfare

For many centuries past Europe has been torn by the wars of its peoples. Actually there have never been any long periods of peace on our Continent. An unfortunate policy of coalitions resulted in the European peoples taking up arms against one another and mutually slaughtering the flower of their youth at frequent intervals. An end must be put to that now and an end can be put to it.

Europe is no longer today the uncontested centre of world power as it was a century ago. Vast power complexes have developed outside Europe in the Soviet Union, in the United States and also in Asia. Were the peoples of Europe to continue annihilating one another, they would in turn finally fall an easy prey to these powers outside Europe. Until now there has not been any real opportunity to put an end to these internal European wars because the destiny of whole continents outside Europe also depended upon their outcome. Today the situation is simply that either Europe unites in combating these extra-European power complexes or that it is gradually undermined country by country and destroyed by them. "Hereditary enmities" dating from former centuries cannot and must not be of any importance in view of this world situation.

In former epochs nobody would have believed that a time would come in which one town would no longer fight against another and one small principality against another. It did nevertheless come about on the formation of the various national states in Europe. Today we are faced by the necessity of reaching the next stage, that of the unification of Europe.

The establishment of this final European peace is our greatest and most important war aim and it is combined with Germany's struggle against the extra-European powers.

Transferred to a map, the adjoining sketches show where the centres of European warfare lay during the period from 1100 to 1900. Whilst the world was being partitioned, Central Europe served throughout the centuries as a Continental battlefield

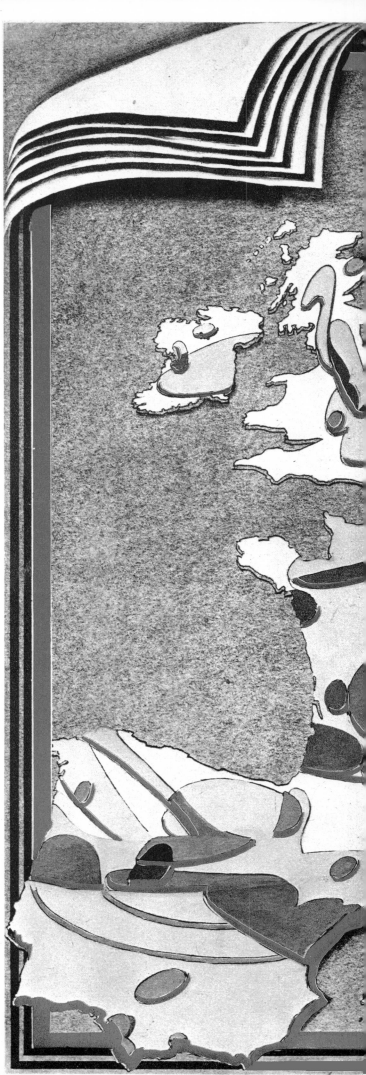

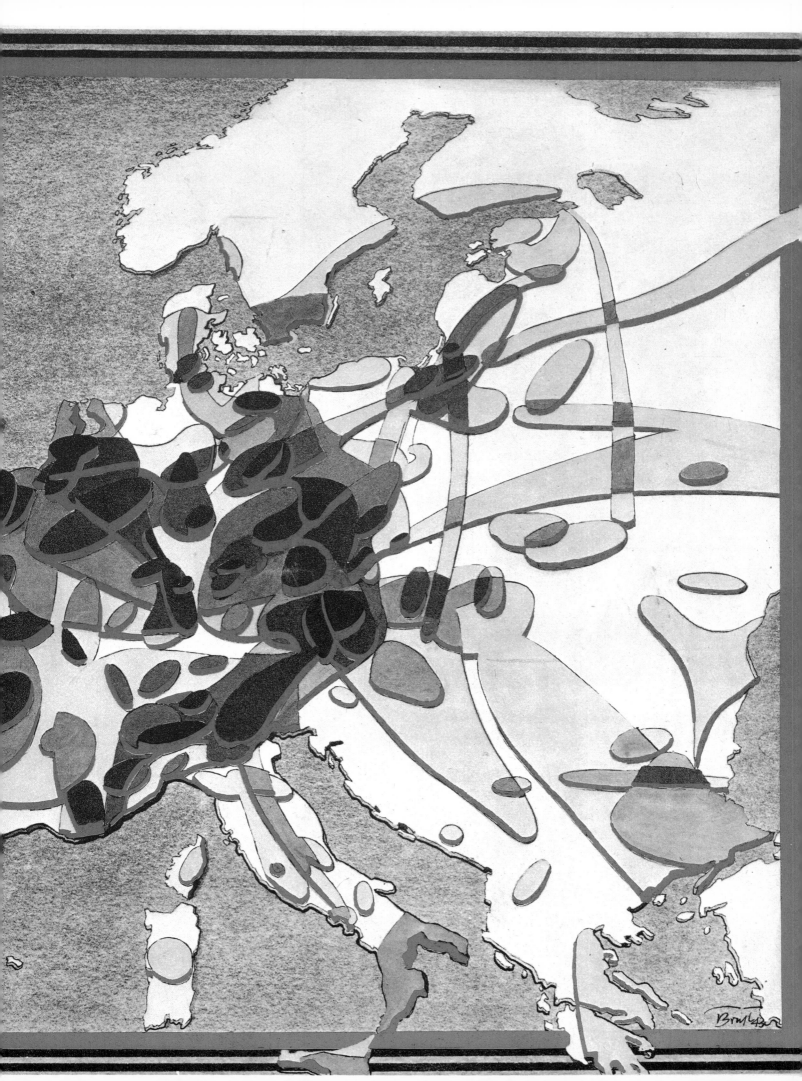

The flight of a shell: *a shell fired from a 15 cm. field howitzer marks its passage in the sky*

Photographs: PK Front Correspondent Hanns Hulm....n

The moment of firing a 21 cm. mortar: *the gunner is just discharging the shell with his left hand while protecting his ear with the right*

PK. front correspondent Hanns Hubmann, who took part in the advance on Leningrad, here shows a few sections of the ring encircling the biggest Soviet port

Kronstadt under fire from German long-range batteries. *The powerful sea fortress about 18 miles from Leningrad is the last and most heavily fortified naval port of the Soviets in the Baltic Sea and is of immense strategic importance on account of its key position before Leningrad. With his long-range camera, the front correspondent took a photograph from Peterhof of one of the German attacks on the fortifications, shipyards and docks of Kronstadt and on the units of the Soviet Navy which had taken refuge in the bays of the island*

Soviet steamers in flames. *Using the narrow sea route, the Soviets tried to break through the ring round Leningrad in order to supply the city with provisions. German reconnaissance planes recognized their purpose in time and German dive bombers set the ships on fire. This photograph was taken from the village of Uritzk*

The last road from Moscow to Leningrad *is in German hands as a result of the rapid advance of the German troops. The Soviet artillery vainly tries to hold up the march of the German infantry by heavy fire*

Encircled Leningrad photographed from a distance of 2½ miles. *From the foremost German lines near the village of Uritzk, the silhouette of the encircled city with the Isaac Cathedral is clearly visible. The factory chimneys of this city of 2 million inhabitants are still smoking. But the vehicles and the tram in the foreground are already in the fighting zone*

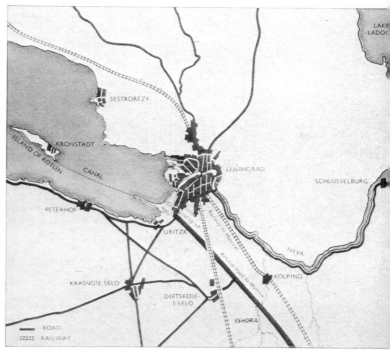

The environs of Leningrad. *While the German troops coming from the south have closed around the city, Finnish units have cut it off from the north*

Schlüsselburg, the gate to Lake Ladoga. *With the fall of Schlüsselburg, the old fortress on the Neva, the Soviets were deprived of the last possibility of supplying Leningrad by sea. The ring is closed. The German flag is already fluttering from the church, but the Soviets are still trying to set fire to the city from the opposite bank of the Neva*

Lying in an advanced position *opposite Kolpino, the strongly fortified factory city of the Soviets, two wireless operators are transmitting the reports from the foremost lines*

ks of the River Ishora, *a tributary* *eva, had been mined. But this did* *vent the German formations from* *the river. German soldiers, using* *icks tipped with iron, clear the* *of mines* Photographs: PK. front *ndent Hubmann, Drawing: Seeland*

From his camouflaged position, *the German observer tensely watches all the movements of the enemy along the outskirts of Kolpino. The security of the ring round Leningrad depends on him too*

Légion des
Volontaires
Français
contre le
Bolchevisme

FOR EUROPE...

"Signal's" PK. Correspondent, Hanns Hubmann, paid a special v
to the French Volunteer Legion on the Eastern Front and w
through an engagement in a wood with two companies of Fre
infantry. His report shows how the companies carried out th
task in spite of most difficult terrain and desperate resista

In billets: letters before the attack...

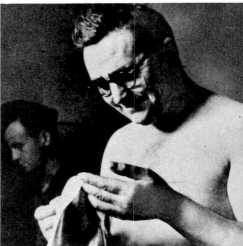

"I am Private Jollyboy," was how one of the first men introduced himself, the acquaintance of whom our correspondent made in the French Volunteer Legion. In the next day's
fighting he showed that he was a particularly dashing soldier. The oldest legionary (below) introduced himself differently: "Comte de Gournay, Corporal." He is a rich man, a
large estate owner and business man, and acts as Mayor of
Gournay in Normandy. But he wants to be doing his duty
in the front rank when the future of Europe is decided

Our Front Correspondent, Hanns Hubmann, makes the
acquaintance of the men in the French Volunteer Legion

Léon, the youngest in the Legion, speaks fluent Russian

"It is not sufficient to propagate a political opinion,
you have to fight for it," said Lieutenant Jacques Doriot
of the Volunteer Legion, who is the founder and leader
of the Parti Populaire Français. In 1935, Doriot who
until then had been a prominent communist, redis-
covered his native country. A political fighter, he
now takes his place in the same ranks as old
warriors of the French Army like Sergeant-major
Maurice Huet who is the bearer of four decorations

Spain's "Blue Division" on the march

They are determined to take part in the final struggle against the enemy of the whole world

The old symbol of victory of the Falange is repeated on the ground and at the top of the staff of the standard carried by every battalion of the Spanish volunteers who have arrived in Germany

On the right: **To the rhythm of the Spanish national anthem** battalion after battalion of Spanish volunteers march into a camp in South Germany where they are issued with their service equipment. From here they will move to the European front in the east

For the second time against the old enemy. As the badges on his left sleeve show, this volunteer was wounded six times in the fighting against the devastators of his native land. But he cannot rest until the world disgrace of Bolshevism has been destroyed for ever

Photographs: Reinke

Heavy guns are taken over. The "Blue Division" is an independent army unit of trained soldiers of all arms. It will only take a short time to teach these men how to use their new weapons and to prepare them for active service

"We are happy". Three brothers from Copenhagen with their company leader in the SS training camp in Upper Alsace. They have fulfilled all the conditions relating to questions of race and health and are now enjoying the manly open-air life in the camp in the woods

"I want to fight for the new Europe"

"Signal" visits the Germanic volunteers serving in the **SS**. Among them are Flemings, Dutchmen, Danes, Norwegians, and representatives of other Germanic countries

On the dagger of an SS officer the volunteer swears the oath. He pledges loyalty to Adolf Hitler, the leader in the fight for a new Europe. The picture shows on the left Björn J., the secretary of the Norwegian Minister of Labour, and on the right Erling H., an electrician from Copenhagen

Much of their time in the Training Camp is devoted to sport. Almost all the Olympic events are practised. The winner of this obstacle race said: "Our time here is like a holiday for us. We are given a good physical training. It is Prussian drill, but the German organization is agreeable"

A practical lesson in German. On the first day of their training the sergeant writes up the German words of command

For the first time: the Germanic salute. *The man with his hand raised is Karl F., a student from Antwerp, one of the best amateur boxers of Belgium, a champion light heavyweight*

The Dutch have a definite gift for shooting. *Josefes K., formerly a business employee at The Hague, is being trained as a sniper in the use of telescopic sights*

The military training *teaches the volunteers up-to-date tactics. Complete familiarity with the ground and the art of camouflage are essential for success*

"Veronica" or the most beautiful hour of the day: *Practising a German soldiers' song*

General Vlassov stands out among the leaders of the various nationalities fighting as volunteers. In the world press his name has frequently been bracketed with Moscow which he defended as a Soviet general. When he realized that the gulf between the Soviet programme and the real interests of his nation were not to be bridged, he resolutely faced the consequences. The photograph shows the general watching the manœuvres of a volunteer unit

AN ARMY...

Russians, Ukrainians, Georgians . . . members of all the races and tribes in the east have streamed in continually increasing numbers to the German armies for enrolment in a Volunteer Army which is fighting shoulder to shoulder with the Germans against the Soviets. This army has at its disposal infantry, cavalry, artillery and engineers, that is to say troops and weapons of all kinds. They have shown surprisingly quickly that the true soldierly spirit can soon be kindled in them when a great idea is at stake. SIGNAL here shows a few examples of their operations and their life as soldiers

No Cossack without a horse. Even in modern mechanized warfare, the Cossack is inseparable from his horse which makes him the master of time and space. He can attack the enemy as fast as lightning and can withdraw from him again just as fast

Right in the frontline, of course, they dismount and the horses are removed from the field of fire. If the operation, as on this occasion, is successful, prisoners march on their way to their first interrogation in front of the frisky mounts (picture below)

PK. Photographs: War Correspondents Pabel (2), Nieberle (1), Artur Grimm (3), Mossdorf (3

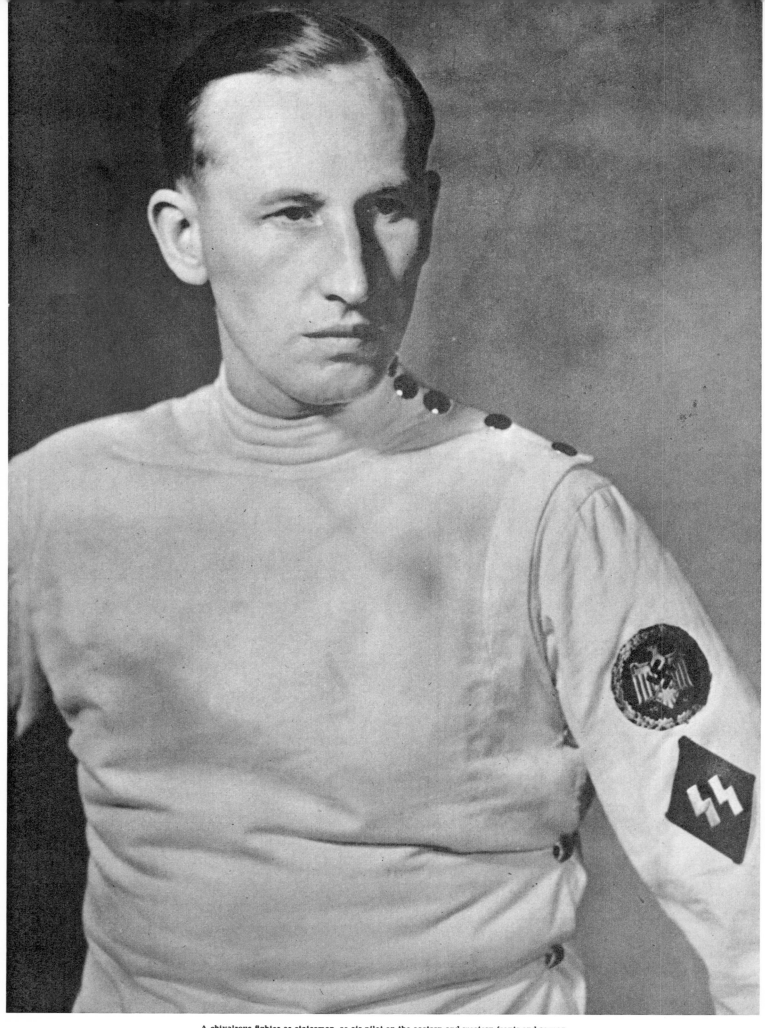

A chivalrous fighter as statesman, as air pilot on the eastern and western fronts and as man—
the sportsman *Reinhard Heydrich was a good swordsman too. He was one of the best European fencers*

What does a soldier require when he is on leave?

1. A ration card

In the food card office at home a man on leave is given priority of treatment. For 14 days leave he receives cards for about 10 lb. of bread and cake. 2 lb. of meat. 1 lb. of butter. 1 lb. of provisions. macaroni etc.. ½ lb. of jam. ½ lb. of legumes. 1 lb. of sugar. ½ lb. of coffee mixture. ⅛ lb. of pure coffee. 2 ozs. of tea. ¼ lb. of nuts. further ¼ lb. of chocolate. 2 eggs and 4 pieces of cheese. soap. shaving soap and soap powder. With this bunch of cards he hurries off . . .

2. His mother

... to his mother, who as every mother on earth has naturally a feeling that her darling will arrive today. He lives at home with her. First of all he takes his pack off and then goes to ...

3. His friend

... the place where he was formerly occupied, where he finds his friend, who has been given army leave for a longer period, because the business, an architect's office, has work of military importance on hand

4. His fiancée

His fiancée, in common with all women and girls without children, is working in a firm of military importance. But she will be given holidays as long as the soldier is on leave

The life of a young man is built up by three spheres of life of inner feeling. They are love for his mother, friendship and love for a girl. The inner feelings of a soldier are nourished by the value of the sentiment he receives from these sources. His mother's, his friend's and his fiancée's letters are precious possessions, which he stows away at the bottom of his pack. What a difference there is between the life of a soldier today and the mercenary of former centuries. In those days the mercenary's home was his regiment and where the regiment went, there the soldier was at home. Today the soldier carries his home with him. He is no longer a mercenary but a representative of his home, a son of his country, who only goes to foreign countries in order to be able to return home again. The thoughts of a young soldier can always vary between the love of his mother, his friend and his fiancée, because the modern organisation of the field post keeps him constantly in touch with home circles.

Every German soldier is authorized to receive 14 days leave and the commanders of the army during war always try to satisfy the soldier's peace time right. When the soldier goes on leave, the sentimental dreams of his innermost feelings in those three spheres of life again become reality. Once again he holds his mother, his friend and his fiancée in tender embrace and he returns contented back again to his hard post of duty.

Then everything will be done by itself:

Most of his leave is naturally spent with his fiancée. She brings the soldier, who has for so long only enjoyed men's society, back under the enchanting spell of woman. Whilst looking at the shop window of a Berlin ladies' clothing shop, she tells him of the worries that every woman now has with her clothes cards

A quick photo for his comrades at the front. His comrades get to know what his fiancée looks like, but at the same time they can see that the Column of Victory is still intact

With his fiancée:

Everything without coupons. During the interval in the foyer of the Berlin theatres light refreshments are served such as lobster salad etc., all of which can be had without coupons

International Variety is still going strong, the shows at the Scala are still up to the high level of pre-war days

The way home at night in the dark and bumpy omnibus. At this time of the night in Berlin only very few people are still abroad. This does not worry either of them; they are just as happy as if they were sitting in their wedding carriage

In the "Red Barricade" fighting zone

Glimpses of the Battle of Stalingrad
by Front Correspondent Lieutenant Benno Wundshammer

The author, who for many weeks took part in the raids on Stalingrad carried out by a squadron of dive-bombers, has paid a visit to the zone of fighting which the airman otherwise only sees from a great altitude. He describes a phase of this fighting concerning which a German officer says: "Stalingrad is a fortress, but it differs in one essential from a real fortress. A real fortress has a system, the secret of which can be discovered. It can then be attacked according to a plan. Stalingrad has no system, Stalingrad is a conglomeration of fortifications, you are faced every hour by fresh problems. That is what makes the fight so difficult..."

Two photographs typical of the fighting in and round Stalingrad

Between the groups of houses in the town and the bank of the Volga in the background, tanks aad artillery have cleared a piece of ground. A small group of tank grenadiers is slowly and cautiously making its way forward to the Volga in order to take up a fresh position

Another group of tank grenaadiers has reachad a trench in the middle of the town where it is subjected to fire. The men do not dash forward to the assault but remain under cover until the tank following them has put the enemy pill-box out of action by shellfire Front Correspondent Herbert (2)

"**H**ave a look at things from down below!" the commodore of my squadron of dive-bombers had said, "and be back in two days' time!"

I am in the advanced observation post of the Air Corps and from there I can see ruined houses, a roof, a stereo-telescope and in the distance a long row of houses behind undulating country and copses.

The scene of the fighting lies where the iron water-tower stretches its finger above the smoking hill. So this is "Target area Dora" which we were attacking only yesterday.

In the town

An acrid smell of burning greets us. The carcasses of horses, their bellies swollen, fill the air with the stench of putrefaction. Prisoners and fugitives totter towards us. Then we enter the town. I have already seen many towns gutted by the fires of war, yet I have never seen greater destruction. The complicated technical installation of a modern industrial town lies a chaos of burnt and broken ruins. Whole railway stations are only a tangled confusion of rusting iron. A dead soldier is lying by the roadside. Even in death he still holds his sub-machine gun tightly in his grasp and I cannot bring myself to take it from his rigid hands. We creep past ruined houses. The enemy has an uninterrupted view everywhere, and now and then shells come howling across from his heavy artillery. The German soldiers have established themselves in cellars and vaults buried under a heap of ruins, where they cook their food and are ready for action day and night. An infantryman gives me the following account: "Every house was a fortification. The enemy fired from the storeys of the houses and the cellars. They were usually in small parties of 15 men under the command of an officer or commissar. They would not come out of their holes at any price! We laboriously crawled up to them and threw hand grenades at them as they fired. Then they lay down and died. When the German planes blew up one row of houses after another, the Bolshevists built new fortifications out of the ruins during the night and held us up with new barricades which really filled us with amazement!"

Leaping from one piece of ruined wall to the next, we stalk forward to the Volga Terrace. In the middle of the river the enemy is still occupying well camouflaged positions behind bushes and in woods. They observe every movement on this bank. Our men are lying in pill-boxes watching the river and not worrying their heads about anything except perhaps their food.

100 yards from the enemy

An armoured wireless transmission and receiving car belonging to the Air Force Signallers, which is engaged on important tactical tasks in the infantry front line, gives us a lift. I am not in a position to say any more about the work done by these men. The mere fact must suffice. The commander of the car is a lieutenant, and as chance would have it, I recognize him as the corporal who trained me as a recruit.

"We are driving to the northern part of the town, we can get close up to the front line there!" The car rumbles off, every other noise is drowned by the clanking of the caterpillar tracks. We follow roads worn by heavy traffic. On both sides of us are artillery positions. The guns roar at regular intervals. Gradually everything becomes more desolate—we can see only shellholes, carcasses, smashed vehicles, tanks and guns. There is apparently no movement on the battlefield. Here and there a cloud of white smoke rises unexpectedly from the mountains of débris and then the lieutenant says: "Grenade-throwers!" We can hear nothing.

Our untrained airmen's eyes are not yet able to distinguish details. To the accompaniment of a great din, we drive through a town of spectral ruins. Only rarely do I see infantrymen. They are wearing steel helmets and bend low as they run. When they take cover as quick as lightning in a crater, another cloud of white smoke is always due the next moment.

The car pulls up among some half burnt out wooden houses. We leave it there. The enemy is only a few hundred yards away. Invisible! That is the greatest surprise for us. The chaos of ruins appears deserted and it is only here and there that we are able with difficulty to make out the entrances of dug-outs where the infantry have taken up their positions. A surprised "landser" stares at us until a hissing whine causes him to disappear into the earth.

No-man's-land in Stalingrad. *The foremost position during the fighting for Stalingrad seen and photographed through the stereo-telescope by the Air Force lieutenant and SIGNAL front correspondent Benno Wundshammer. While he was in the city the struggle for the vast gun factory "Red Barricade" was in progress. The gigantic workshops rise up behind the miserable workers' dwellings. The position of the foremost German troops is indicated by the arrow*

When an open city is converted into a fortress and not evacuated . . .

"Signal's" reporter comments on the picture on the left: *"Over and over again we are appalled by the state of the civilian population of this city. A street in north Stalingrad is being subjected to heavy fire from enemy grenade-throwers when suddenly a civilian emerges from his hut. After weeks of fear and anxiety he has to flee with his goods and chattels. Women come toward us, 400 yards from the firing line. What do they want? Terrified by the erratic grenade fire one of them has lost her children who are hiding in a cellar somewhere. The other is crying. She has had nothing to eat for three days. We give her bread. Slowly, women, old men and children trickle through our advancing line of fire and collect before the city along the roads used for our reinforcements and prepare to march westwards (picture above). This stream of misery already reaches as far as the banks of the Don, hundreds of miles in extent . . ."*

The "Red Barricade" fighting zone

We cross a communication trench. A glance across the parapet reveals the Volga as it flows behind fences and factories. Skyscrapers burning with a vermilion glare are silhouetted against the blue sky. An M. G. is slowly crackling somewhere, bullets whistle through the gardens. The grenade-throwers roar dully. Then come short, clear, sharp detonations. Snipers!

We take cover in a cellar. In the dim light I can make out a box of hand grenades, sub-machine guns and a Very pistol with cartridges. Such an arsenal of weapons ready to hand is a great comfort. A ladder leads up to the loft of the wooden house, which has no back wall. An N. C. O. reports when we reach the loft. A stereo-telescope operated by a lance-corporal has been brought into position in the front of the sloping roof. I look through the glass at the streets where the enemy is ensconced only 100 yards away from us. I see only wooden huts and behind them a large factory, the gun factory "The Red Barricade", from which that whole part of the town derives its name. The lance-corporal says: "The houses are occupied by the Russians." I can see nothing. Nobody. Just over there I catch a glimpse of a slight movement. "Yes, that's one of them," says the lance-corporal. "And in front there, exactly above the yellow blob of clay, is our most advanced post."

For a matter of seconds there is a

dull gleam from a German steel helmet. The battlefield is deserted just as though there were nobody here at all. Only the detonating grenade-throwers and the staccato crackle of invisible M.G.s betray the struggle that is in progress. Well concealed, full of endurance and cunning, the antagonists observe one another.

I stare at the factory. White smoke is pouring out of the workshops. The lance-corporal explains: "We discovered a Stalin organ and several grenade-throwers there." However much I look, I can see nothing but a small cloud of dust here and there among the destroyed furnaces. The lance-corporal consoles me by saying: "That is quite enough. We don't need any more than that." A horrible roar causes us to throw ourselves down in a confused heap. There is a sudden ear-splitting explosion. "That was quite close," the lance-corporal says as he gets to his feet again. Twenty yards to our left a wooden hut goes up in flames—the lance-corporal is once more seated behind is stereo-telescope and the N.C.O. is at the telephone.

We creep, jump and crawl back. Again there is a roar followed by loud explosions above us and white clouds of smoke. A.A. guns with fuses set high are joining in the ground battle! Shell splinters crunch into rotten wood. Two infantrymen pass by carrying a third whose head is hanging down motionless. His fine fair hair moves in the wind. We go on. Behind the next brick wall I see a soldier writing a letter on a box. He takes no notice of the artillery and the impacts of shells, he has something more important to do.

When I ask him how things are, he answers: "Quite O.K., thank you! Rations are good and plentiful and, besides, things are pretty quiet today. But it warms up in the afternoon. The dive-bombers attack ahead of us then. Damn plucky lads, they are!"

I have not the courage to tell the man that is exactly what I think of him. He would not believe me.

A section of the highway *used by the fugitives seen from the air. A knot of fugitives has realized that empty German lorries on their way to the rear can take the civilians out of the danger zone. Opposite a demolished Soviet tank, the last lorry in the column is being loaded with the possessions of the fugitives, while the others wait for the next chance of a lift*

63 degrees Fahrenheit of frost

A storm boat races across the Dniester . . .

. . . the first of many. Under the hail of fire the men at the steering wheels guide their outboard motor-boats through the muddy waters of the broad river. Every muscle is tense, every eye is fixed on the goal: the blind spot on the steep slope on the enemy bank of the river. There, the torpor of the brave infantrymen will give way to stubborn warlike ardour — for beyond the river is the Stalin Line in the Ukraine

Photographs: PK Hackl

Lieutenant Jäckel's orders are to attack the Volga ravines in Stalingrad. He identifies the objective on a reconnaissance photograph

The last Soviet "artery" in Stalingrad. *For months the struggle for Stalingrad went on and step by step, at the cost of much bloodshed, the city was wrung from the grasp of the Bolshevists. With the stubbornness of despair the Soviets hold on to a tiny strip along the western bank of the Volga. Deep rifts, the Balkas, run down to the river and simplify the problem of reinforcements and supplies for the enemy. With bombs of the heaviest calibre our dive-bombers hammer ceaselessly at these natural "communication trenches" annihilating considerable numbers of troops even before they can be sent into action. The picture shows one of these ravines after a bombing raid. On the island in the river Soviet A. A. batteries trying to hinder the attack by the Air Force were bombed at the same time. On a more distant arm of the river shown in the top right-hand picture the reader can distinguish a ferry used by the enemy every night*

Deadly blows at the Balkas. *The German airmen show great skill in hitting the ravines that are packed with troops. According to reliable statements by prisoners, the daily losses of the enemy vary between the strength of a battalion and a regiment*

"*Far below we see the olive-green shimmer of the river and the gleam of the sandbanks as Lieutenant Jäckel's machine dives to the attack*"

RAVINES ALONG THE VOLGA

A report on the fight for Stalingrad by Front Correspondent Lieutenant Benno Wundshammer

"*Above the Volga ravine the clouds from the exp sions disperse beside the burning oil tanks as we beg our return flight. Once more we had hit the mark*"

*"Above the city our Vees spread out to lessen
the danger from the A. A. Flying in cur-
ves we move forward towards our objective"*

*As we dive," writes our reporter, "I see a vast
tory among the ruins of which the Bolshevists
e still hiding. It is the "Red October" works.*

*nding, Lieutenant Jäckel is congratulated by his
des and presented with a few bottles of something
In half an hour he is due to make his 601st take-off*

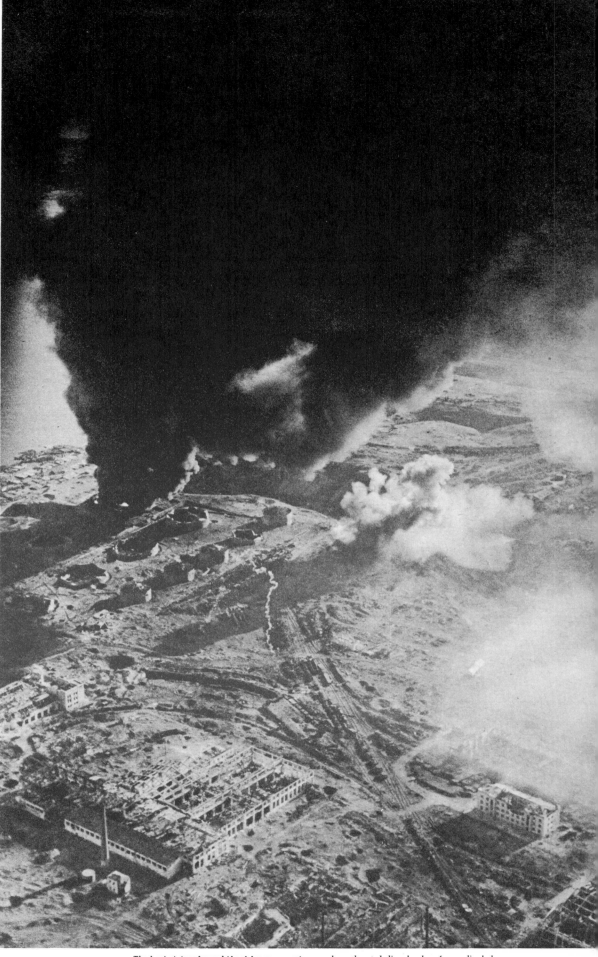

The best picture brought back by our reporter.
Commenting on this photograph, Lieutenant
Wundshammer told us: *"After our return I developed the films in the squadron dark-room and
this is the best picture of the attack. I took it immediately after our machine, flying as Number Two
behind Lieutenant Jäckel, pulled out of the dive.
We are moving off flying close below the heavy
banks of smoke from the burning oil tanks and in
the ravine a mushroom of smoke is just rising
above the exploding bombs. As we dived down
alongside the rising pillar of smoke Soviet fighters
attacked us, coming unexpectedly out of the swathes
of smoke. We kept up a hail of fire to occupy
the enemy while our pilot dropped all our
bombs direct on the objective. It was not long
before German fighters were with us and after
a short battle in the air brought down a JAK 1
fighter. The pilot baled out and landed behind the
German lines among the debris of ruined houses*

MAJOR DR WILHELM EHMER:

EUROPE'S SHIELD

CONCERNING THE SPIRITUAL FOUNDATIONS OF THE GERMAN ARMY TRADITIONS

For the second winter Stalin's armies have been attacking Europe's Eastern Front in a battle of truly Continental dimensions and Continental importance. The soldiers of the German 6th Army together with a Croat regiment and two Rumanian divisions defended Stalingrad to the last man, thus binding several Soviet armies and enabling a new and strategically more favourable front to be established. The sacrifice they made can only be explained by a soldierly spirit, the foundation of which is here interpreted by a contemporary soldier and philosopher

The battles of material during the last two years of the first World War had played a large part in establishing the view that the individual soldier was once and for all doomed to disappear from the battlefield as a unit having a will of his own. Mechanical war, the war machine crushing everything in its path, was supposed to have taken his place. This opinion was held by many military writers, particularly by French, British and American theorists, but it also made itself felt in the measures adopted by General Staffs. We will here quote two examples. When the German Army was disarmed in 1918, particular care was taken to ensure that it possessed no heavy weapons, no heavy guns, no tanks and also no planes, for these had been the principal weapons employed in the battles of material. It was consequently believed that this prohibition more than anything else would render Germany defenceless. The second example is the Maginot Line. If mechanical war was going to decide the victory in the future, it was only necessary to establish a tremendous wall of heavy weapons to be invincible for all time.

It would be interesting to investigate whether the Germans, too, would have adopted this "material view" if they had not been forced by Versailles to do without the most important weapons. We doubt whether the German theorists and practical experts would in such a case have recognized the superiority of war material over the soldier. The spiritual foundations of the German military tradition had always been too firmly established in the nation itself for that. Had not, too, the individual German soldier, by defying the material superiority of his enemies for so long, proved that determined men scornful of death are superior to blind material?

Endowed with soldierly virtues by destiny

The Treaty of Versailles forced Germany where her Army was concerned to rely upon that strength which no dictate could forbid—the spirit. Where there was a lack of external means, the internal ones were mobilized and where the employment of material was restricted, the abundantly flowing spring of ideas was exploited.

The historical comparison: Leonidas, the Spartan General

Fighting to the last man, he defended the gate to Greece, the Pass of Thermopylae, against the Persian invasion in the year 480 B.C. Nurtured by the spirit of such sacrifice, the Attic naval alliance, the first great political alliance of the Greeks, came into being three years later. The Persian danger was now finally overcome. Athens began to flourish. The hour of the birth of European culture had come. The sacrifice had borne fruit

TRAVELLER, SHOULD YOUR ROAD LEAD YOU TO SPARTA, TELL THEM THAT YOU SAW US LYING HERE AS THE LAWS WILLED IT

Inscription on the national monument erected by the Greeks in memory of Leonidas and his soldiers

The "victors" of the World War clad themselves in a heavy coat of armour and dug themselves in behind lines of fortifications built with the greatest cunning and bristling with weapons, whilst the tiny German Army consisting of but 100,000 men became the guardian of the great spiritual German soldierly tradition and at the same time developed this tradition by drawing the necessary conclusions from the experiences of the World War. The difficulties of the situation did not cause it to throw in its hand or to despair, on the contrary, they aroused all the soldierly virtues, strength of character, determination, inventiveness and courage, all of which are foundation stones on which the German soldierly tradition has been built from its very beginning.

Peoples which have to fight for and secure their existence on a poor soil under hard conditions regard soldierly virtues as the expression of an attitude forced upon them by necessity. The two German races, which were the first to develop a genuine soldierly spirit, had to carry out tasks of a warlike character. The Prussians were obliged to wrest from their country, which had been so ungenerously treated by nature, the foundation for a modest existence as a nation and, moreover, also had to defend themselves against strong and more favourably placed neighbours. The Austrians, being the inhabitants of the frontier marches, were forced to become soldiers in order to defend themselves against the southeast. In both cases, therefore, it was not the whim of a despot which established an army and imbued the people with soldierly conceptions, but their historical fate, nature itself, which stood as godparent at the cradle of both the Prussian Army and the old Austrian Army. After again covering their colours with immortal glory during the first World War both have been organically incorporated by different processes in the young National Socialist German Armed Forces.

The Prussian Field Marshal Hellmuth von Moltke, the first Chief of the Great General Staff, once characterized soldierly virtues as follows: "Courage and self-denial, devotion to duty and willingness to make sacrifices, even of life itself." If we

... Generals Pfeffer, Hartmann and Stempel together with Colonel Crome and a handful o f soldiers standing out in the open on the railway embankment ...

THE MONUMENT OF STALINGRAD

This and the following descriptions, some of which have been illustrated by Front Correspondent Hans Liska, are based on radio messages from the German 6th Army, the accounts given by the last wounded to escape from Stalingrad and the last field-post letters brought out of the lost city by the last plane. Among them are the reports of eye witnesses such as the driver of a troop transport lorry who scorched along at breakneck speed through advancing Soviet tanks spraying 300 Soviet infantrymen with M. G. fire only because he wanted to rejoin his unit in Stalingrad. Three cooks were busy for the last time in their field kitchen when surprised by Soviet tanks. To defend themselves they snatched a few grenades lying nearby and leapt at the tanks demolishing a couple of the giants. Then they went on with their cooking. A German plane, compelled to make a forced landing among the ruins of Stalingrad, alighted in Soviet territory. Was it madness when the crew was rescued by those grenadiers who themselves were trapped in the city? What did it mean when officers and men harnessed themselves to their gun to pull it 12 miles through the snow to Stalingrad because they had neither horses nor petrol, a gun for which they had scarcely any ammunition? What kind of men were they who knew for weeks how everything would end and who nevertheless wrote home: "You know what the situation is like here, Father, and you know the solution. You can depend on it finishing honourably ...'

apply these ideas to civilian life as it has developed under the modern liberal system, we immediately see that we really have to do with definitely soldierly qualities. Instead of courage, liberalism prefers skill in business in order to make a way in life, it prefers comfort to self-denial, duty is often felt to be only an unpleasant compulsion and when sacrifices have to be made, it is material goods which are surrendered with the hope of avoiding the possibility of being exposed to personal dangers.

The German soldier places his faith in courage, self-denial, devotion to duty and the willingness to make sacrifices not for any material advantage but simply for the sublime conception of the fatherland and for the honour and greatness of his people. In his will, Frederick the Great wrote that it is man's destiny to work from his birth until his death for the weal of the community to which he belongs. We might add in the spirit of that great king: Not only to work but also, should it be necessary, to fight and to die. In the three wars during which he won the vital foundations of the national power for his people, which numbered only three millions and was faced by a coalition numbering 50 millions, Frederick in any case acted according to that precept. Frederick the Great was, moreover, anything but a fighter by nature, he was a highly cultivated and extremely sensitive man devoted to philosophy and to the arts. He combined with rigid discipline, unconditional obedience and an unshakable sense of duty, a self-sacrificing spirit scornful of death, determination even in apparently desperate situations and that mental liveliness which a generation later found expression in the achievements and creations of men like Clausewitz and Yorck, Gneisenau, Scharnhorst and Heinrich von Kleist.

At the same time a decisive step forward was taken. The defeat suffered in 1806 at the hands of Napoleon's Revolutionary Army had shown that the old Prussian military spirit had become rigid and was incapable of adapting itself to the new era. It required rejuvenation. Scharnhorst and Gneisenau saw plainly that military leadership could no longer remain a privilege of the nobility, but that it was necessary for fresh blood to bring a new stimulus into the army. They consequently created a genuine national army in the face of great opposition from various quarters. Even today it is still worth while reading what they wrote in their memorandum to Frederick William III concerning the necessity of throwing open the career of officer not only to the middle classes but to every German who had proved his worth in the face of the enemy.

Those thoughts, indeed the whole of that epoch, can be compared with the events of our own days. Prussia-Germany required six years, from 1806 to 1812, in order to recover her strength after her great fall and it was in a similarly short space of time that the new German Armed Forces were created from nothing. Just as in those days, the rich abundance of the nation's strength makes it possible for every capable soldier to climb to the highest positions in the services without this resulting in any depreciation in quality. In both cases the foundation consisted of the same soldierly virtues adapted to the requirements of the age, supplemented today by a new element, field-grey socialism as experienced for the first time in the sufferings undergone in the trenches and under the drum fire of the first World War.

Soldiers of a new state . . .

For the German soldier the most profound human experience of the first World War was the comradeship, the human bonds uniting him to his fellows in his misery and during the fighting, the feeling of an indissoluble community of destiny in the face of a hostile world superior in material resources. It was from this spiritual and mental factor that the Socialist idea on a national basis, National Socialism, was born in the postwar period. It was not the invention of a theorist but the practical application of experience gained in four years of war, the application of a new conception of life moulded during those years in the sphere of politics. Adolf Hitler, himself a soldier who proved his worth during the first World War, gave that experience and that conception of life both shape and expression. After the collapse of the old structure of society of the monarchic period, he carried out what was in accordance with the essential development and the meaning of German history. That is why although he originally had no resources of power at his disposal, he was able during the course of time to overcome all obstacles supported solely by the increasing faith of the people in the rightness of his intentions and his doctrine.

The soldierly elements in this development must be kept in mind in order to pass a correct judgement on the phenomena of our day. Everything ever said or written by Germany's enemies regarding a conflict between the Party and the Army in Germany is either objectively wrong or malicious calumny. The Party is the political branch and the Army is the military branch springing from one and the same trunk. The National Socialist Party has adopted many features of the soldierly tradition, for example, the principle of leadership, the rigid organization and discipline. The Army as reorganized since 1935 is imbued and inspired with the political-revolutionary spirit of the National Socialist creed.

Both were to a very considerable extent the result of pressure from outside. They owe their existence to the fact that the sated victorious powers of Versailles wished to keep the German people—the people with the biggest population in Europa and culturally one of the most important—in a state of impotence for all time to come after first disarming it and financially plundering it. To do so they used various means including such States as Poland and the artificial creation known as Czechoslovakia. Such a state of affairs was intolerable for the German people with the consequence that the re-establishment of its Armed Forces was carried out in the spirit of the new political order and at a speed verging on the miraculous.

The final struggle of the southern group in Stalingrad: the last "hedgehog" in front of the OGPU buildings

THE LAST DAYS...

The sacrifice for Europe of the German 6th Army and a Flak division, 2 Rumanian divisions and a Croat regiment

This hedgehog in the square in front of the OGPU buildings and a second hedgehog in the tractor factory a few miles away were the last strongholds defended by the Germans and all that remained of the "Stalingrad pocket" at the beginning of February 1943. People no doubt are inclined to think of other pockets during this war and draw comparisons. And it is right that they should do so. Kiev was surrounded by the Germans on 20th September 1941 and, 6 days later, 665,000 prisoners were counted. There was the famous pocket of Briansk and Wiasma closed by the Germans on 8th October 1941 and evacuated 10 days later by 663,000 prisoners. It was glorious early autumn weather at that time and the Germans were dealing with the remnants of armies. The Stalingrad pocket was held by one German army, 2 Rumanian divisions and a Croat regiment for almost 80 days. From the commander-in-chief

PK. Drawing: Front Correspondent H. Liska

down to the last private, everyone in Smlingrad knew that they, the pier supporting the entire front, had to hold out to the bitter end. In the middle of November 1942 the pier was cut off in the rear by the flood. The dead flat terrain swept by snowstorms and frozen hard as stone with the thermometer registering 35° centigrade below zero, offered no tactical barrier. But transporters could still land bringing rations and ammunition and evacuating the wounded. Five to six Soviet armies kept storming without a break, artillery and bombs hammered the besieged ceaselessly, the ring was closing in. At Christmas it was no bigger than the city of Stalingrad proper. The possibilities of landing and provisioning from the air became smaller, the daily rations were reduced from day to day, every shot fired and every drop of petrol was irreplaceable: systematically the enemy razed every remaining wall to the ground. In the cellars and subterranean passages the soldiers and the wounded had their quarters. It was the beginning of January. The men suffered

privation and hunger. At the same time, however, one single assault made by these soldiers against the northeastern front cost the Soviets 800 dead before the main fighting line of a tank division. Up to 20th January 100 enemy tanks had been destroyed. The losses in men and material by far surpassed the figures of the encircled forces and the time lost was irreplaceable. The days went by and the men in Stalingrad fought on. When the two last hedgehogs were driven together in the heart of the city the southern group hoisted the Swastika from the OGPU buildings, the symbol of the square. Without reinforcements, ammunition or rations they fought on with bayonets until February. Then they destroyed everything that could be of use to the enemy. The OGPU buildings collapsed in a gigantic explosion, the flag disappeared in a cloud of smoke, the tomb closed over the last defenders. When everything was quiet again, the noise of battle could still be heard from the tractor factory. The end had not yet come.

EUROPE'S SHIELD

In this case, reference to the German powers of organization explains but little, the decisive fact here was the spririt employing those means of organization. The German Army had not played any part in the internal political chaos between 1918 and 1933. It had watched over the military heritage and added to it the experiences of the first World War. It now became the heart of the new Army which received a further impulse from the revolutionary impetus of a political rejuvenation. This amalgamation between the best military traditions and the new ideas and the belief in new conditions of existence then made possible the amazing victories won by the German Armed Forces since 1st September 1939. They must not be interpreted only in the light of technical progress in war or material organization, for Germany's antagonists also had them abundantly at their disposal. Had they not their Maginot Line, did not armies at first far superior in numbers encircle the Reich prepared for war at a moment's notice and did they not possess the resources of the whole world? The Polish Army was swept away in only 18 days, the Maginot Line was overrun and France vanquished in something less than seven weeks, the British suffered one defeat after another from Narvik to Dunkirk and from there to Crete, the Bolshevist armies, far superior in numbers and material, were thrown far back into their own country. All this must be ascribed to the mental and spiritual strength of the rejuvenated German Armed Forces which the ohters had nothing equivalent to oppose with. The fact that Germany this time also secured strong reserves of material for herself and from the very outset adopted better precautionary measures regarding raw materials and food supplies than in 1914, was a natural consequence of the experiences during the first World War. The decisive factor was, however, and still is the ideas and ideals with which the German Armed Forces are imbued and which provide them with the strength to gain the victory.

... and political soldiers

Ever since the democracies so despicably threw away the magnificent chance they had in Versailles of carrying out a really just reorganization of our Continent, Germany has undertaken to provide tortured Europe with new possibilities of existence. It is in this sense that the German Army feels that it is, indeed, the executor of a political will. The view, which used often to be asserted, that the soldier must be "unpolitical has given way to the conviction that he must be political through and through, that is to say, that he must be completely imbued with the importance and the value of the ideas now championed by National Socialism. It was not the lust for conquest which caused Germany to take up arms, this war has been forced on her by the destructive aims of her enemies. The German soldier is convinced of this to the very depths of his innermost being and that is why the German Armed Forces form an invincible bloc having as, its spiritual foundations the sublime ethics of a soldierly tradition. It is, moreover, inspired by the belief in the high mission of protecting the Reich and thereby also the whole of Europe against the attacks of the capitalist Powers in the West and above all against the horrors of Bolshevism.

Every German soldier knows that this is in the true sense of the word a life and death struggle. Not one of them has any illusions on that point so that the determination to hang on and to deal the enemy heavy blows wherever possible is only increased.

The distorted description which enemy propaganda customarily gives of the Reich's Armed Forces cannot stand up to a dispassionate investigation by a really neutral observer.

Germany has today in the real sense of the word a national army in which every capable soldier carries a field marshal's baton in his pack. He has not sacrificed any of the important values of his great soldierly tradition, on the contrary, he has gained many new ones. Courage, self-denial, modesty, discipline and the willingness to make every sacrifice are still the highest virtues. The principle of being more than you seem to be is still in force. The German still fights chivalrously as he always has done and does not employ the cruel methods of a brutal mercenary with which he has become acquainted during this war from his antagonists such as the shelling of military hospitals and attacks on planes engaged in rescuing men in distress at sea, air raids on open towns carried out by the British in order to terrorize the population and the terrible maltreatment of prisoners by the Bolshevists. The populations of all the territories occupied by the German Army are unanimous in their praise of the exemplary·conduct and discipline of the German soldiers. One is continually surprised in such countries at the friendly relations between the men and officers in the German Army. For every German officer it is a natural duty to take a human interest in his subordinates. Here there are no clear-cut class distinctions, no social abyss exists, they all feel themselves equally pledged to a common duty. Military rank and discipline do not suffer in consequence for a single instant, they remain just as rigid as ever before.

In the service of Europe

It is consequently sublime spiritual values tested and chastened throughout the course of centuries, consolidated in many wars, handed on from generation to generation and continually inspired with new life which have enabled the German soldiers to achieve what they are now performing in the defence of a whole continent. They are the best manly virtues which every nation ought to appreciate that has not fallen a victim to the empty hurry and scurry of a noisy, materially-minded civilization as the Americans have done. Undoubtedly there are many other valuable conceptions of life besides the soldierly one, but in the struggle for existence the latter is the solid foundation without which a people must in the long run collapse when exposed to heavy crises. For the soldier who is forced to kill and destroy is also hazarding his most valuable possession, his life. By so doing he leaves behind him the sphere of dull utility and rises into a region where the conduct and value of a man are reckoned according to unchanging standards.

The most sublime example of this is the sacrifice of the troops fighting at Stalingrad which enabled the allied armies on the Eastern Front to build new dams to hold up the raging Bolshevist torrent and continue to preserve Europe from the annihilating rule of the Soviets. Cut off from all possibility of receiving reinforcements, surrounded

The Alcazar of the steppes ... *The remnants of the 11th Army Corps under General Strecker of the Infantry have established themselves in the tractor works. The fitting shop forms the centre of the defence. The enemy have slowly worked their way forward to within 20 yards systematically destroying the walls and iron girders. Then they throw hand grenades and mines among the ruins. The defenders have taken up positions in subterranean passages and erecting pits. Driven forward by their tanks, the Soviets repeatedly force their way into the fitting shop where they are annihilated with bayonets and spades in hand-to-hand fighting. Wounded men fight on. Men suffering from severe frostbite pass the ammunition up to the others. There is not much of it left... They still have a wireless set. On 30th January, the tenth anniversary of the Greater German Reich, they listened with its help to the Führer's proclamation amidst the detonations of bursting shells, the noise of crumbling walls and the groaning of the wounded. The last defenders of Stalingrad reported this, their last ceremony, by wireless. "...and perhaps for the last time we raised our arms to give the German greeting." Those were the concluding words of their message*

Is Europe a fiction?

Does a common European destiny really exist or do the European peoples employ the word Europe only when it appears suitable to them in order to disguise their motives? SIGNAL publishes on page 11 an article dealing with this subject by Giselher Wirsing. During these decisive weeks it particularly concerns us all:

We, the Europeans!

Attemps to demoralize ... *Even at an early stage, the Soviets sought to demoralize the encircled German Army and its allies. They installed loudspeakers in the front lines and advised the soldiers to surrender as the struggle was hopeless. Pamphlets like the one here reproduced rained down on Stalingrad from Soviet planes guaranteeing the soldiers, both officers and men, their lives and good treatment if they laid down their arms. It was also asserted that 70,000 men had already surrendered. The "mass photograph" of German prisoners intended to confirm this statement is obviously a bad forgery and places the Soviet promises in their proper light. The same groups are repeated several times on this photograph (compare the white circles joined up to one another!). It is a composite photograph. Every appeal to the Germans to surrender including two official ones were answered by force of arms until the last bullet had been fired, the last document and the last rifle destroyed*

70 000 deutsche und rumänische Soldaten und Offiziere haben sich gefangengegeben!

70 000 Eurer Kameraden sind lebendige Zeugen dafür, daß die Rote Armee den Befehl Nr. 55 des Volkskommissars für Verteidigung der Sowjetunion, **Stalin**, strikte durchführt. Dieser Befehl garantiert den deutschen Offizieren und Soldaten, die die Waffen gestreckt haben, das Leben und gute Behandlung.

70.000

„Ein Soldat, der sich in einer aussichtslosen Lage gefangengibt, handelt nicht ehrlos, sondern vernünftig... Die Kriegsgeschichte kennt viele Beispiele, wo die tapfersten Soldaten und Offiziere die Waffen streckten, wenn weiterer Widerstand aussichtslos war."

Aus dem Aufruf des Kommandos der Roten Armee an die im Raum von Stalingrad...

KATYN –
A RECORD

How twelve European experts drew up a report, described by SIGNAL'S war correspondent Hanns Hubmann

A witness. The 74-year-old farmer. Kieselor. who whispered to Polish chauffeurs at the beginning of this year: "Just go and have a look at the Katyn Forest." relates to the European commission how in the spring of 1940 he for months observed the arrival of Polish officers at the station of Gniesdova and for months heard shots from the Katyn Forest. On the left of the photograph. Professor Naville of Geneva. on the right. Professor Speleers of Ghent

Victims of the Soviets

The Swiss delegate, Professor Dr Naville of Geneva, stated after the conclusion of the investigations at Katyn: "We have conducted what was probably the world's most tragic post-mortem examination. Polish officers had been murdered. The motives from this mass murder are rooted in a cruel philosophy, the will to destroy the bourgeois world, an aim full of danger for the whole of Western culture. We legal doctors went to Katyn to seek and proclaim the truth of the matter. This time it was not difficult to see the truth. It will be in the interests of all Europe and it is our duty to make known this truth to Europe and the whole world."

All killed by a bullet in the back of the head. Dr Orsós. Professor of Legal Medicine and Criminology at the University of Budapest. Hungary's representative on the European commission appointed to investigate the mass graves of Polish officers in the Katyn Forest near Smolensk. selects an Ogpu victim in one of the mass graves for dissection

KATYN — A RECORD

The official report of the European experts of world repute, drawn up at Smolensk on 30th April 1943, was signed by the 12 members of the commission: Dr Speleers (Belgium), Dr Makov (Bulgaria), Dr Tramsen (Denmark), Dr Saxén (Finland), Dr Palmieri (Italy), Dr Miloslawich (Croatia), Dr de Burlet (Holland), Dr Hájek (Protectorate), Dr Birkle (Rumania), Dr Naville (Switzerland), Dr Sublik (Slovakia), Dr Orsós (Hungary)

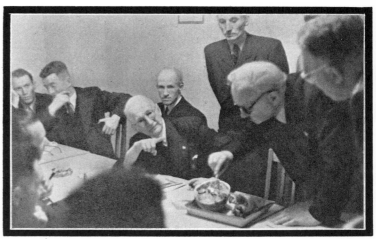

Hands bound — a bullet in the nape of the neck. *The report states: "The binding of the hands is in accordance with what was discovered in the case of the bodies of Russian civilians who were also exhumed in Katyn Forest and had been buried much earlier"*

One of the most important discoveries. *Professor Dr Orsós of Budapest, demonstrating to the commission, said: "We have here a tufaceous limestone incrustation in several layers on the surface of the cerebral mass, which has already become homogenized like clay. Such a transformation is observed only in the case of bodies which have been buried less than three years"*

Bankbook and certificate of award. *The Polish Brigadier-General Smorawinski still had in his possession not only his pass but the certificate awarding him the decoration "Virtuti militari" and his bankbook*

Burial with honour. *The two Polish Generals, Smorawinski and Bochaterewicz, whose bodies were discovered, being put into coffins in the presence of the commission preparatory to being given burial with honour*

Katyn— a record

One layer after another. *The bodies of the murdered men lie close together and on top of one another. When this photograph was taken, two layers had already been removed. The remaining three layers are also being exhumed*

A grave containing 2,500 bodies. *The largest of the seven mass graves already opened is L-shaped and measures 26 feet wide, one arm of the L being 91 feet long and the other 52 feet long. Five layers of 500 murdered Polish officers were buried here by the Soviets*

Professor Orsós of Budapest carrying out a dissection. *The Hungarian expert dictating his report in the presence of Professor Saxén of Helsinki, Dr Markov of Sofia and Professor de Burlet of Groningen*

Corpse No. 800. *Professor Dr Palmieri of Naples dissecting the head of a 50-year-old major — three shots in the nape of the neck, many splinters in the brain*

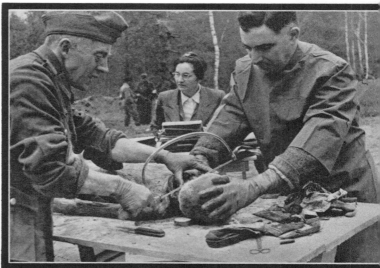

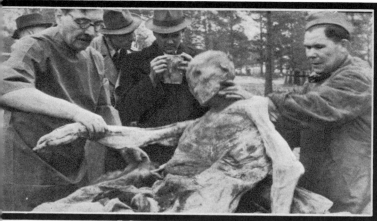

orpse's clothes are removed. *Professor Dr Hájek of Prague has found documents in the uniform of the murdered officers. They are here being examined by Professor Dr Subik of Bratislava (in rear) on the left and Dr Wodzinski, the Polish Red Cross's representative. "The subalterns lay at the bottom and the generals at the top" said the Polish doctor*

shot in the back of the skull. *The Croat, Professor Dr Miloslavich of Agram, member of the "London ety of Legal Medicine" and famous as an expert in the U. S. A., where he is called "Doc. Milo", showing results of his investigations to Professor Dr Buhtz of Breslau, who conducted the exhumations*

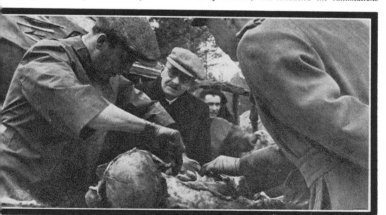

Nine bodies examined. *Dr Tramsen of Copenhagen dissecting. His work is being carefully followed by Professor Dr de Burlet and Professor Dr Saxén*

The nationality ascertained. *Professor Dr Naville of Geneva recognizes the uniform of one of the murdered men to be that of a Polish officer* ↓

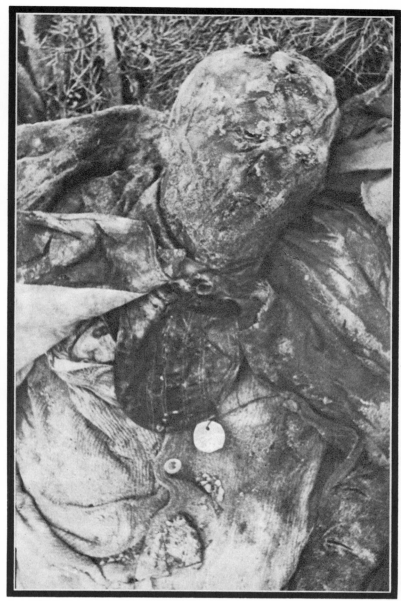

There was also an army chaplain among the victims. *The body of Zielkowski still bore the band indicating his office. In his winter clothes, which indicate the time of year in which the murder took place, were found his rosary (picture below), a small portable altar which he had made for himself at the Kozielsk camp in 1940, that is to say, shortly before his assassination, a prayer-book and a visiting card*

Kozielsk 1940.

One of the men belonging to a unit holding a "dug-out village" on the Eastern Front. The position forms a part of the front in the same way as the vertebrae form the spine. Men are required here who are tough because they know what is at stake. This man's gaze travels past the approaching Soviet tank to the prospect of a future which justifies every sacrifice

A glance at this man's face tells everybody capable of reading faces that he had never dreamt he would once be numbered among the toughest men at one of the centres of fierce fighting in the greatest struggle in history. This man's courage can be seen in the earnest strength of his eyes which are full of knowledge and confidence

Cover! The enemy is just laying down a barrage

This concerns you, too!

. . . Dear friend, just take a look at these pictures! They show you something which is by no means out of the ordinary among us in the front line. A dug-out is being fought for somewhere on the Eastern Front and after the fluctuating fortunes of the engagement, the Germans are still in possession of it. Such actions have been taking place for years now and they form the daily life of our men at the front. Can you imagine what that means? For you life still runs on quietly along its normal channels — we know, of course, that many large towns are exposed to extremely heavy air-raids and yet you must admit that most of you, in spite of everything, live a different life from that. And, moreover, we are pleased you do. You must realize, however, that these nameless soldiers, who all have perfectly normal names and are not mentioned personally in any military communiqué, are out in the front line for you! Have you ever thought what it means day after day; year after year, to keep on dashing out from cover or the security of a dug-out into the murderous hail of shells from the enemy's guns and into the death-bringing no man's land where whistling bursts of M. G. fire are the only music with which these men are still acquainted? Do not run away with the idea that these soldiers have only one desire— to be soldiers! I know how much yearning for beauty and happiness is hidden behind the mask of soldierly bearing and I know how much unlavished tenderness is stored up in these hands which for long have been clasping their weapons with inexhaustible courage. It is easy, it is even intoxicating to perform a bold deed or an exacting duty if but once To do so, however, year after year with faith in your heart is a far greater thing! PK. Photographs: War Correspondents Ohlemacher and Scürer

We understand the passionate tension in this soldier's face as he loads when we think that he has to carry out the movements with the greatest precision as quickly as possible. The concentrated energy with which the necessary actions are carried out is the energy of the soldier who realizes what the outcome of the struggle will mean

The gaze of the man, who looks fixedly but fearlessly at the low-flying Soviet planes roaring towards him proves that he is accustomed to danger and has learnt to suppress all feeling of fear. Only moral strength such as is founded upon the knowledge of a high ideal renders men capable of self-sacrifice

Grenadiers ready for hand-to-hand fighting: Bolshevists are approaching in the fog

Leaping on to an enemy tank which has broken through. Every scrap of cover is utilized

THE SEED OF THE THIRD WORLD WAR

By Giselher Wirsing

If the Russian Bolshevists could only pull down Britain, ruin its prosperity, plunge it into anarchy, obliterate the British Empire as a force in the world, the road would be clear for a general butchery, followed by a universal tyranny, of which they would be the heads and out of which they would get the profit . . . England is not Russia. One tenth of the dose of Bolshevism which has ruined and changed Russia would kill England stone dead.''

The speaker who had pronounced these words at the Alexandra Palace in London was greeted with a storm of applause when he left the platform. His speech was intended to warn the British people that in consequence of the menacing development of the Soviet Union, a second World War would become almost inevitable. The speaker had said this with a grim expression on his face and accompanied his words by the drastic gestures of a prophet firmly convinced of his mission. The date was 19th June 1926 and the speaker was Winston Churchill.

We are now standing at the crossroads of this second World War. Humanity is groaning. Millions are rotting in their graves. The burden on all the peoples of the earth taking an active or passive part in the struggle is daily becoming heavier. But the hope still prevails that European culture will nevertheless be preserved unbroken in the midst of this flood. During the last few months, however, a threatening thundercloud has formed over the yawning chasm of the second World War. Its heavy shadows have plunged the last green islands still lit up by the rays of the sun into a dim light. It is the shadow of the third World War.

That is the true state of affairs. We are not talking deliriously. We on no account get up in front of the European forum and give free rein to our thoughts. On the contrary, we speak of the prospects resulting inexorably from the course of this war for every individual who is able to perceive them. These prospects indicate that the future of our life, our existence and our culture in this Continent of Europe depends principally on whether this second World War will result in a long period of peace and put an end to the bloody world struggle which began in 1914. Were this not the case, the dragon seed of a third World War would be sown of which the European Continent would again form the centre. The pessimism felt by more than one important person at the end of the first World War would have been justified. Other happier continents farther from the centre of impact of the Great World Powers may then perhaps survive such a third World War. It would leave us, the Europeans, impoverished, humiliated, degenerated, no better than cave-dwellers. Who could doubt this in view of the two World Wars which the generations living at present have to contend with? Surely nobody can be so blind to reality.

For months past we have been emphasizing in this periodical that the subterranean war within the war being fought out on the one side between the British Empire and the United States and, on the other side, between those Powers and the Soviet Union, is no less important than the open war being waged by those three Powers against Germany, Italy, Japan and their allies. Naturally it is difficult for the contemporary to understand without prejudice the fundamental laws governing history in a time of general upheaval. It is in the consistency of human nature to regard the forces at work in the contemporary age as static phenomena. We of the 20th century are particularly inclined to do so because behind us lies the glittering surface of the calm lake of the 19th century—that epoch when great things took place, it is true, but which when compared with all the other centuries of modern history, particularly in Europe, was nevertheless an epoch of stability and long periods of peace. The standards by which we have to measure our own age are completely different and it is consequently no use for us to cast furtive glances over our shoulder. The correct decisions essential for the preservation of our European existence and, above all, of our culture, can only be made, on the contrary, by all European peoples if they thoroughly understand and quite objectively reckon with the immense dynamic force of our age. We do not laud it. It is only a tremendous force which has unleashed the transition from the old to the new age. But it cannot be denied as the events of the last few years show. That is why the subterranean wars already being waged between Britain, the United States and the Soviet Union are so important. If we grasp their significance, we can also distinguish the contours of the future and act accordingly.

The third World War, which would be fought out for the most part on European soil, is inevitable if the British—American—Soviet coalition wins this second World War. This is the deeper significance of this war within the war which so far has been concealed under a cloak although only thin. As far as the human mind is at all able to see into the future, that is the grim truth which, beyond all our present sufferings, is revealed like a shrunken and hollow-eyed skeleton to our inquiring glances. It is worth while rereading the sentences said by the United States Vice-President Wallace in which he frankly asked the question whether the seed of the third World War is not being sown now (cf. text printed below).

Wallace pronounced these sentences, it is true, in order to warn his own camp against dangers. His immediate intention, however, is unimportant.

Henry Wallace, Vice-President of the U.S.A. said concerning the third World War:

"We shall decide some time in 1943 or 1944 whether to plant the seeds of World War number three. That war will be probable in case we doublecross Russia. That war will be probable if we fail to demonstrate that we can furnish full employment after this war comes to an end and if Fascist interests motivated largely by anti-Russian bias get control of our Government. Unless the Western Democracies and Russia come to a satisfactory understanding before the war ends, I very much fear that World War number three is inevitable. Without a close trust and understanding between Russia and the United States, there is grave possibility of Russia and Germany sooner or later making common cause."

"Of course, the ground for World War number three can be laid by actions of other powers even though we, the United States, follow a constructivist course. For example, such a war would be inevitable if Russia should again embrace Trotskyism, ferment a world-wide revolution or if British interests should again be sympathetic to anti-Russian activity in Germany and other countries. Another possible cause for World War number three might rise out of our willingness to repeat mistakes made after the World War number one. When a creditor nation raises its tariffs and asks foreign nations to pay up and at the same time refuses to let them pay in goods, the result is irritation of a sort which sooner or later leads first to trade war and then to bloodshed."

(Speech made in Delaware on 8th March 1943)

The important thing is the automatic dynamic direction being followed by the initiative of the Great World Powers. If Wallace's words are thus critically examined, we discover that there is not the slightest chance that the Communist Soviet Union would ever abandon the policy of the third Internationale and of the Comintern. The pathos of Communism as conceived by Stalin is thus bound up with it no less than the Communism of Lenin or Trotzky. Nor can England, as Wallace demands, abandon Europe to Bolshevism, should it prove victorious, if she does not want to be annihilated herself as no less a person than Churchill himself stated at Alexandra Palace. Nor will the United States, however, be willing to turn voluntarily from the path of a world imperialism along which they are being driven by high finance which holds sway at home. Neither the intentions of one or other of them nor any "good will'' can do anything to alter the imminent tendencies of the Great Powers in the camp hostile to Europe. The grotesque phenomenon of the brutal treatment meted out by Stalin and his people to the demands of the Polish and Yugoslav émigré Governments in London prove even to the most incredible that a victory of the Soviets would mean the bolshevization of the whole of Europe. That alone would be the inevitable seed of another World War with Europe as the battlefield. The map on the opposite page roughly indicates the situation at its commencement.

This would consequently at the same time be the result of the policy of disintegration which Britain is striving to pursue in Europe. This would be the result of a continuation of that unbounded chauvinism which has so often led to new civil wars on the Continent. Is it asking too much if in view of the forces which, were they to be victorious, would reduce our Continent to an inferno in consequence of another struggle between themselves, if we call upon the peoples of Europe, first of all to examine closely what is really happening? We are not carrying on a controversy with anybody. The problems with which we are faced are far too big and too serious for that. But we realize that here and there in Europe, people are trying to withdraw into their shells, that people are living in the cheap hopes of being left untouched by the storms raging past us.

If the German armies together with the efforts being made by all European peoples succeed in driving back Bolshevism on the Eastern Front and establishing frontiers for the Continent which are firm and secure at all points of the compass, the danger that Europe will become the battlefield of the world for the third time will simultaneously have been banished. This European Continent, united in its sovereign peoples, will then stand as a power factor between Sovietism and Americanism as it will also stand between the Soviets and Britain. These Powers at least will not then be able to clash on European soil as anticipated by Wallace. That is quite clear. If we succeed in doing this, Americanism, even if it gains possession of the British Empire, has no base from which to inundate this Continent and turn it into the extreme limit of the extension of its power across the oceans. If we succeed in making this a joint European achievement, then peace will be established at the end of the second World War.

That is the question with which the peoples of the European Continent are now faced. Herein lie our dignity and the greatness of our future.